IMAGES
of America

SOUTH FAYETTE TOWNSHIP

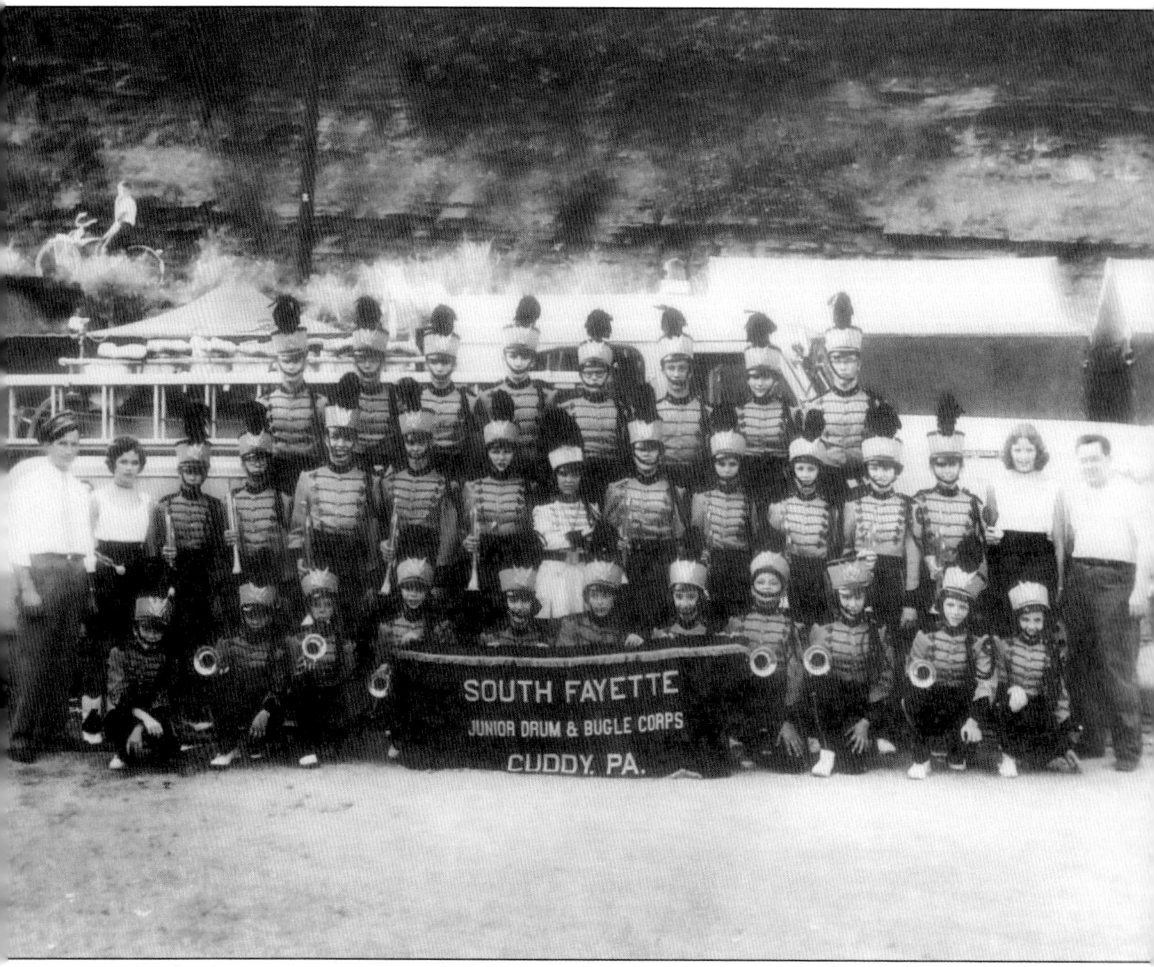

Pictured is the South Fayette Junior Drum & Bugle Corps from Cuddy, a group of student musicians sponsored by the fire department in the mid-1940s who would play in local parades and at fireman's carnivals. (Courtesy of the Historical Society of South Fayette Township.)

On the Cover: When the South Fayette High School marching band was formed, many students were involved in that and the drum and bugle corps disbanded. (Courtesy of the Historical Society of South Fayette Township.)

IMAGES of America

SOUTH FAYETTE TOWNSHIP

Charlotte Smith on behalf of the
Historical Society of South Fayette Township
Foreword by John L. Kosky Jr.

ARCADIA PUBLISHING

ISBN 978-1-4671-2318-1

Published by Arcadia Publishing
Charleston, South Carolina

Printed in the United States of America

Library of Congress Control Number: 2014950427

For all general information, please contact Arcadia Publishing:
Telephone 843-853-2070
Fax 843-853-0044
E-mail sales@arcadiapublishing.com
For customer service and orders:
Toll-Free 1-888-313-2665

Visit us on the Internet at www.arcadiapublishing.com

To the residents of South Fayette Township, your past was remarkable, your present is always developing, and your future is limitless.

Contents

Foreword

Having grown up in South Fayette Township since 1929, I recommend this book's accurate depiction of the township I still call home 86 years later. South Fayette has seen a great influx of families to the area through the years, and the pictures displayed within the following pages provide a glimpse of the township's historic past. Many of the buildings and landmarks identified are still prevalent throughout the township. I think this book is a must-read for all residents of and visitors to South Fayette Township, present and past, whether to inform about the robust history of the township or to rekindle fond memories from the past. My hope is as you read through the pages and identify through your journeys one of the existing landmarks, that you close your eyes and let your mind take you back to another era. Enjoy.

—John L. Kosky Jr.
Class of 1945

Acknowledgments

This book began as homage to the past in an effort to memorialize the township's founding, its rich sports, its farming and mining histories, and its hearty citizens who have carved out a unique reputation for excellence in its small corner of Allegheny County, Pennsylvania. The Historical Society of South Fayette Township, begun in 2004, has started the work of preserving this heritage so that present and future residents will know and enjoy its unique qualities. The township has changed since its colonial days, now known more for the awards garnered by its school district, a state champion basketball team in 2010 and football teams in 2013 and 2014, and a prizewinning high school marching band. But the spirit of its resourceful and enterprising colonial founders still resounds among those who continue to make a modern-day South Fayette Township a "great place to live, work and play."

Community members who have contributed photographs, stories, memories, facts, and history are Geri Casciola Adair, Marylee Ainsworth and the South Fayette Band Alumni Association, Emil "Patsy" Battistone, Teresa and Louis Berceli, Emily Williamson-Brady, Fred Cardillo, Matt Cochran, Colussy Chevrolet, Debra Conoscuito Deep, Keith Delaney, Frank DeThomas, the Fatigati family, Armando Ferri, John Franjione, Florence Joy Hayes, Linda Collins Garrett, Midge Brown Gilson, Marion Campbell Grafe, Lisa Knez, John Alan Kosky, John L. Kosky Jr., Carol and Bob Kurchena, Joanne Petrillo, Kay and Bob Rank, Mark Schneider, Mike Shuck, and others. Except where noted, all photographs are from the Historical Society of South Fayette.

Thanks also go to Ryan Tomazin and Shad Wachter for their scanning assistance; to Linda James, Kevin Sutter, and Matthew Shuck for their photography skills; and to Abby Walker and Lily Watkins of Arcadia Publishing for guiding this project along. Everyone's input and enthusiasm has been invaluable, enlightening, and gratefully welcome. The coordinator of this book also appreciates the loving support of her family during the compilation of this project. Every day, we all make history in our own ways. This book celebrates the history of South Fayette's ancestors and its present-day residents by saving everything in a written format for future generations.

Every effort has been made to obtain correct factual information and to acknowledge all contributors to this archival endeavor.

INTRODUCTION

The area currently known as South Fayette Township was originally claimed by both Virginia and Pennsylvania. In 1788, it was finally decided that this area would be part of Allegheny County, Pennsylvania, not Augusta County, Virginia. It originally was assigned to Moon Township, as Allegheny County was divided into seven townships at the time.

In 1790, Moon Township was deemed too large, and a new township named Fayette was defined in western Pennsylvania. The new township was named after French general Gilbert du Motier, the Marquis de Lafayette. Over the years, this area became again too unwieldy to function properly as one municipality, and in 1842, Fayette was divided into North and South Fayette Townships.

South Fayette is bounded by the Washington County line, Robinson's Run, Coal Run, and Chartiers Creek. The first known resident was a Mr. Miller, for whom Millers Run was named. Miller settled at the mouth of the stream in 1768. When other settlers began to come here, he moved on. The first permanent settler is believed to have been Christian Lesnett, who was born in Germany and first settled in Maryland. An early family story has Christian, then about 41 years old, bringing with him his two sons, Frederick and Frank, who were 14 and 12 years old, respectively, at the time. The township was noted for more Indian attacks than any other section of Allegheny County as the Mingo Indian Trail went right through the township. It was known and always feared as the route of scalping parties. After clearing the land and building a small cabin on a 600-acre tomahawk claim near the creek on Alpine Road/Coal Pit Run, Christian returned to Hagerstown, Maryland, to bring back the rest of the family and left the boys behind to hold the claim to the land. Winter weather and other circumstances prevented the entire family from returning by horseback until one year later. It was a joyful scene to find the boys still on the claim, healthy and safe, and not having seen a single Indian the entire lonely year. In 1770, George Washington supposedly acquired nearly 2,900 acres of land in South Fayette Township in exchange for forgiveness of a debt. This land is now known as the township's Hickory Heights residential community.

Some residents prior to 1820 (and whose relatives still reside in the township) include the families of Dixon, Kelso, Herman, Campbell, Erich, Slater, Sterling, McConnell, Waters, Morgan, Wallace, Brice, Steward, Hopper, James, Herriott, Collins, Dunlevy, Boyce, Hickman, Fawcett, Lesnett, McKown, Nesbitt, Hall, Boyle, South, and Jordan—many of these families have streets named after them.

Though at first a farming community, the area had a few thriving industries. About 1790, Capt. Samuel Morgan built a gristmill, later purchased by Moses Coulter, a German who came here from Baltimore. Coulter sold it in 1812 to William Gilmore but then repurchased it. His son Goodman Coulter converted it to a steam mill, added a sawmill, and later changed it to a steel mill. A fuming mill was built about 1820 on Millers Run by Samuel Stewart, who manufactured sickles. Other family names at this time included Rowley, McKee, Matthews, Brown, Mitchell, Scott, White, Walker, Ewing, McElheny, McGraw, and Fink.

Another prominent citizen was Col. Joseph Noble, whose daughter Elizabeth married George Vallendingham, a surveyor and friend of George Washington. Both men staked 1,000 acres at Robinson Run and cleared enough to farm. Colonel Noble ran pack trains of grain and flour from Robinson Run/Noblestown to Millers Run to Chartiers Creek where it crossed into Bridgeville and met Forbes Road near McKeesport. This was called "Noble's Trace." The first shipment of flour sent from Coulter's Mill to New Orleans by riverboat was made by Mike Fink of Sturgeon about 1800. Fink had a reputation for hell-raising among keelboat men and inspired the name of nearby Fink's Run, a feeder creek that flows into Robinson Run. Another prominent business was the Diamond Flour Mill, owned by Joseph Campbell.

Coal and oil were discovered in the township between 1860 and 1910. The population jumped 250 percent, with a great many different ethnic groups coming to work here, including those of Scots-Irish, German, and English lineage, the backgrounds of the original settlers. Mining became a big industry. The first mines were opened on the farms of Samuel H. Cook and James Wallace, producing 200,000 tons of coal annually. Other mines were Laurel Hill Mines and Coke Works (established in 1872), Star, Oakridge, Pennsylvania Coal Company, Parrish Coal Mining Company, Chartiers Block Coal Company, Boyce Mines, Grant Mine, McConnell Mines, Jackson Mine, Cherry Mine, and the Pittsburgh Union Coal Company. The Willow Grove Mines (established in 1866 from the estate of James T. Wood) had a daily capacity of 500 tons and employed more than 400 men.

The area's 19 mines are now exhausted and closed, and very little industry has moved in, but with the new highways and accessibility to the city of Pittsburgh 12 miles away, the township has become more of a residential community. It has a total area of 20.4 square miles with topography of mostly wooded, small hills and floodplains on four streams. It is bordered by Bridgeville and Upper St. Clair to the east; Cecil Township (Washington County) to the south and west; McDonald Borough, Oakdale Borough, and North Fayette Township to the northwest; and Collier Township to the northeast. The population in 1930 was around 9,147 people, and in 2010, it was around 14,416 (*Census of Population and Housing*, US Census Bureau), living in the zip codes of Morgan, Cuddy, Sturgeon, Oakdale, McDonald, Cecil, and Bridgeville.

One

Churches and Cemeteries

South Fayette Township, although small, can count nine active churches, one "closed" parish, and nine cemeteries within its borders.

Yet many residents also travel to nearby Collier Township, Cecil Township, Scott Township, and other neighboring communities to attend Mass at St. Barbara's, St. Mary's, Our Lady of Grace, SS. Simon and Jude, St. Margaret's, or St. Patrick's or services at Bridgeville United Methodist, Bethany Presbyterian, St. George's Orthodox, Beth El Synagogue, and others.

In addition to the five historic churches detailed on the following pages, five new churches have been built since 1960—Calvary Full Gospel Church, at 538 Hickory Grade Road (the "Church on the Hill" built on 35 acres donated by the Hickman family); All Saints Episcopal Fellowship, at 850 Boyce Road; Kingdom Hall of Jehovah's Witnesses, at 3482 Washington Pike; Crossroads United Methodist Church/Bridgeville Campus, at 3191 Washington Pike; and Lakeview Christian Life Church and Academy, at 1 Lakeview Place.

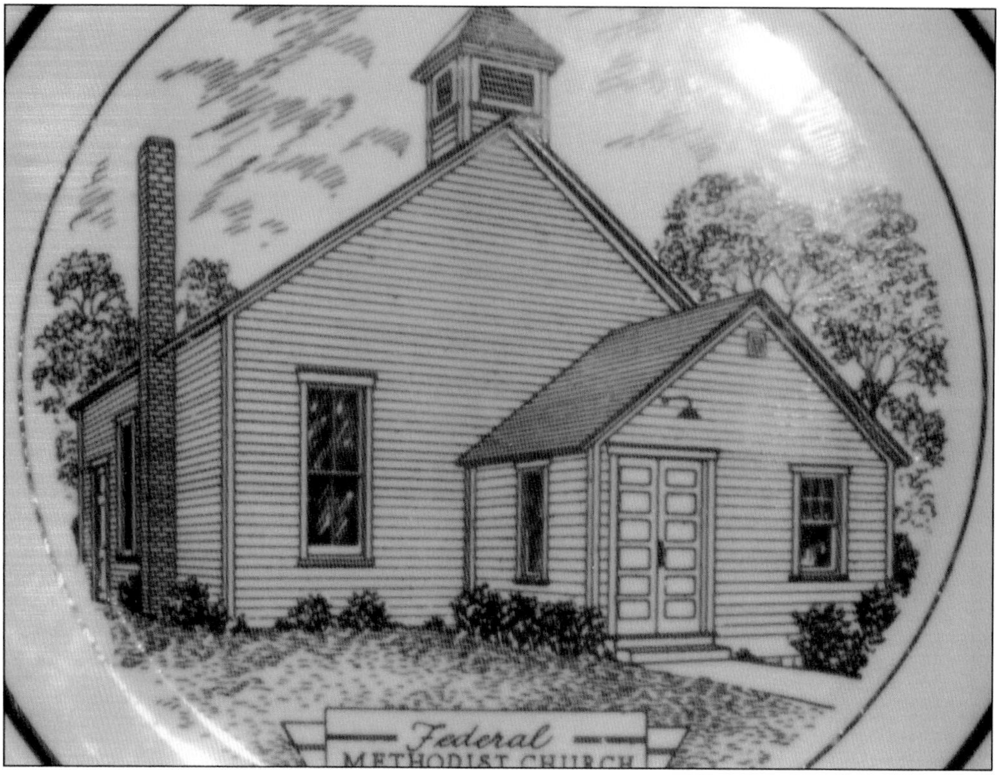

After securing donations from local mining families in the area off Thoms Run, also known as Beechmont, Hickman, Federal, Rosevale, and Burdine, the church building at 811 Dutch Hill Road, Oakdale, was dedicated on land given by the Herriot family in September 1891. In 1948, Federal United Methodist Church began sharing the same pastor with Noblestown United Methodist and now shares with Midway United Methodist. The church has only about 45 members but continues to be active, sponsoring several community events.

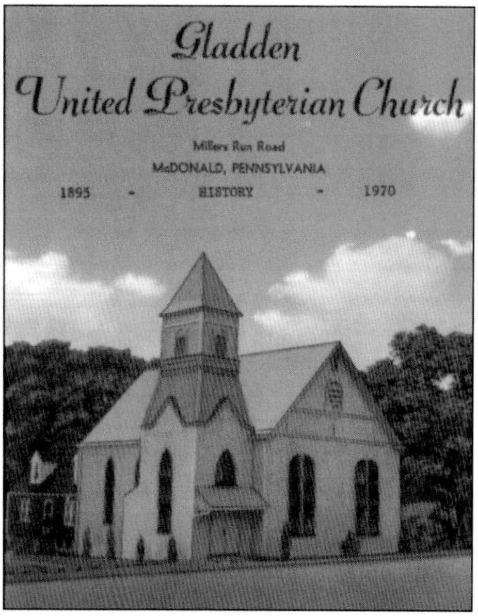

In 1893, Thomas Gladden offered his land to build a church at 747 Millers Run Road. Gladden United Presbyterian was dedicated in 1895. He gave $100 for a 600-pound bell to be placed in the building's bell tower. When the original church was demolished in 1973, the bell was too heavy for the roof and it currently rests on the porch of the Christian education building. A pipe organ, donated by Andrew Carnegie, was used by the church from 1901 to 1948.

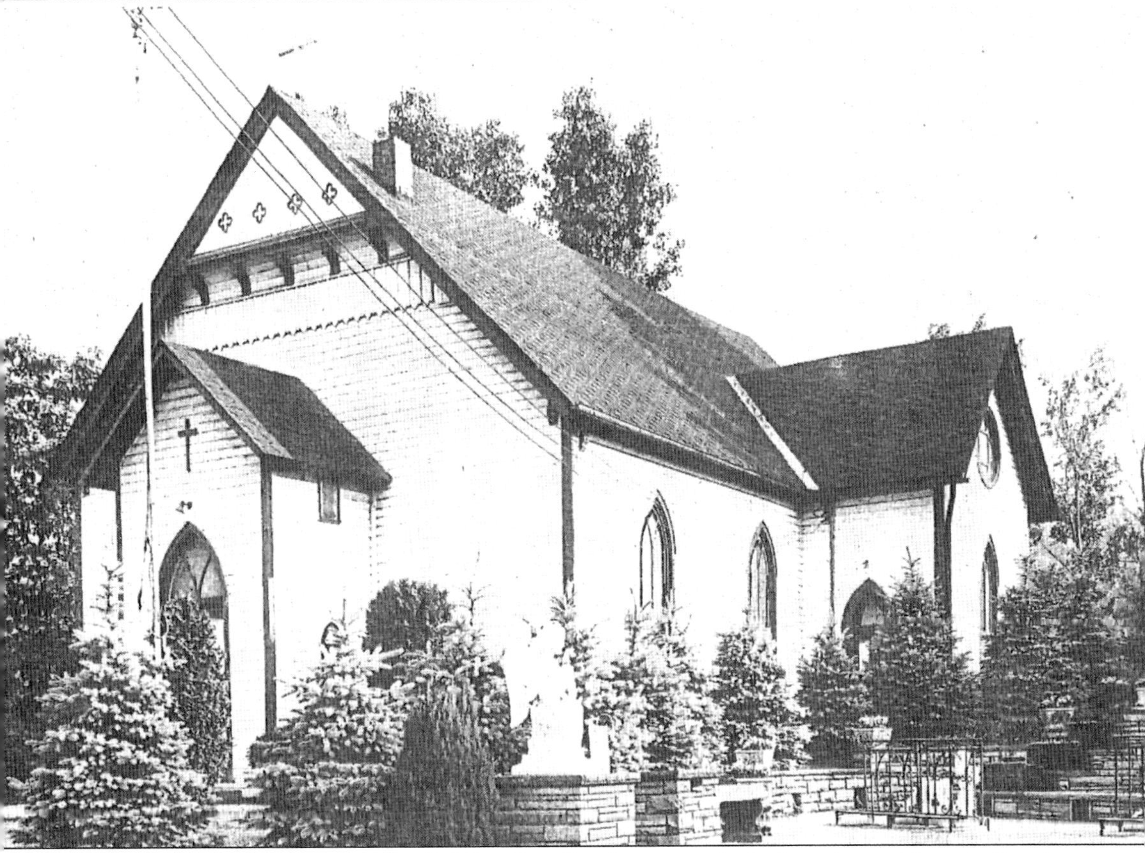

Established in 1915 at the corner of Millers Run Road to serve the Lithuanian residents in South Fayette, St. Anthony Roman Catholic Church originally was in a building formerly occupied by a Methodist Episcopal church and purchased for $4,000. After a remodeling, St. Anthony's was an extension of the Bridgeville Catholic parish called St. Agatha that was established in 1894. The parishioners donated money and time toward constructing the Our Lady of Fatima Shrine and grotto, placed between the church and the rectory. A parish hall was dedicated in 1959. A crisis erupted in 1960 when a proposed interstate highway would have bisected the church's property, but after many meetings and the intercession of His Excellency Bishop Leonard (now deceased), the highway was relocated, and the parish remained for 35 more years. St. Anthony was merged with St. Agatha in 1994 to establish Holy Child Parish, a Catholic faith community encompassing Bridgeville, South Fayette, and parts of Collier and Upper St. Clair townships. Originally, the parish maintained both church sites, but St. Anthony's closed on September 8, 2007, and was torn down completely in 2012.

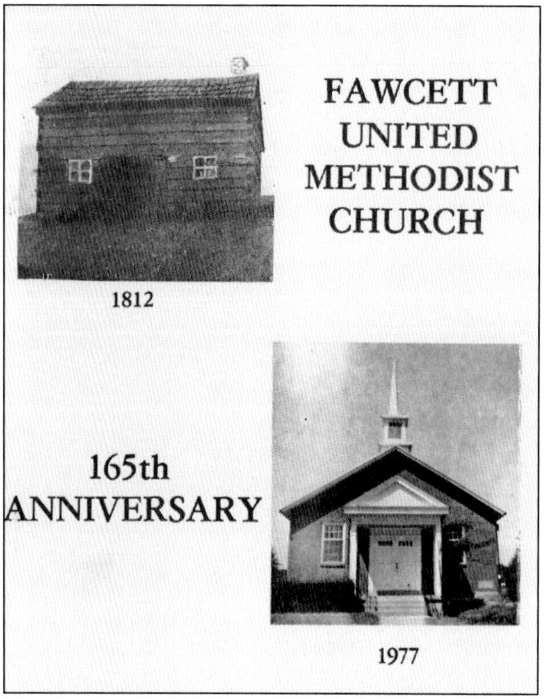

Although now located at 346 Fawcett Church Road, Fawcett United Methodist Church actually began in 1793 on Morgan Road in John Fawcett's home, which was a preaching point on the Ohio circuit. That land is now the Veterans Affairs National Cemetery of the Alleghenies, which contains a Fawcett-Boyce-Hickman plot. This continues to be a small congregation. Pictured are the original 1812 log building and the 1945 version.

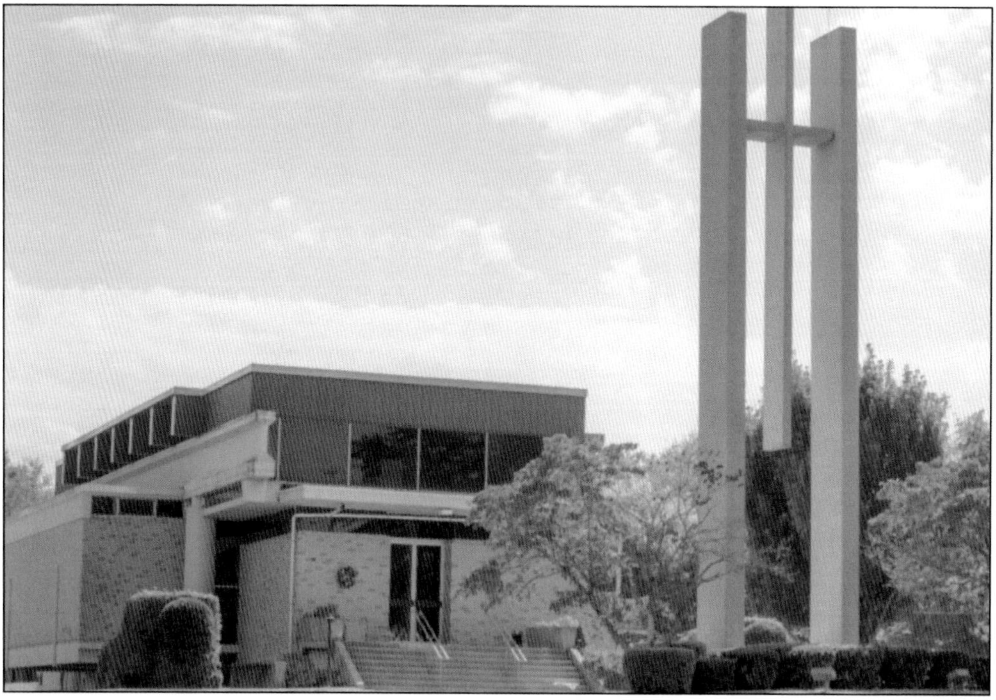

Zion Lutheran Church began in 1898 with a group of German immigrants meeting in the C.P. Mayer Building, later relocating to larger quarters in Poellet Hall on Washington Avenue and then to 347 Prestley Road. Expansion required purchasing land in 1960 at 3197 Washington Pike, South Fayette, completing the present-day church in 1968 and adding a preschool in 1980. Services were in German until 1920, when English was adopted. (Courtesy of Linda James.)

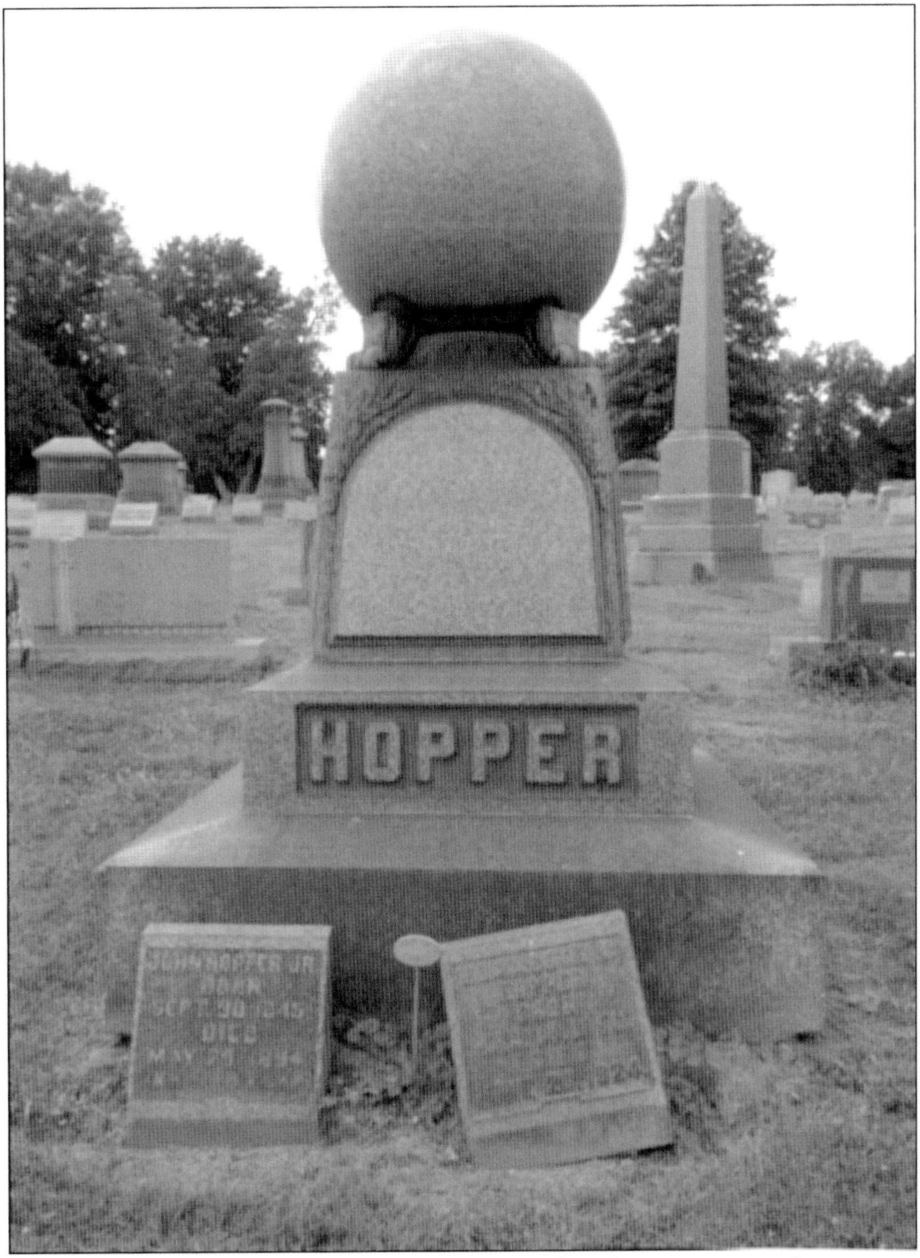

In 1884, Melrose Cemetery, on Washington Pike, received its charge as a nonprofit, nonsectarian cemetery. One of the first large monuments (pictured here) was purchased and brought in by a team of horses pulling a cart. The cart got stuck hub-deep on the muddy road, and more horses and men had to be called in to move the stone to its foundation. Many local family names will be found here, along with 150 victims from the 1918 flu epidemic. This cemetery is the ending location of the annual Bridgeville Memorial Day Parade in which many community organizations, churches, and the South Fayette Little Green Machine Marching Band participate every year. A service is conducted here by several ministers and sponsored by the Bridgeville American Legion. The South Fayette Coal Company Melrose Mine ran directly under this cemetery. (Courtesy of Linda James.)

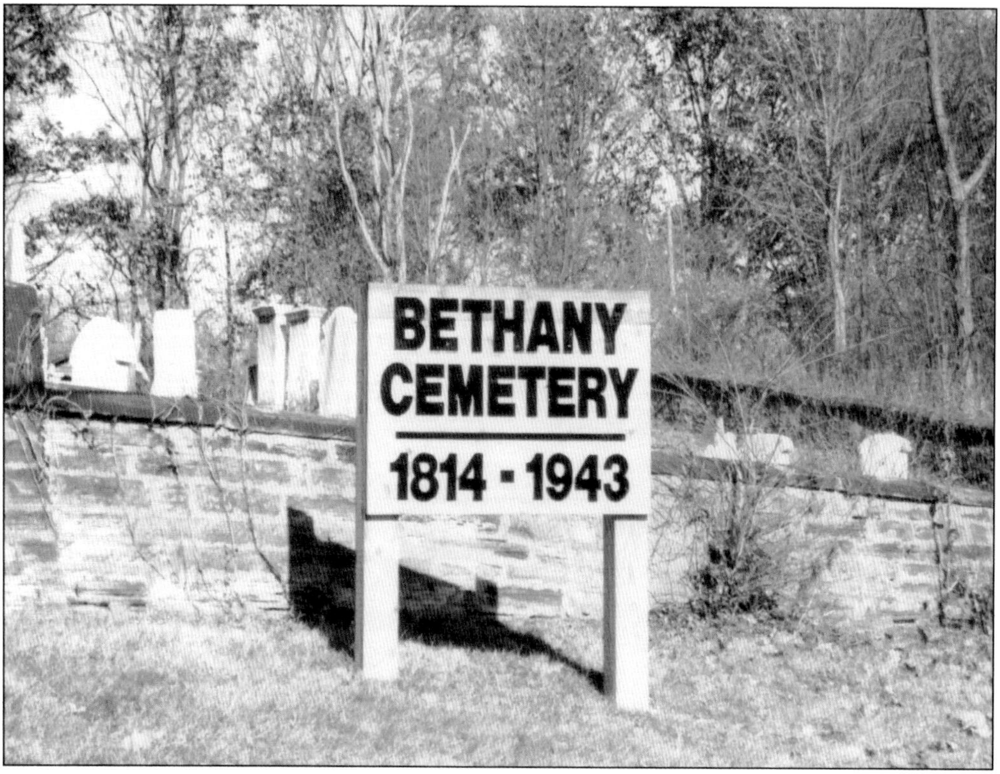

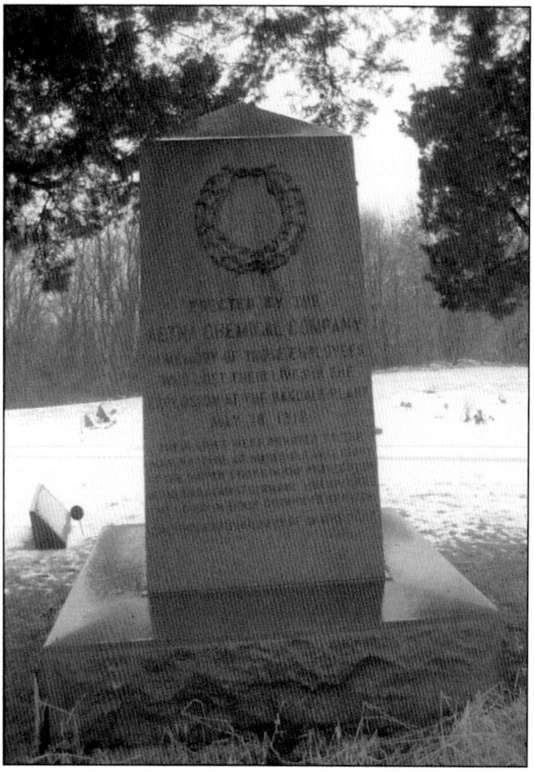

Bethany Cemetery is located on Presto-Sygan Road on the site where the first Bethany Meeting House was built in 1815 on land purchased for $40.77. Bethany Presbyterian Church of Bridgeville still maintains it, noted for its old stone wall along the road. Frederick Lesnett, a Revolutionary War veteran, is buried here. There is also a headstone with the inscription "Unknown Colored Civil War Soldier." Burials took place here from 1814 to 1943.

Opened in 1892 off Union Avenue, Oakdale Cemetery is the final resting place of Rev. John Wilson McCleland, founder of the Boys' Industrial Home of Western Pennsylvania, which operated for 70 years until its closing in 1972. There also is a large four-sided monument, approximately 10 feet tall, with text as follows: "Erected by the / Aetna Chemical Company, / in memory of those employees / who lost their lives in the / explosion at the Oakdale plant / May 18, 1918."

Located near Oakdale Cemetery on Union Avenue Extension, the small Old German Cemetery originally was on land desired by a group of German Lutherans, including members of the Metz and Brinkman families, to hold a church. Quickly running out of money, the families never built the church, and it instead became a burial ground. A significant section is set aside to honor members of the Grand Army of the Republic (GAR). (Courtesy of Linda James.)

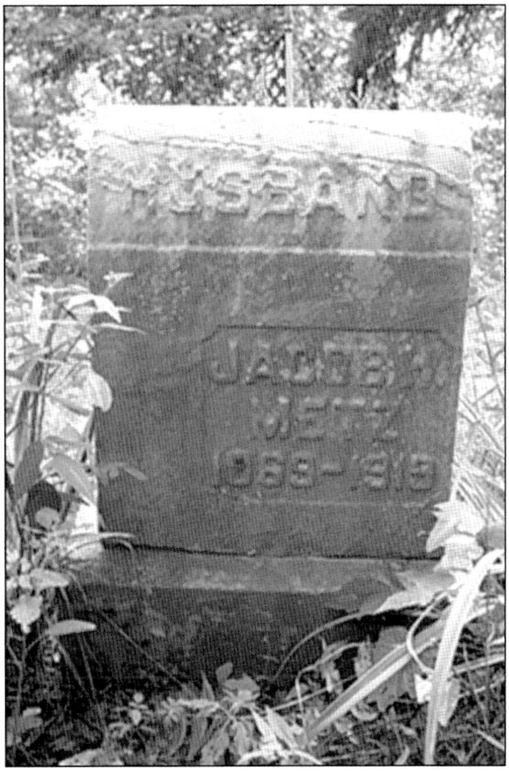

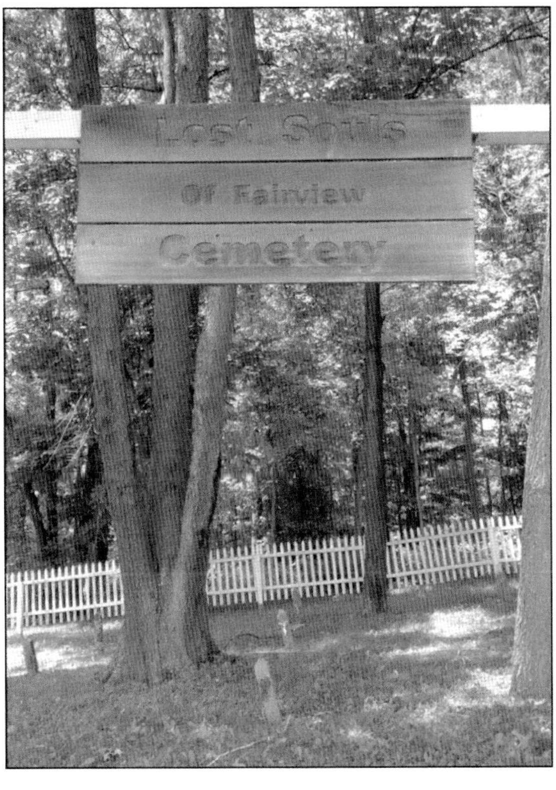

The tiny fenced-in Lost Souls Cemetery at Fairview Park remains from when the property was owned by Mayview State Hospital. The cemetery was operated between 1913 and 1918, and it is unknown how many residents were actually buried here during that time. These were considered paupers' graves, and coffins were not used. The 28 current grave markers were renovated in 2002 as part of Todd Lewis's Eagle Scout project. The township maintains the site now.

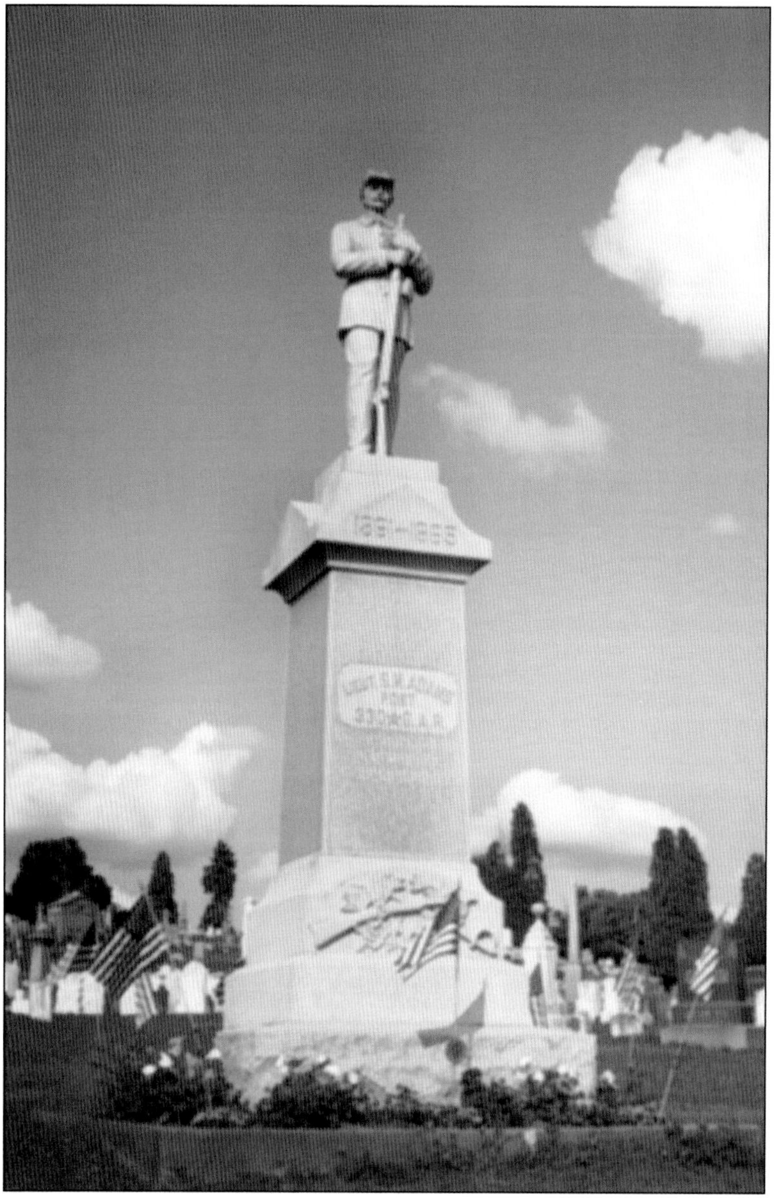

Located on Robinson Run Road, the Associate Reformed Church of North America (later known as Robinson Run Presbyterian Church) members first worshiped in a tent in 1772 until a log church was built there in 1790. A brick church was built around 1833. In 1902, the church was demolished by a great storm; the congregation relocated to nearby McDonald, but the Robinson Run Cemetery remains. A large monument dedicated to Elizabeth Gilmore was erected by the Daughters of the American Revolution; Gilmore was a nurse in the Continental Army who served at Valley Forge with George Washington during the long winter of 1777 and died in 1824. The famous Pennsylvania Bucktails were formed at the cemetery in 1862. The group got its name from an initiation custom requiring recruits to demonstrate proficiency with a rifle by producing the tail of a buck. There are 13 Revolutionary War veterans, 52 Civil War veterans, 17 Spanish-American War veterans, 213 World War I veterans, and many veterans from World War II, the Korean War, and Vietnam War buried here.

St. George's Antiochian Orthodox Church began with the arrival of Syrian immigrants to Carnegie who then moved their church to Bridgeville, first occupying a small building on McLaughlin Run Road for about 25 years and then moving to the church's present spot at 610 Dewey Avenue on land purchased in 1940 from Dr. Clarence McMillen. Because of World War II, the church was not finished and dedicated until 1950. The church's cemetery, however, is located in South Fayette Township at 3093 Washington Pike, next to St. Agatha Cemetery and up the road from Melrose Cemetery. The 13 acres were purchased by Murray Toney and Abe Monsour for around $800; a large section of the land was used for years to host the church's Fourth of July three-day picnic. The church is in the midst of a major fundraising campaign to move its building from Bridgeville to the former picnic grounds next to the cemetery. (Courtesy of Linda James.)

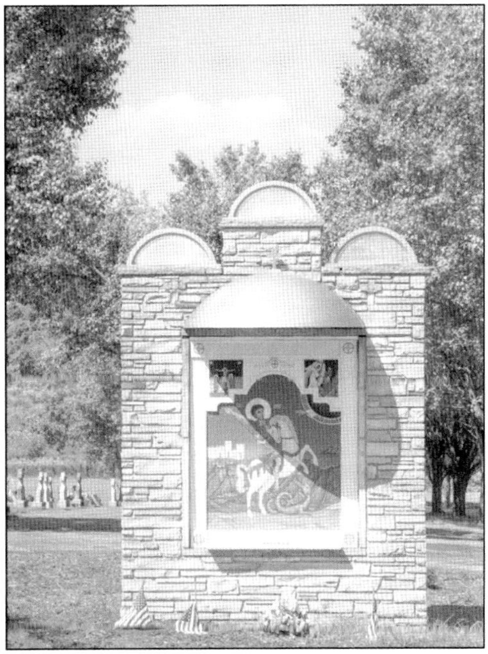

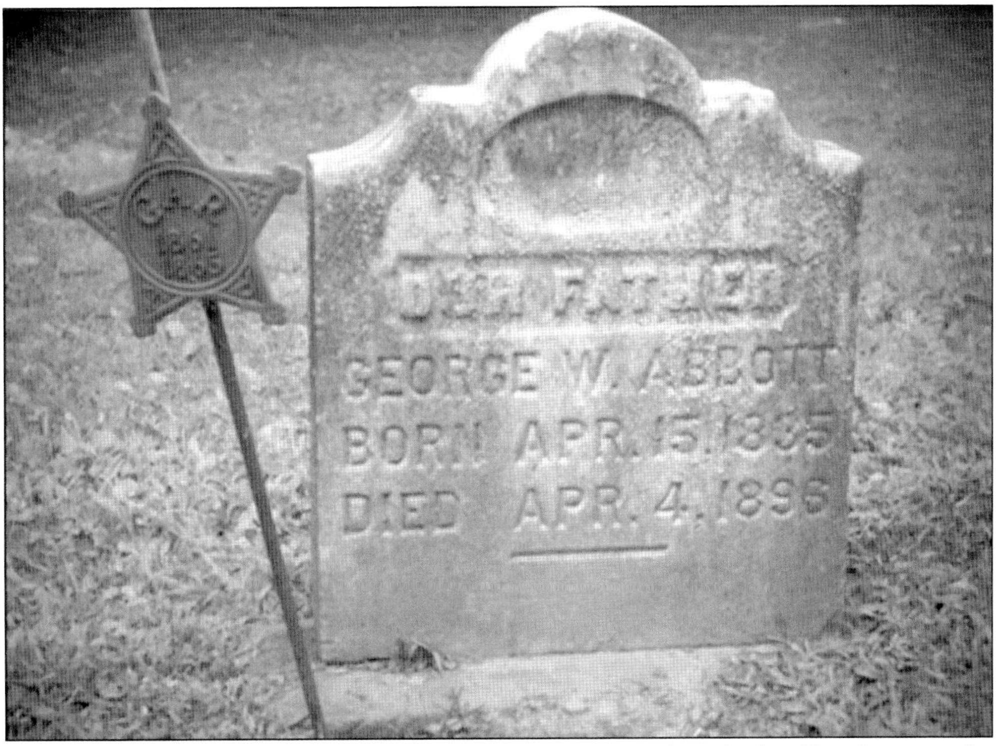

The small Fawcett Methodist Cemetery, next to Fawcett United Methodist Church, sits on the border between Washington County and Allegheny County. The cemetery is in Washington County, but the church is in Allegheny County, in South Fayette Township. There are about 45 gravesites, with the last burial in 1949. Family names include Boyce, Lesnett, and Hastings. (Courtesy of Linda James.)

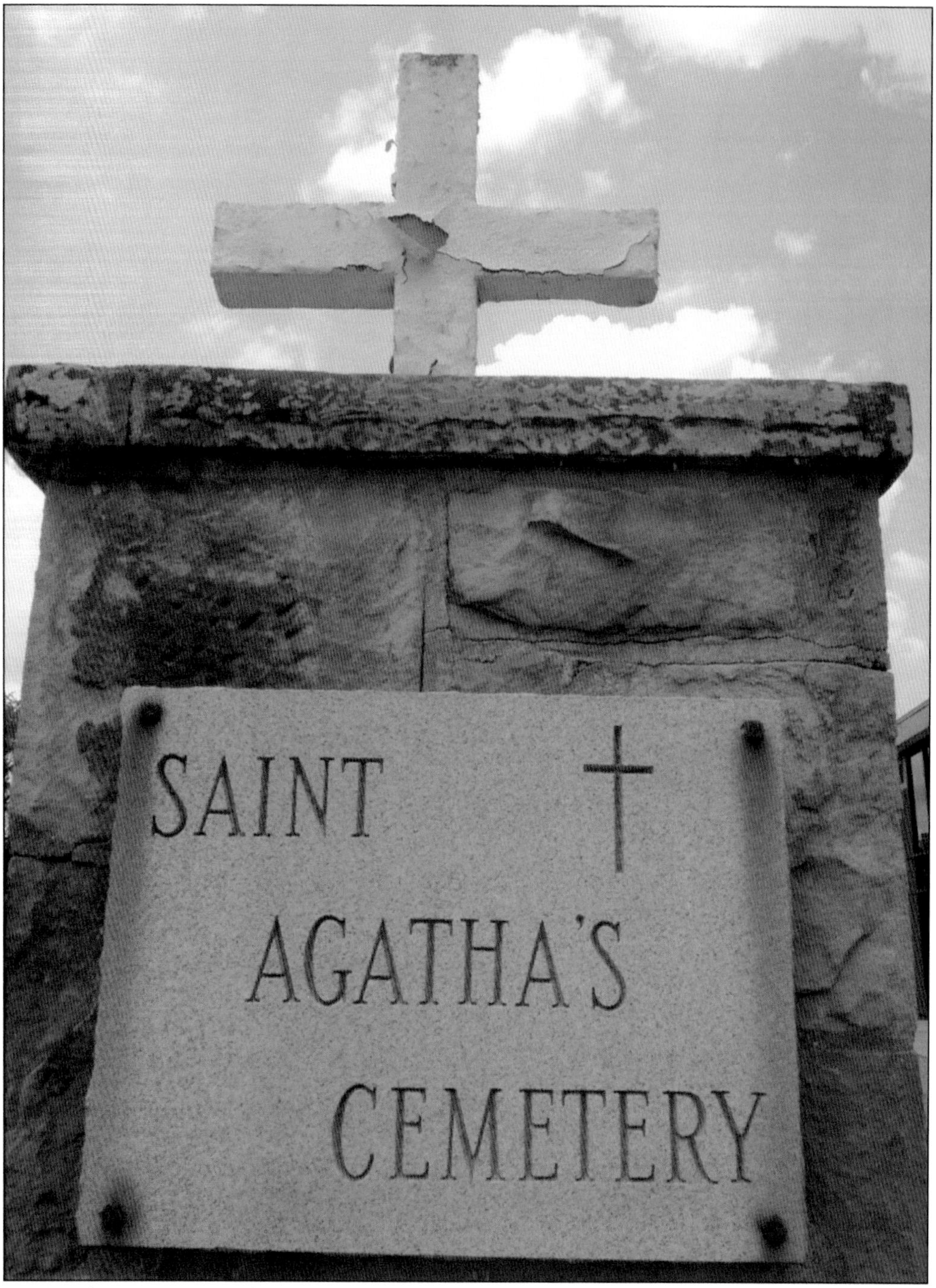

St. Agatha Cemetery is the middle of three cemeteries located on Washington Pike (heading towards Boyce Road and Upper St. Clair, first is Melrose, followed by St. Agatha, and then St. George's). The cemetery also has a mausoleum. It is affiliated with Holy Child Roman Catholic Parish of Bridgeville, the merged parish from St. Agatha Church of Bridgeville and St. Anthony Church of South Fayette Township.

Two

Communities and People

More than 100 years ago, oil wells were being drilled over the township hillsides. Coal mines were flourishing in the Millers Run Valley, with a mine in Sygan, one in Morgan, three in Treveskyn, Maude Mine in northern Gladden, Standard Mine in central Gladden, a mine in Derby, and the big Creedmore Mine in nearby Cecil.

Gladden, named for Thomas Donaldson Gladden, lies in the valley of Millers Run. Composed of three sections, Gladden proper was in the central section, the northern part was called Pump Station, and the southern part was called Derby. The miners' homes were scattered along the valley. The Wabash and the Pennsylvania Railroads serviced the Millers Run Valley, carrying freight and passengers. Miners made their purchases at the company store on Sygan Hill or National Hill. In the early years, Gladden had several outdoor bake ovens for families to use.

Sturgeon was originally settled by Henry Sturgeon, who bought the land warrant in 1800 from his neighbor Judge Hugh Henry Brackenridge. Predominantly farmland, the area was first called Arlington, later Willow Grove. Morgan was named after John Morgan, who had the original land warrant in 1787, later patented by Moses Coulter in 1811. Battle Ridge Road was named for the numerous battles with Indians, tracing its origin back to the French and Indian Wars. The area is rich in natural springs. Mohawk Road was named for the numerous issues between early settlers and Mohawk Indians. Cuddy had three large coal mines. Mules were used to transport coal to the surface. A local stable owner was named Cuddahey, the name was shortened to Cuddy, and the stables were referred to as Cuddy Stables. Some people think this is how the area got its name. The neighboring Treveskyn area has disappeared and been absorbed into Cuddy.

Likewise, Burdine, Herriottsville, Federal, Beechmont, Blythe, and other town names are gone. South Fayette Township currently has the zip codes of Bridgeville, Morgan, Cuddy, McDonald, Sturgeon, Oakdale, and Cecil. To be even more confusing, parts of Bridgeville and Oakdale are in Collier Township; parts of McDonald and Cecil are in Washington County. South Fayette Township does not have a mayor, but it does have a township manager and a board of commissioners, and in the last few decades, various committees, such as parks and recreation, have been formed to determine the township's destiny.

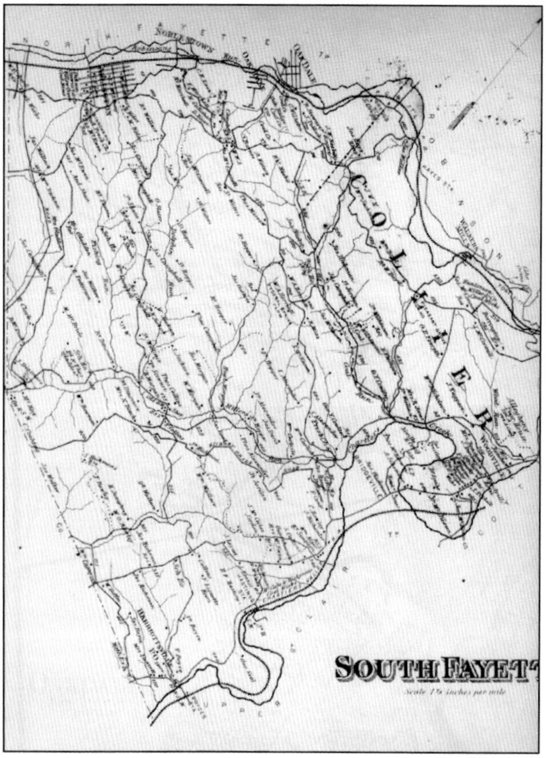

Pictured from the 1878 *Atlas of the County of Allegheny, Pennsylvania* are the land warrants of South Fayette Township.

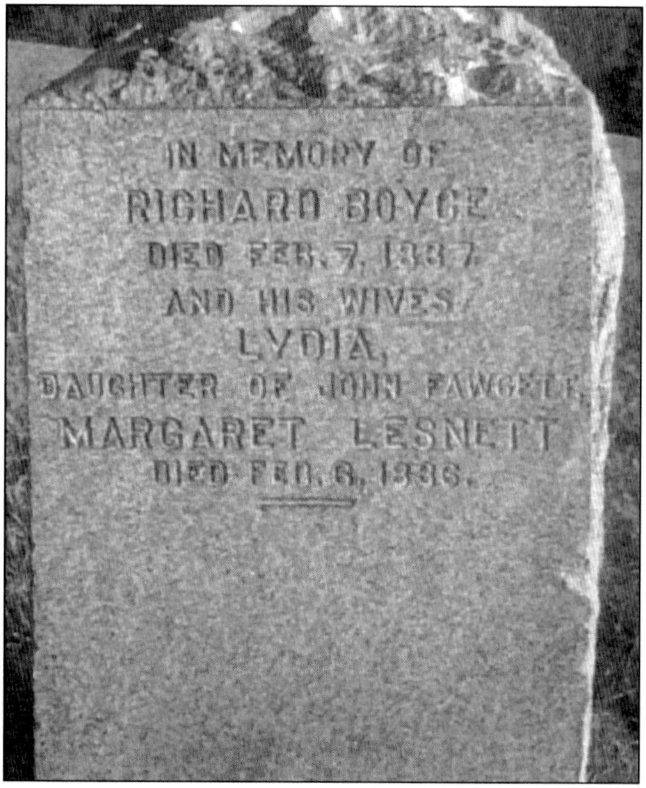

Richard Boyce, born in Ireland, came to America in 1756, married Lydia Fawcett in 1769, and moved to South Fayette Township in 1772 to an area claimed by both Virginia and Pennsylvania. By 1780, he had a Pennsylvania warrant for 377 acres he named "Content" and built his first log home at the intersection of today's Boyce and Mayview Roads. After Lydia's death in 1787, he married Margaret "Peggy" Lesnett, the daughter of another original settler. Richard served in the Pennsylvania militia during the Revolutionary War. His son Christian built wagons under government contract during the War of 1812, and numerous grandsons served in the 1st Pennsylvania Cavalry during the Civil War. Pictured is Richard Boyce's gravestone in the Morgan family farm cemetery.

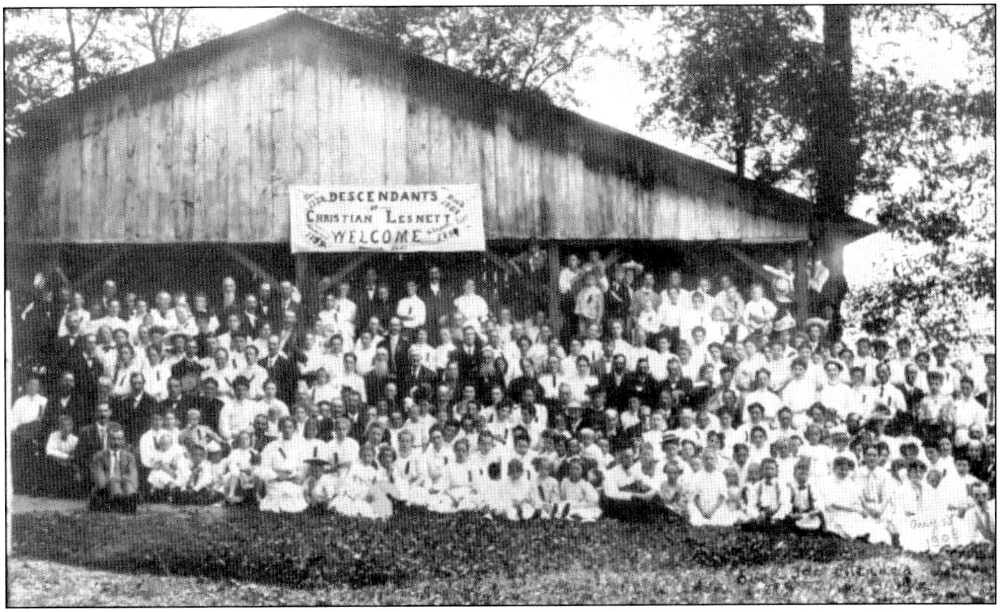

The descendants of Christian Lesnett have gathered for a reunion on August 24, 1909.

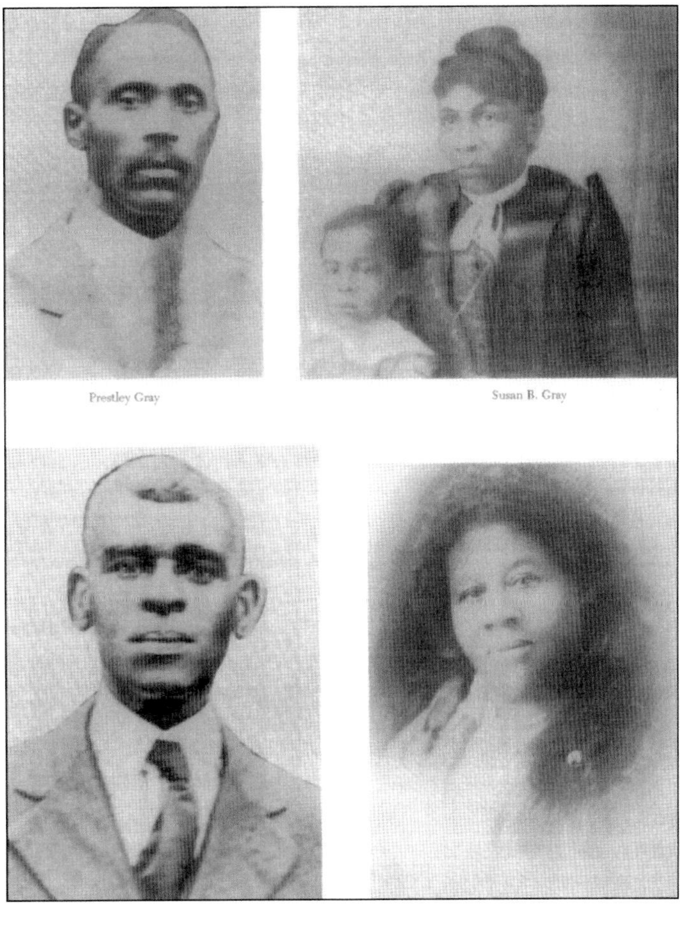

In the spring of 1886, a group of friends met at the home of W.B. Gray, located in the Willow Grove section of Sturgeon, and organized the First Baptist Church of McDonald. The Gray and Bennett families are four of the 13 original founders of the church. The church was built by architect Ballard Henderson of Sturgeon. Decades later, the Jewett Hayes family members, direct descendants of the Grays and Bennetts, moved to Sturgeon.

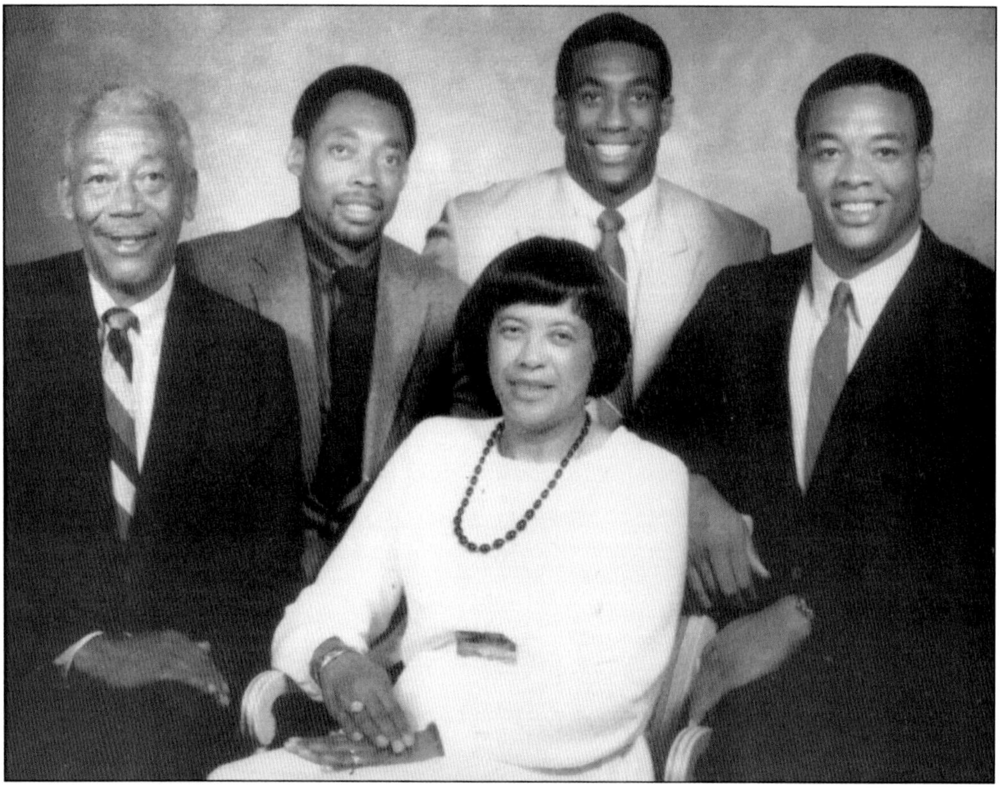

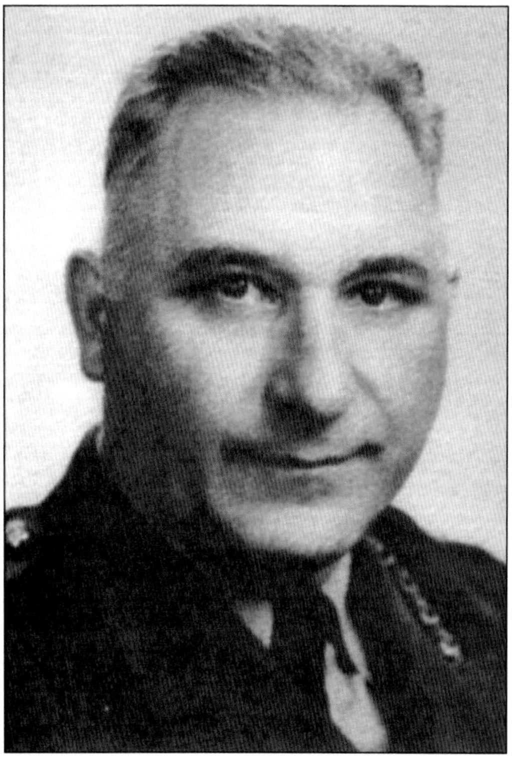

Jewett and Florence Joy Hayes came to Sturgeon in 1959. Their son Jeffrey coached South Fayette Junior High basketball. Sons Jay and Jonathan currently are both assistant coaches with the National Football League (NFL) Cincinnati Bengals. Jonathan also published a book, titled *Necessary Toughness*, about his diabetes. Joy was cochairperson of the Friends of the South Fayette Township Library. Jewett was the first chairman of the township's parks and recreation board. Pictured are (seated) Florence and (standing, from left to right), Jewett, Jeffrey, Jay, and Jonathan.

Henry Bourg Jr. was the township's first police officer. Born in Cuddy in 1898, he married Anna Saussol, and they had 11 children. He also helped start the South Fayette Volunteer Fire Department in 1937, becoming its first president. He went on to become the township's constable. He died in 1961 while at the polls on Election Day. Despite dying, he still received enough votes to win reelection as constable.

From left to right, Sam Migliorini, Armel Kelly, and Blackie Diorio, comprising the first South Fayette Township Police Department, stand proudly before their squad car in 1951.

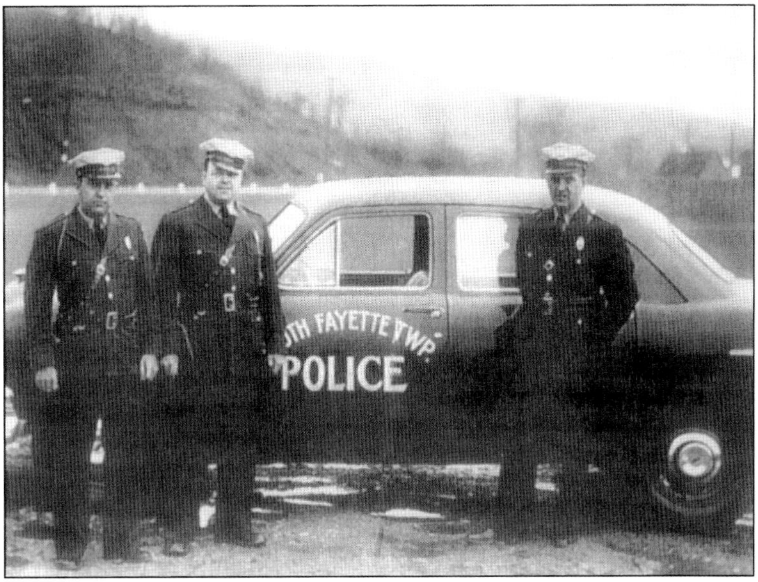

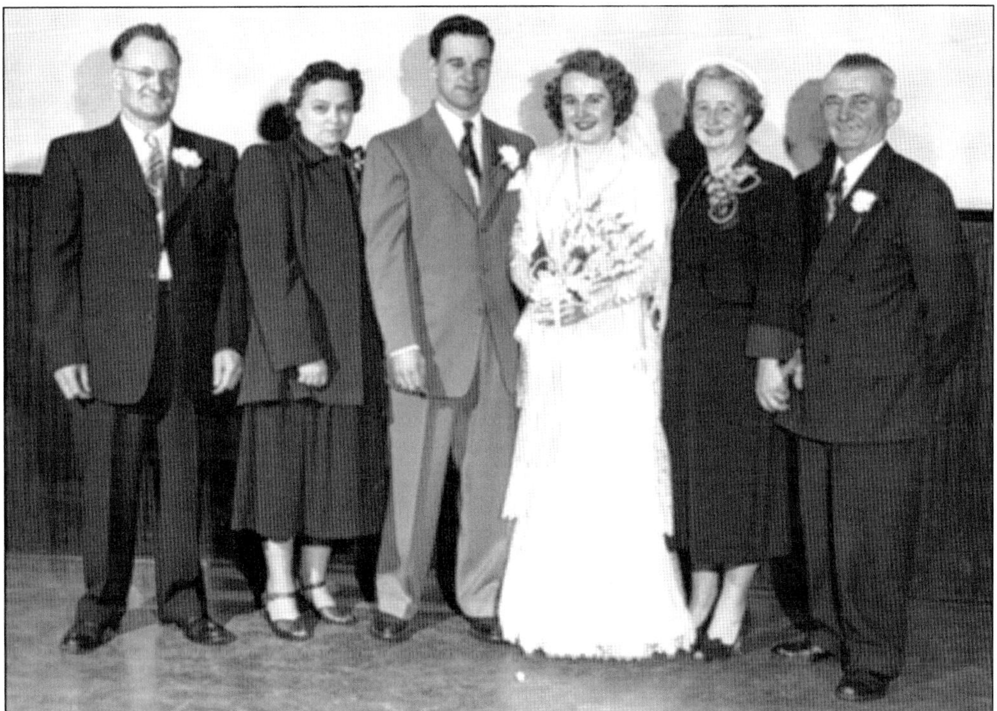

On July 4, 1926, Gaston and Helen Rank opened a confectionery and grocery store on Main Street, Sturgeon, at the site of today's Hunner's Deli. The Ranks are pictured on the left at the wedding of their son Robert and his bride, Kay Taucher. Gaston was a 25-year member of the school district authority, which oversaw school construction, and was president of the Sturgeon Volunteer Fire Department for 20 years. The fire siren sat atop his store until it was moved behind the newly built Sturgeon station. Robert was an executive with Metropolitan Life Insurance and is a retired member of the Oak Ridge Volunteer Fire Department. They also had a daughter, Florence, and another son, Kenneth, who became principal of South Fayette Elementary.

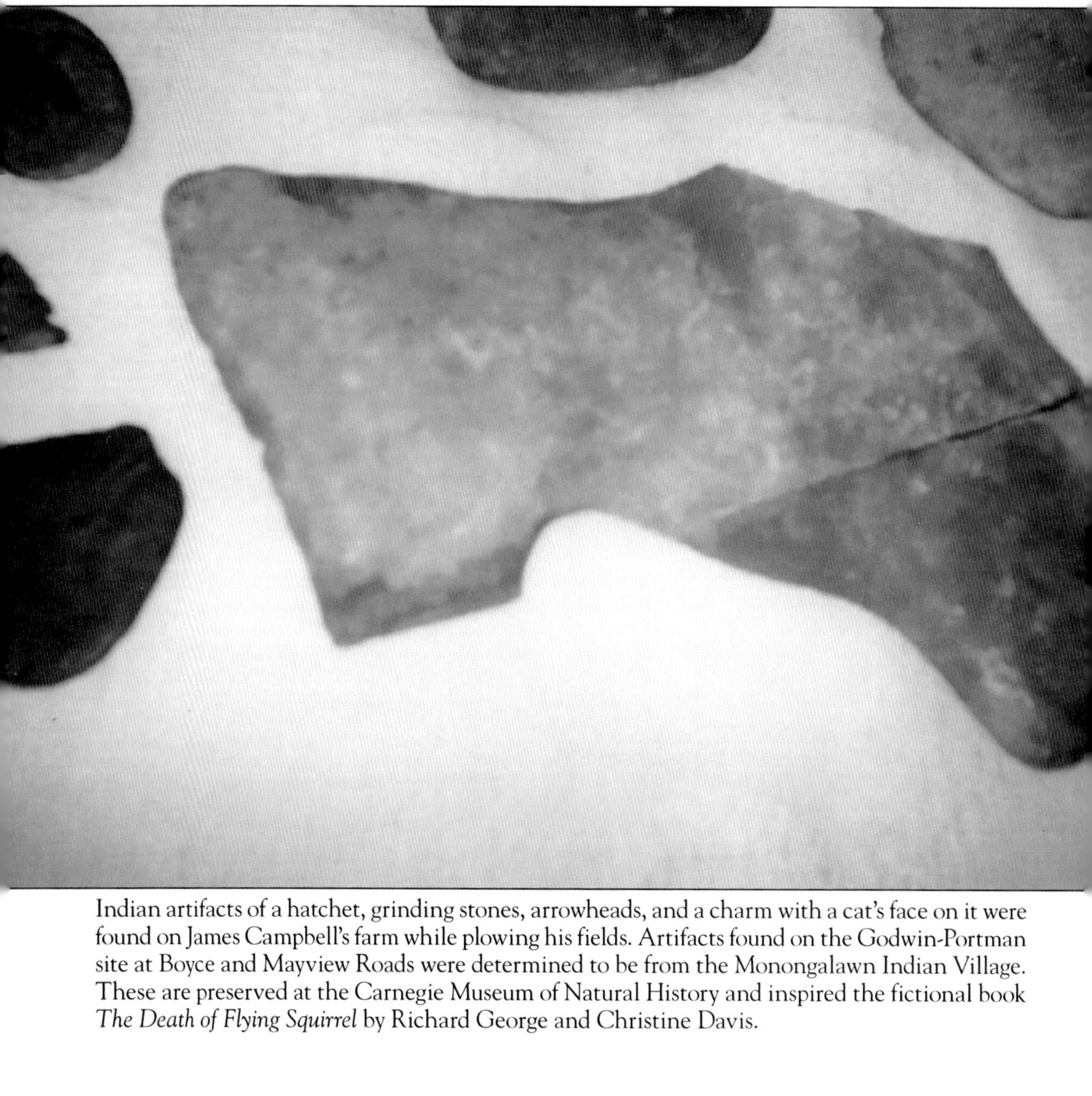

Indian artifacts of a hatchet, grinding stones, arrowheads, and a charm with a cat's face on it were found on James Campbell's farm while plowing his fields. Artifacts found on the Godwin-Portman site at Boyce and Mayview Roads were determined to be from the Monongalawn Indian Village. These are preserved at the Carnegie Museum of Natural History and inspired the fictional book *The Death of Flying Squirrel* by Richard George and Christine Davis.

Michael Matesia and Mari (or Mary) Bonic came to Mohawk Road from Austria in 1902. By 1930, they had 12 children; their house had two bedrooms. The parents slept in one, and all 12 children slept in the other—boys in one bed and girls in the other. Their original name was Matesic, but the boys changed the last letter to *a*, as it sounds more American with it. Pictured are Mildred, Michael, and Mary "Baba" Matesia.

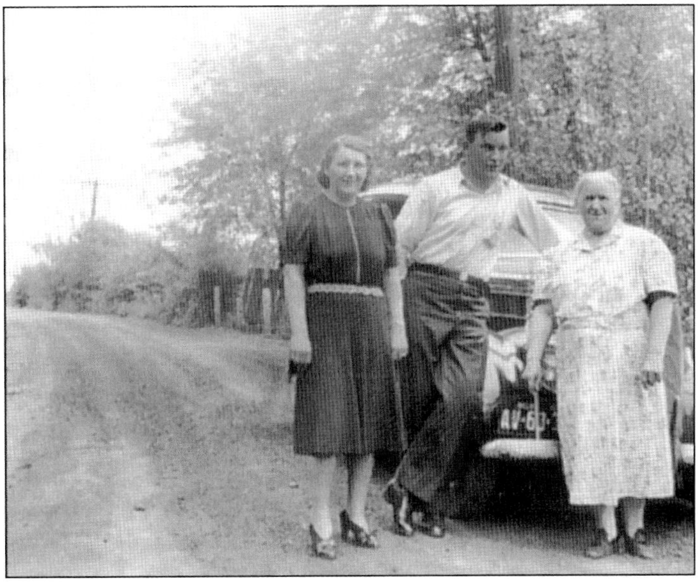

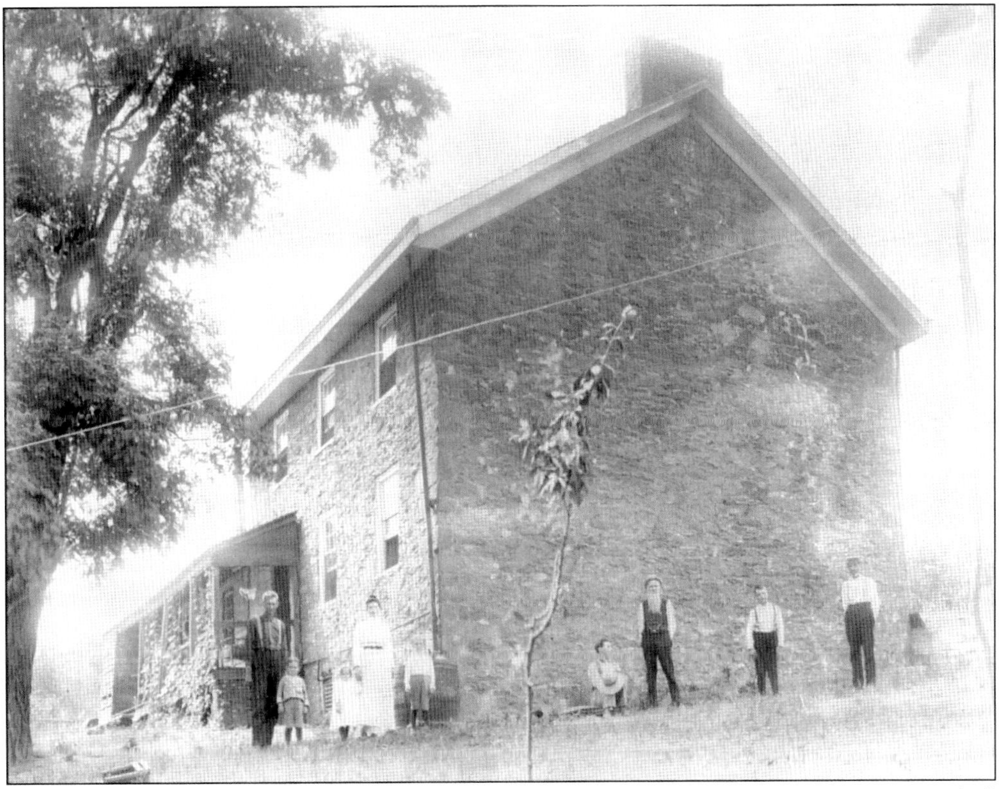

Pictured are, from left to right, T.A. Campbell, son James E. Campbell, daughter Mary Campbell Hastings, Eva McKnight Campbell, and daughter Jessie Campbell Freed in front of the Dunlevy-Campbell House built in 1814 by David and Ida Dunlevy. James married Grace Freed who had one daughter, Marion Campbell Grafe. James was a dairy farmer who shipped milk to Bridgeville Dairy. He also raised tomatoes that were shipped to the Heinz Plant in Pittsburgh to be made into ketchup.

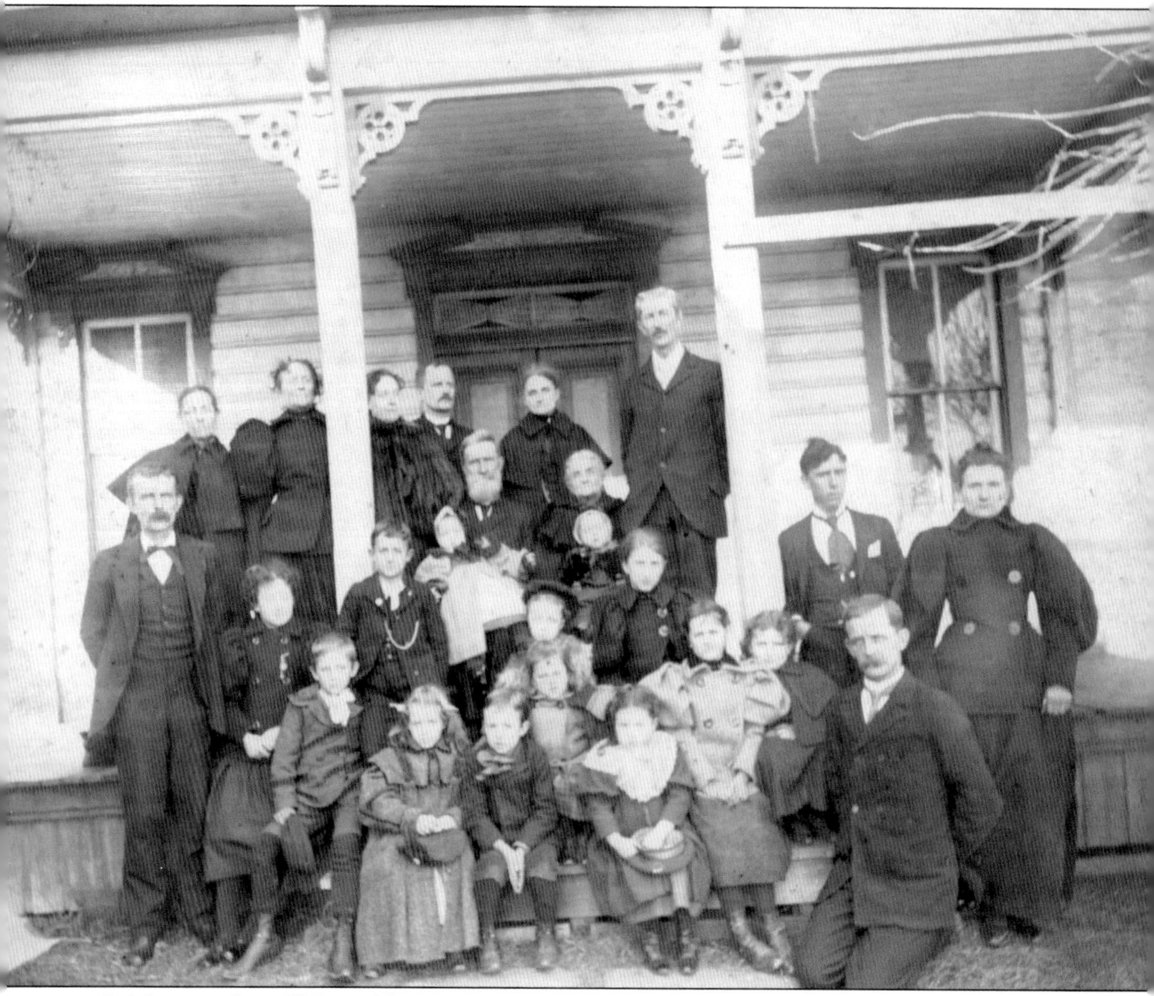

Celebrating their 50th wedding anniversary in 1898, the children and grandchildren of Joseph and Sara Jane (Young) Boyce gathered at the house. Those pictured include Margaret Boyce (Wright), Thomas Boyce, Helen Boyce, Nella Freed, and William F. Boyce; William B. Freed, Grace Freed (Campbell), and Bernie Boyce (Lamberton); Anita Boyce (Billman), Joseph Boyce, grandfather Joseph, holding Dorothy Boyce (Tope), grandmother Sara Jane, holding Ruth Boyce (Allen), Preston Kittering, and May Kittering (Smiley); Caroline Boyce, Rebecca Young, Annie Boyce, Isaac Boyce, Anna Boyce Freed, and John Freed.

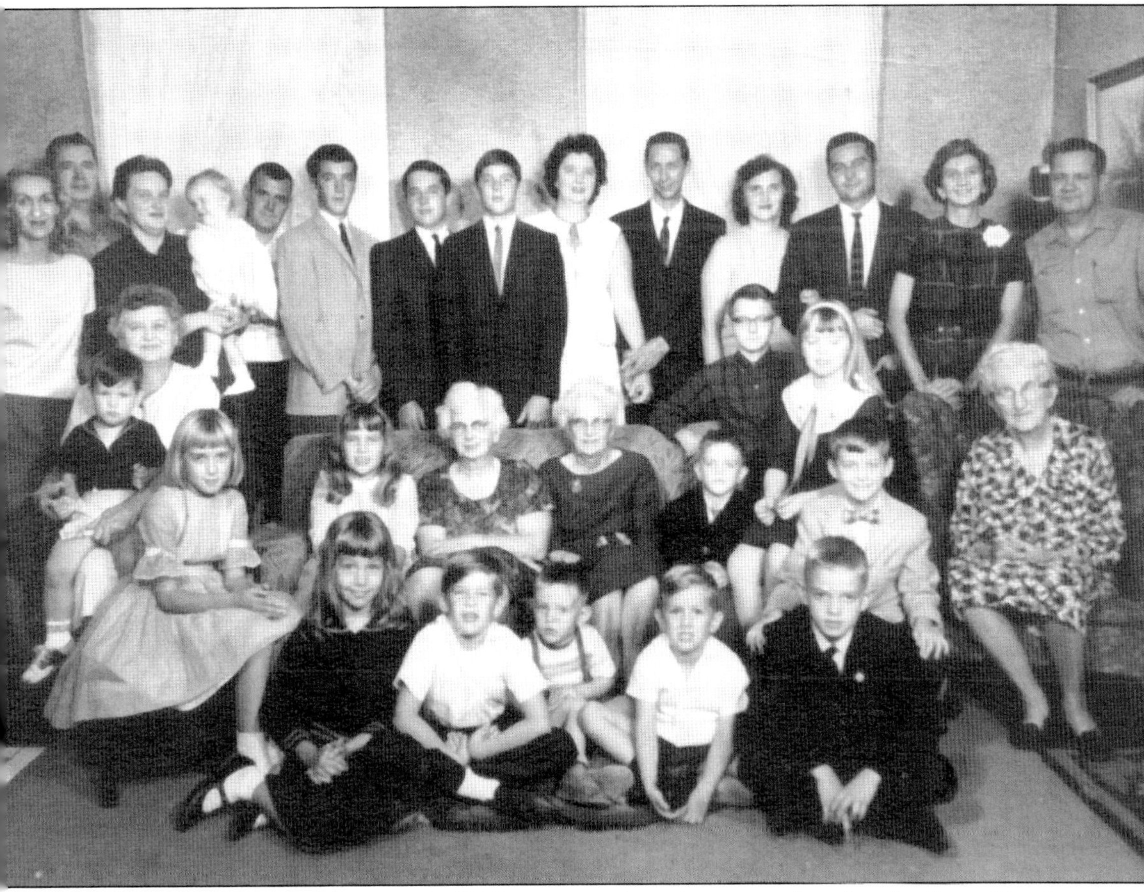

The Freed family held a reunion in 1965. This picture shows how many founding families of South Fayette had intermarried and remained within the township. Those gathered are, from left to right, (first row) Suellen Paxton, Timothy Paxton, Michael White, William Paxton, and David White; (second row) Edward Schweitzer, Jessie Campbell Freed, Jessie Ann Schweitzer, Alice Ann Paxton, Marion Freed McCracken, Grace Freed Campbell, Boyce White, Glen Hagan Jr., Marion Jean White, William C. Schweitzer, and Alice Freed; (third row) Mary Alice Freed Hagan, Glen Hagan, Diane McCracken White, Bonnie Jean White, Floyd White, George Paxton Jr., John Paxton, Jim Paxton, Gail Freed Schweitzer, William Schweitzer, Bonnie Jean McCracken Paxton, Marion Campbell Grafe, and Davis G. Grafe.

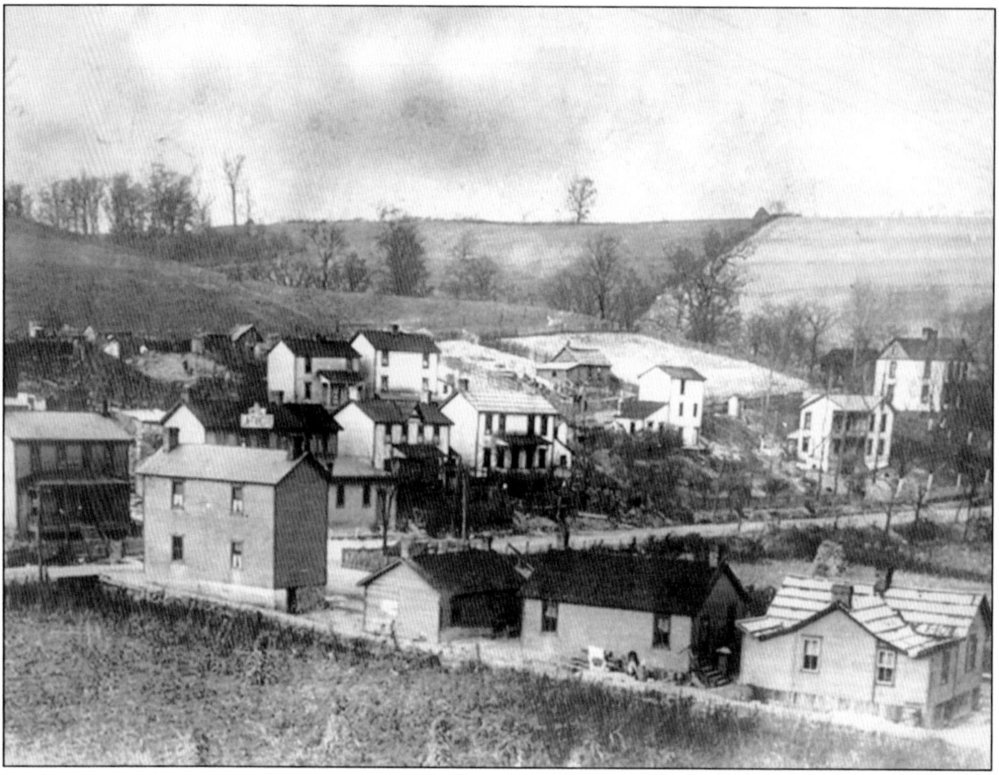

In the 1920s, these were the houses in Gladden. The farm in the background was the Gladden Farm, owned by Thomas Gladden, from which the community gets its name. A few of these houses are still residences today. Albert Packing Company, a meatpacking company currently operating in Taylorstown, Pennsylvania, owned the buildings in the foreground.

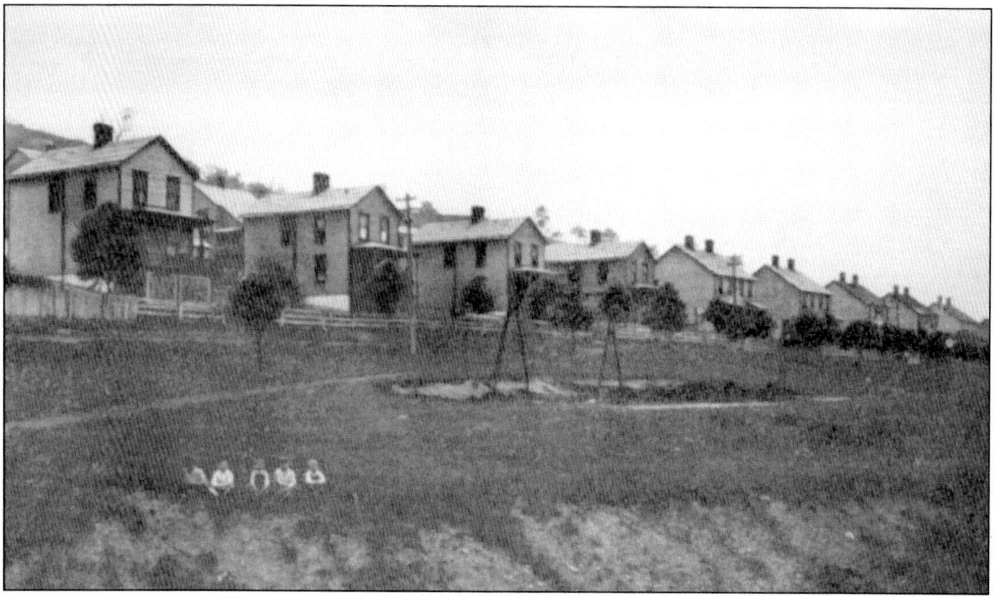

A group of young children sits near the local neighborhood playground along Wabash Avenue, Morgan. Most families living in this area worked at the National No. 1 Mine.

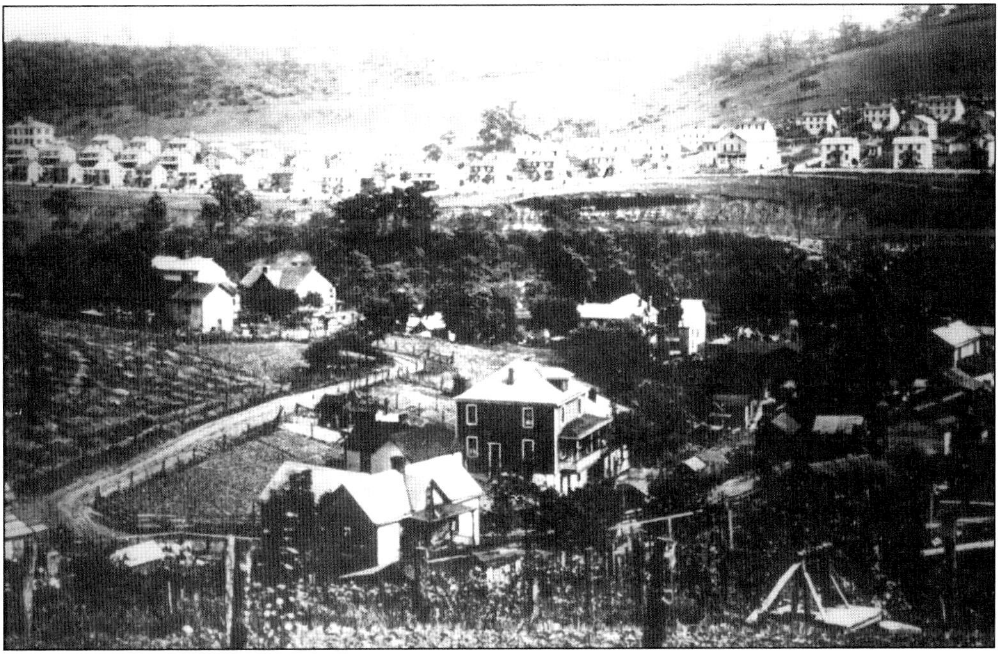

This is a 1920s view from Old Oakdale Road, McDonald. Valley Forest Road is on the left, and National Hill is in the background. National Hill School is visible in the far left. The very last row of homes was demolished in the early 1970s when present-day Route 50 was built.

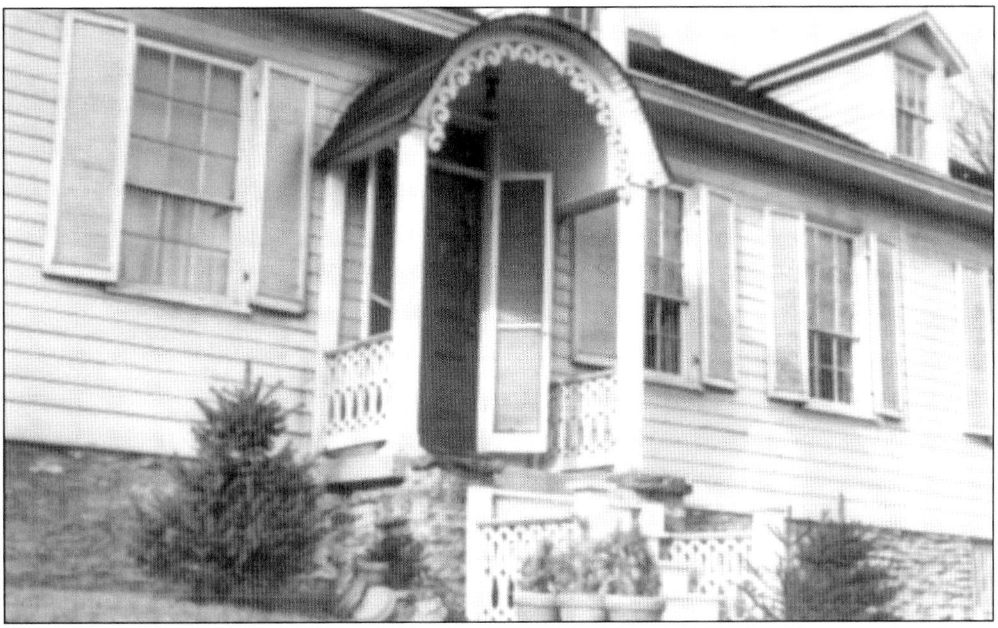

The McClane home, at 698 Millers Run Road, was built in 1796. During this era, the Huron Indians kidnapped two young girls from this home and took them to northern Michigan. Two years later, the girls escaped and returned to the area. Mac McClane purchased the home in the early 1900s. He was the owner of the Katie, Blythe, and Maude Mines in the area. He named the mines after each of his daughters. The home has maintained its original charm and has residents to this day.

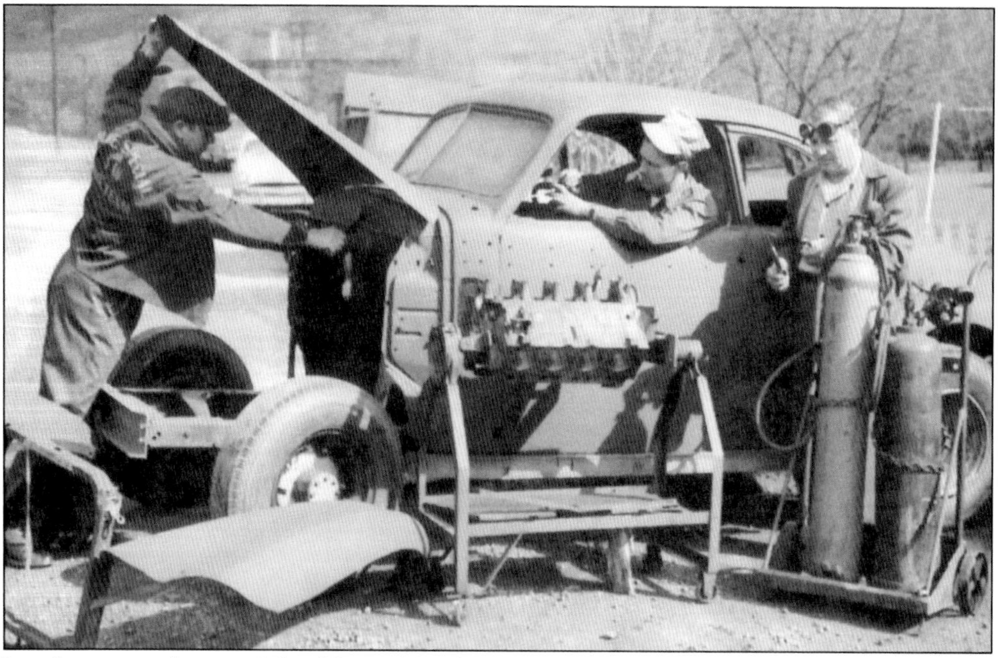

Local racing enthusiasts John "Ginger" Luck is preparing to install an engine as Gene Celento makes modifications. Charles Campbell Jr. is sitting inside the racing car, "The Maude Special." This photograph, taken in 1950, was on Maude Mine Road, next to the Maude Mine Garage. Today, Bell Container Company is across the street from Maude Mine Road.

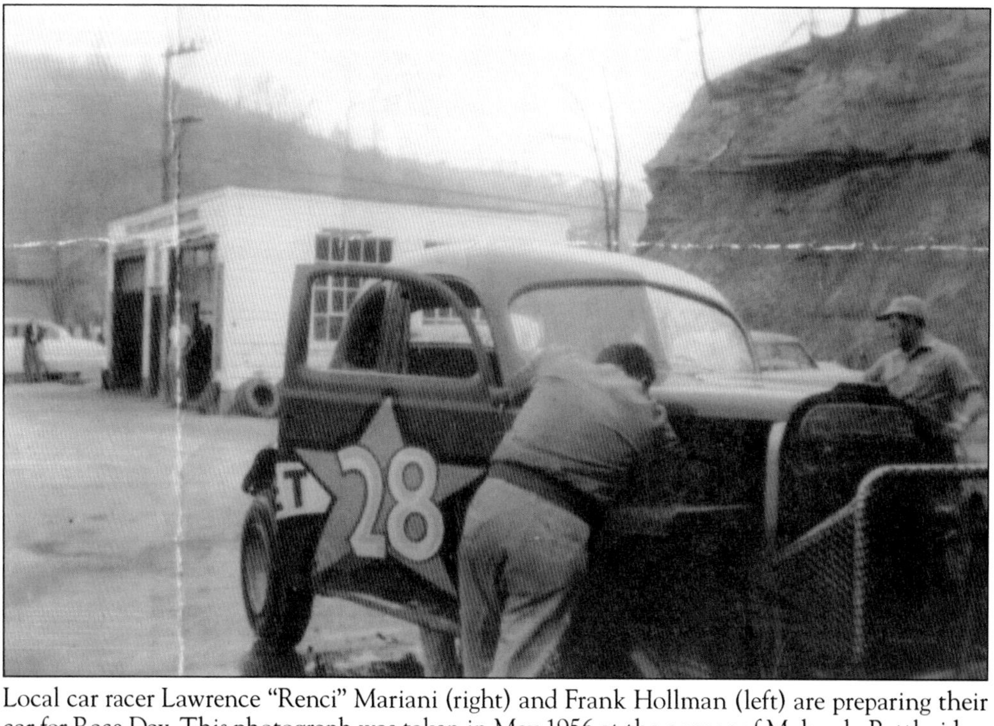

Local car racer Lawrence "Renci" Mariani (right) and Frank Hollman (left) are preparing their car for Race Day. This photograph was taken in May 1956 at the corner of Mohawk, Battleridge, and Millers Run Roads.

The race team of "The Maude Special" is taking a break; members are, from left to right, (kneeling) Rusty Whiteman; (second row) Marshall Mariani, Chuck Campbell Jr., John "Ginger" Luck, Gene Celento, and Rusty Slovick.

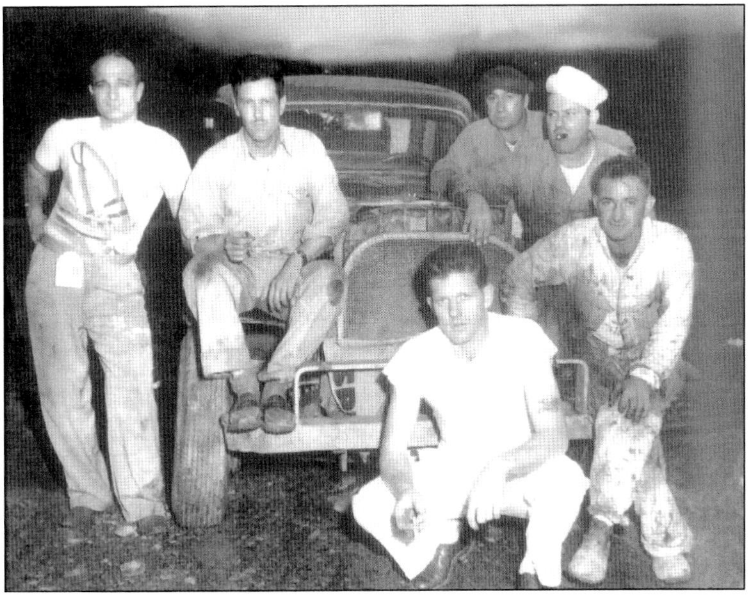

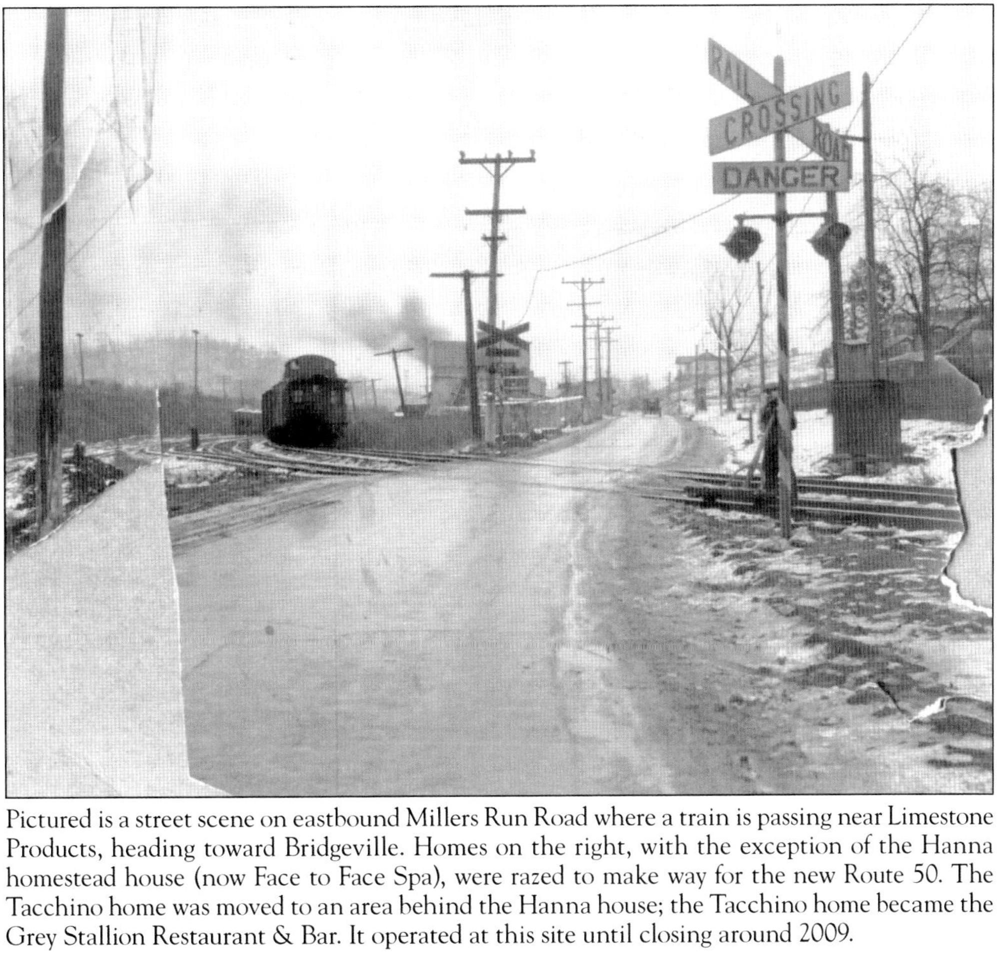

Pictured is a street scene on eastbound Millers Run Road where a train is passing near Limestone Products, heading toward Bridgeville. Homes on the right, with the exception of the Hanna homestead house (now Face to Face Spa), were razed to make way for the new Route 50. The Tacchino home was moved to an area behind the Hanna house; the Tacchino home became the Grey Stallion Restaurant & Bar. It operated at this site until closing around 2009.

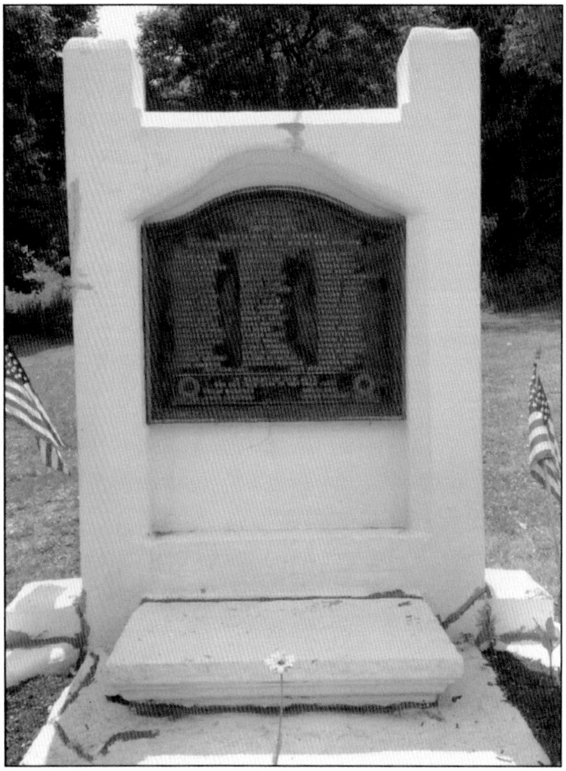

This is the war monument at the edge of Dutch Hill and Thoms Run Roads; it is dedicated to local World War I veterans.

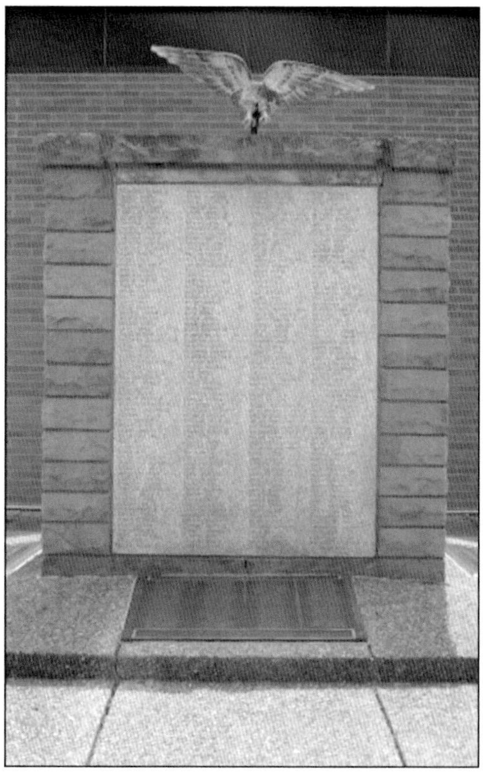

The monument at the South Fayette Fire Department in Cuddy is four-sided and dedicated to those who fought in World Wars I and II, the Korean War, and the Vietnam War. (Courtesy of Linda James.)

The monument at Gladden United Presbyterian Church is dedicated to those who served in the armed forces during World Wars I and II.

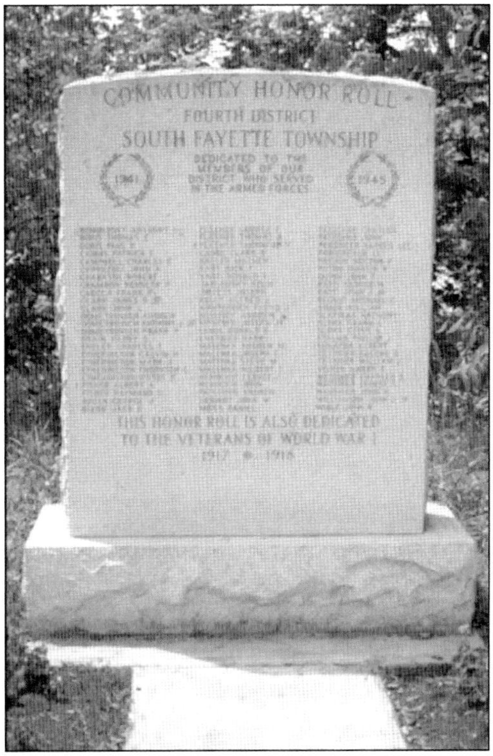

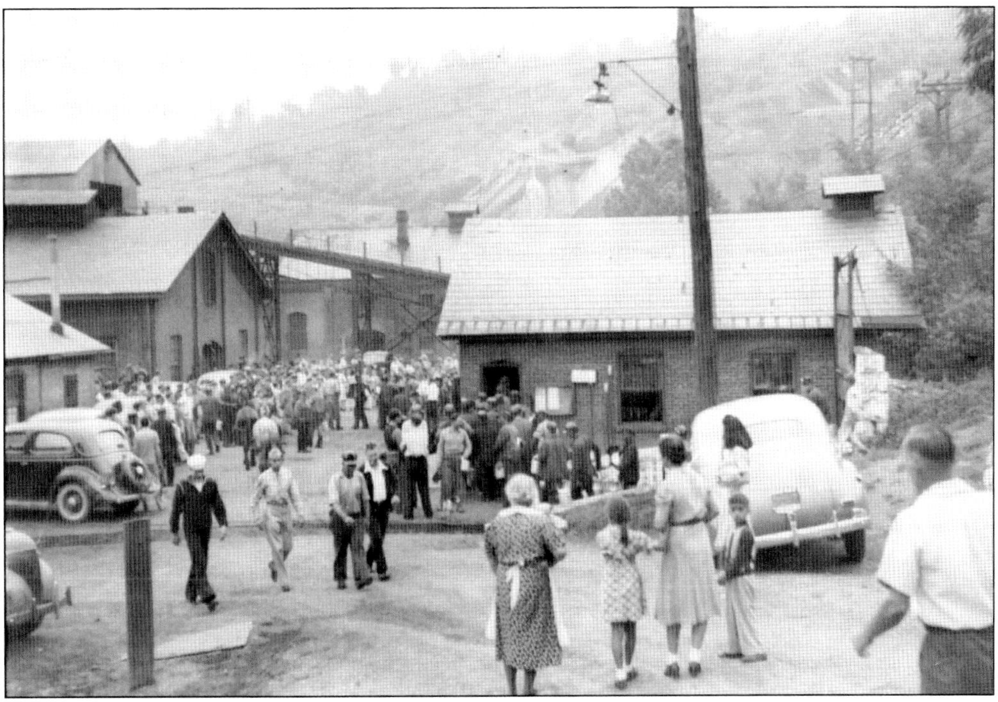

This photograph was taken on VE (Victory in Europe) Day on May 8, 1945, at the National No. 1 Mine in Morgan. Miners and local residents have gathered to celebrate. Today, storage units and office buildings occupy this site off Wabash Street, Morgan.

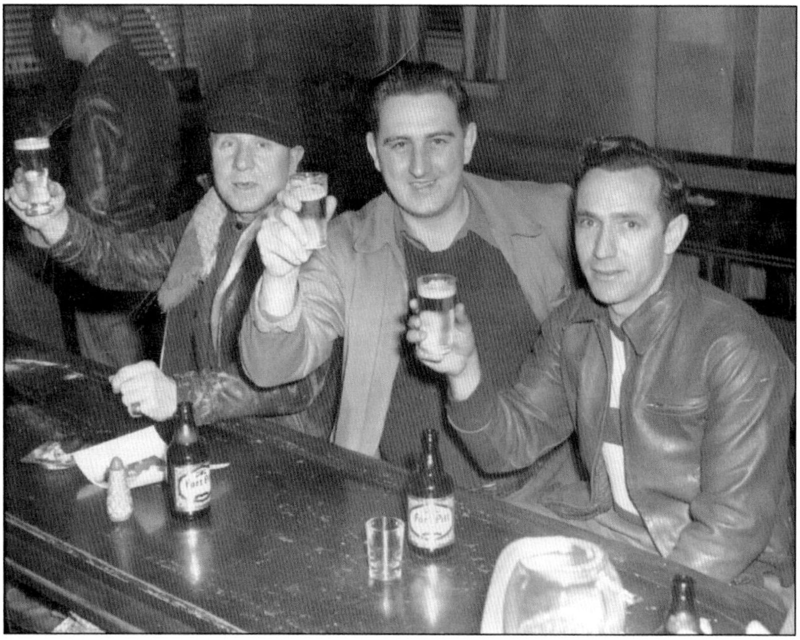

From left to right, Lou Mitchell, Bill Sekel, and Fred Mannering are seen visiting Doc's Café in Morgan.

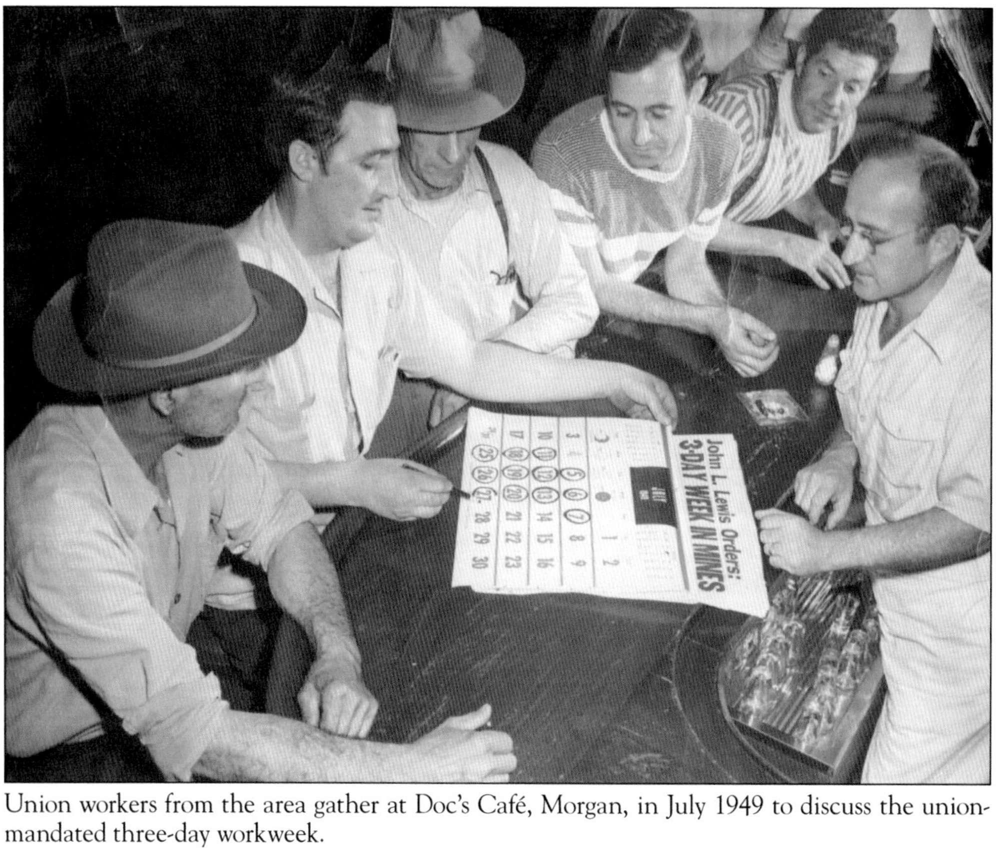

Union workers from the area gather at Doc's Café, Morgan, in July 1949 to discuss the union-mandated three-day workweek.

Charles E. Campbell Sr. was a prominent businessman and resident of South Fayette. He owned and operated the former Maude Mine and many other businesses in the coal, oil, and gas industries.

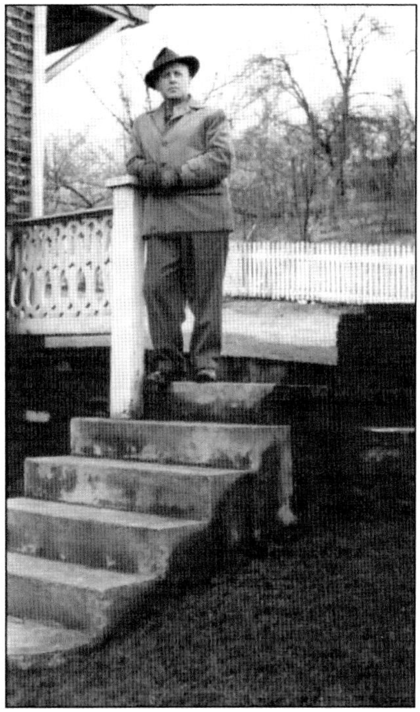

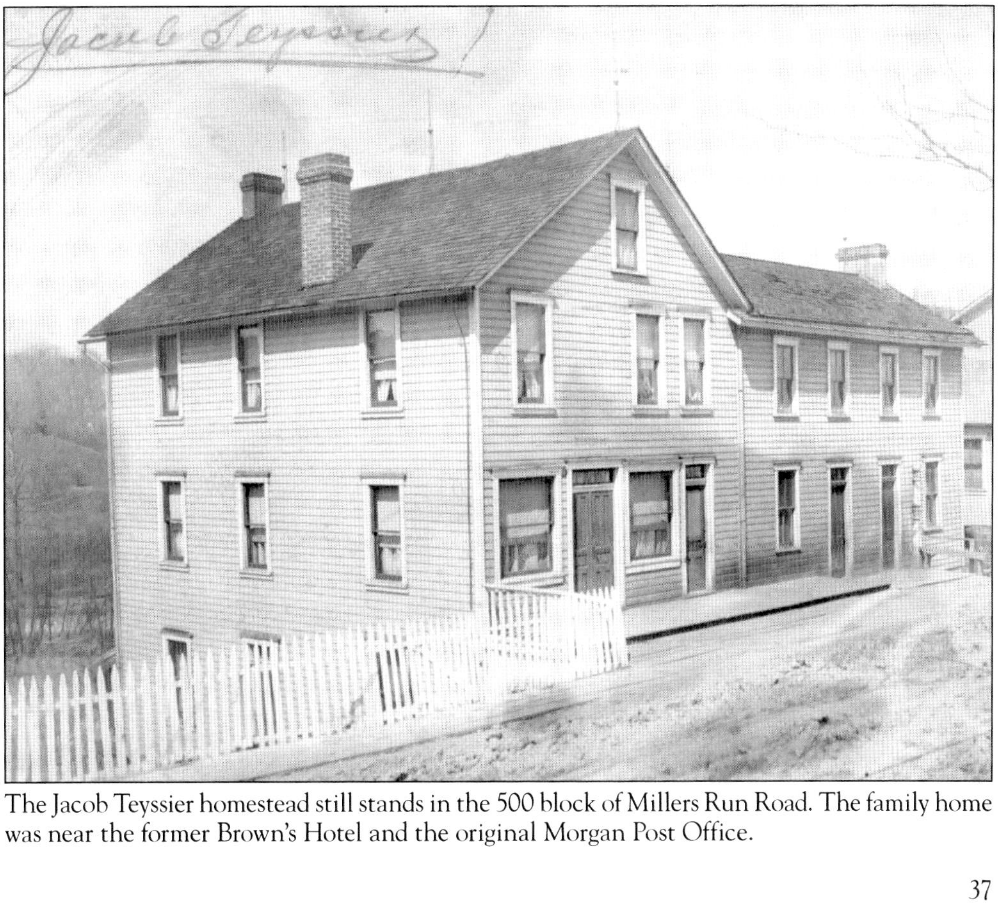

The Jacob Teyssier homestead still stands in the 500 block of Millers Run Road. The family home was near the former Brown's Hotel and the original Morgan Post Office.

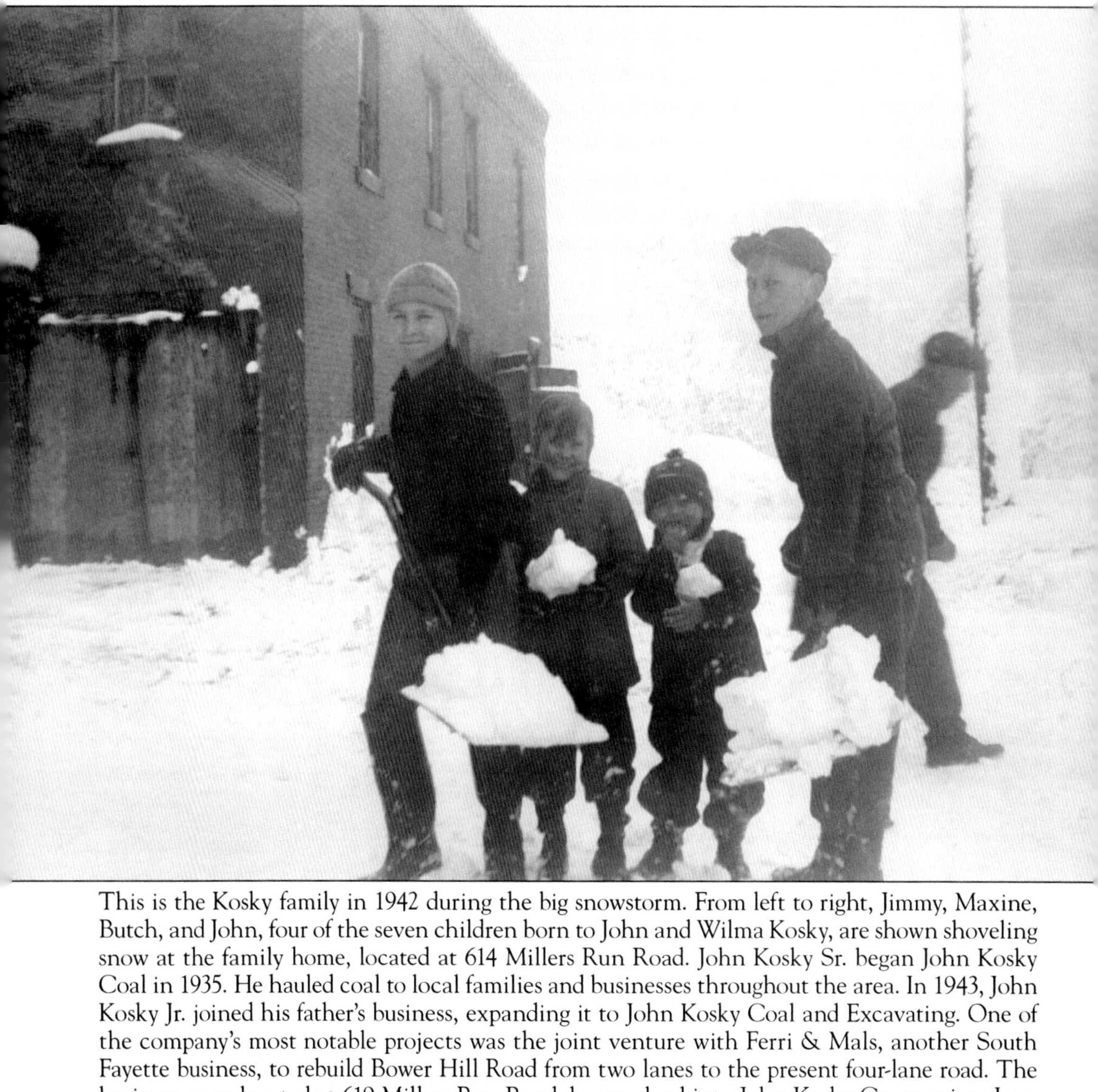

This is the Kosky family in 1942 during the big snowstorm. From left to right, Jimmy, Maxine, Butch, and John, four of the seven children born to John and Wilma Kosky, are shown shoveling snow at the family home, located at 614 Millers Run Road. John Kosky Sr. began John Kosky Coal in 1935. He hauled coal to local families and businesses throughout the area. In 1943, John Kosky Jr. joined his father's business, expanding it to John Kosky Coal and Excavating. One of the company's most notable projects was the joint venture with Ferri & Mals, another South Fayette business, to rebuild Bower Hill Road from two lanes to the present four-lane road. The business, now located at 619 Millers Run Road, has evolved into John Kosky Contracting, Inc., with third-generation John Alan Kosky as president.

This picture of Honey Verish, dressed for her high school graduation in 1939, was taken in the yard of the Quarture family, located behind the Quarture's store. The yard was beautifully landscaped, and many local residents would take photographs of special occasions in this large green space.

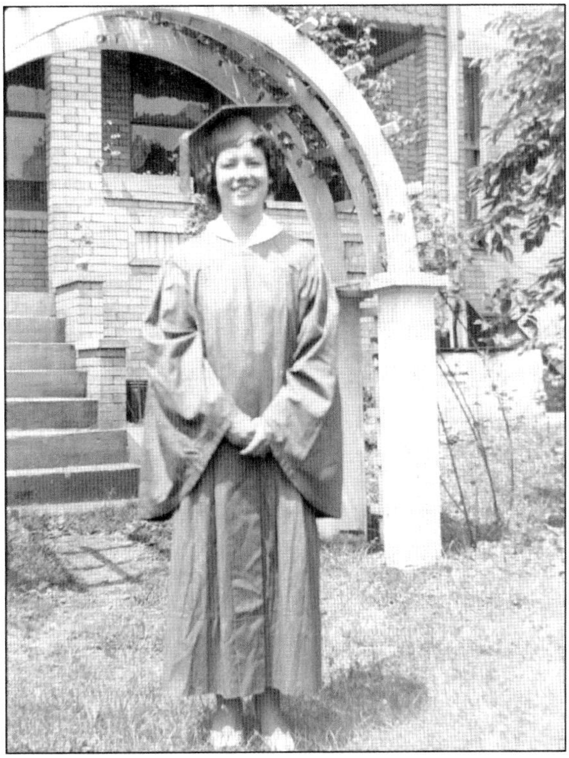

Pictured is Anthony "Doc" Casciola; he opened Doc's Café Dinner-Dance establishment on Millers Run Road in 1946. Doc also coached and managed the Pittsburgh Indians, a local soccer team that won numerous titles.

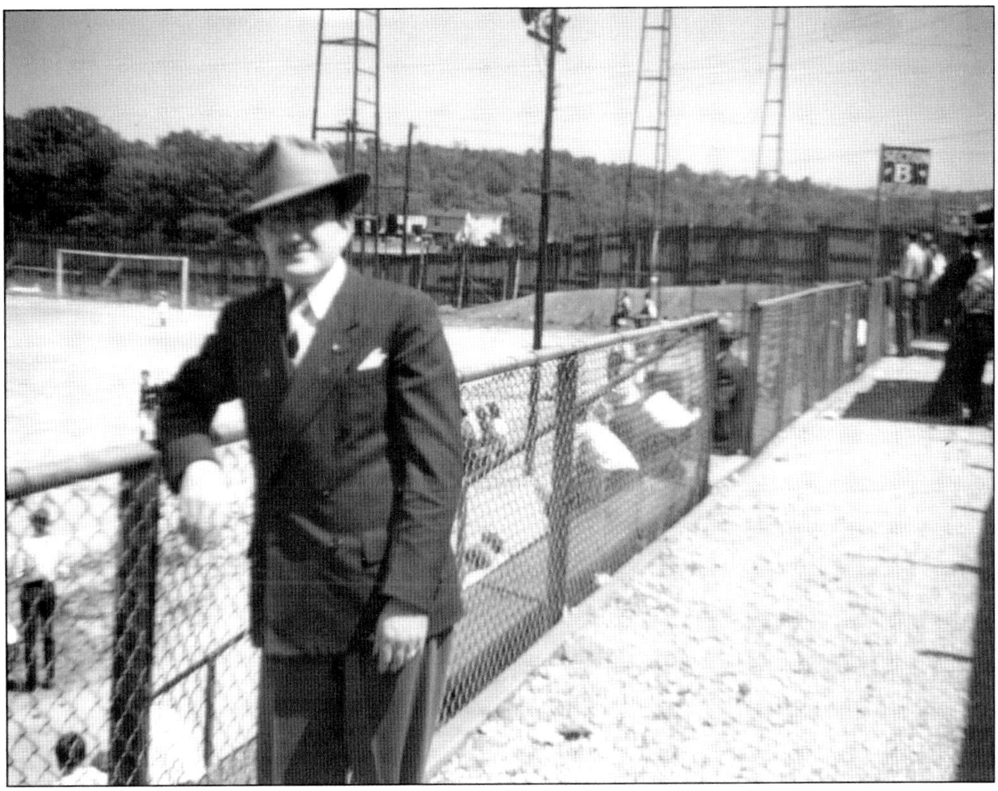

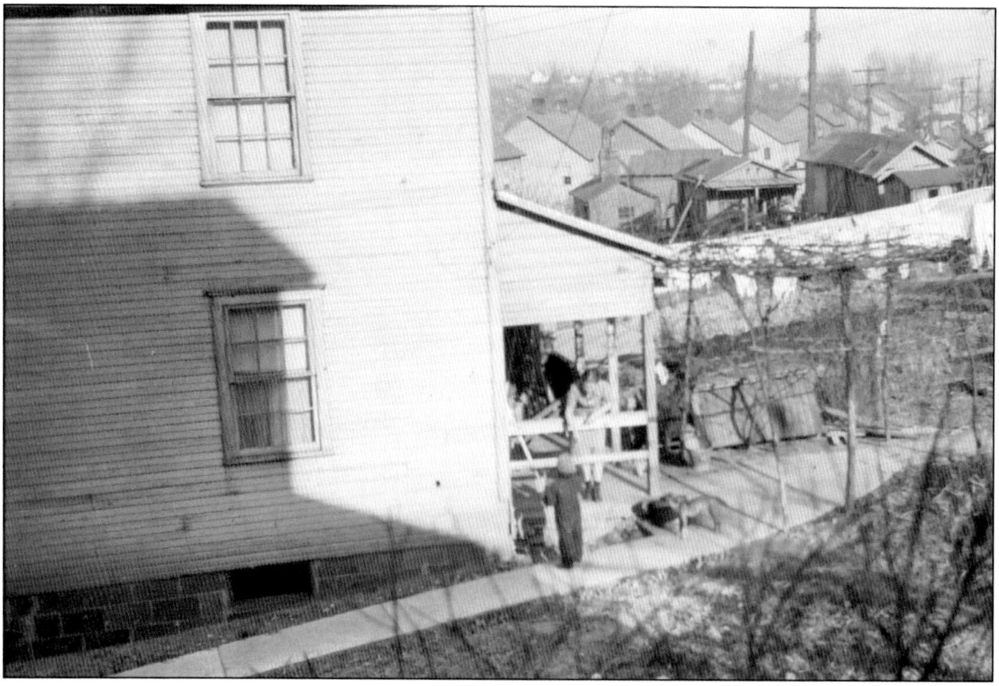

Pictured on wash day is a typical house in the Morgan Blocks, which had been built to house the workers at the National No. 1 Mine. Sygan Hill is in the foreground. In this picture, Rose Simone is giving a cookie to Gene Casciola. Gene grew up to play saxophone with the Bobby Vinton Orchestra, lead his own band, and be inducted into the National Cleveland-Style Polka Hall of Fame in 1999.

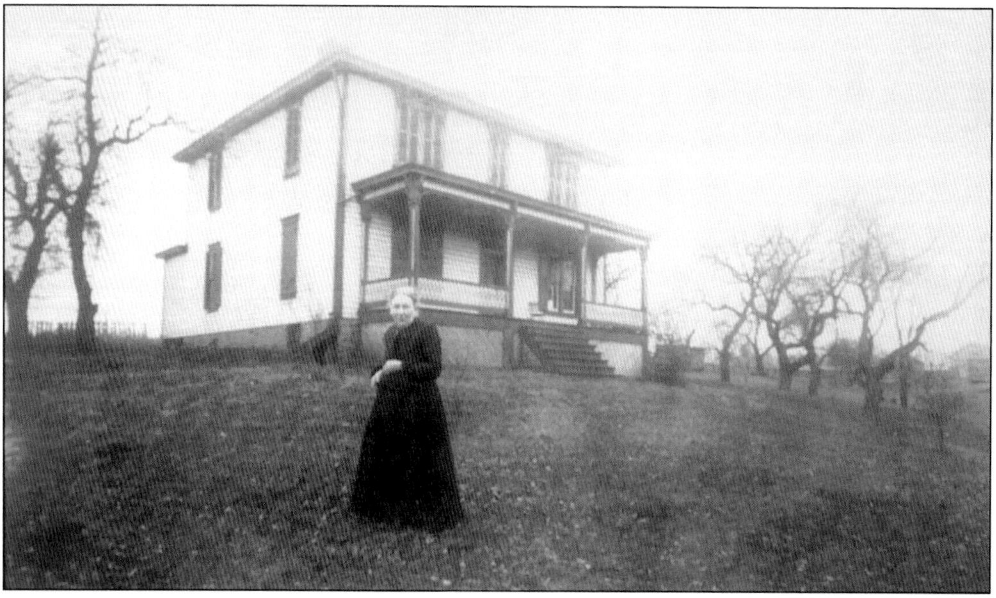

Mary Jordan Collins is standing in front of John Collins's farmhouse on Washington Pike in the early 1900s. The Collins family owned many acres in South Fayette. The original farmhouse still stands on the left side of Route 519 south of Bursca Business Park and is now owned by the Schullek family.

Three

Local Businesses, Mines, and Farming

Besides the 19 mines, most of South Fayette Township remained farmland until the mid-1960s. By 1887, there were 41 coke ovens and at least 60 oil wells in McDonald, with many more in Oakdale, Sturgeon, and Noblestown. Transportation was a growing concern, beginning with the Black Horse Trail (now Washington Pike), which was a stagecoach line from Pittsburgh to Washington. Mail was sorted at Herriotsville (near the county line), and horses were exchanged before the next run. There were the keelboats of Mike Fink and the pack trains of Colonel Noble, as well as "Adams Express," a team of horses and wagons run by Abraham "Thump" Adams, the son of Bob and Anne Adams, freed slaves who built a house on Millers Run Road.

The first train, the Panhandle Railroad, began in 1828 from McDonald and Oakdale to Pittsburgh. The Chartiers Valley Railroad began in 1853 from Canonsburg to Bridgeville to Pittsburgh. Joseph Supan ran a taxi service in the 1920s from Bridgeville to Cecil, and later, there was the Blue Ridge Bus and Community Bus from Hickory to Pittsburgh. In 1953, Community Transit was formed by David E. Brown, Robert Scheibler, and John Kosky Jr. and was located at the National No. 1 Mine mule stable. It ran until 1964, when the port authority took over all transit services in Allegheny County. The first school bus, a classic model 227, was used in 1926 to bring the local students to school.

Although many farms have been replaced with housing, the rolling hills of South Fayette are still home to Rolling Hills Ranch on Hickory Grade Road, which has been in the Earl Porter family since 1959 and originally was just a farmhouse and hay barn. The 70-acre property offers guides for the horses that are available to rent by the hour to ride over the open fields or wooded trails. It also offers birthday parties and boarding facilities.

The areas of commerce within the township were and still are centered on Main Street in Sturgeon, Millers Run Road in Morgan and Cuddy, and, later, Washington Pike heading south toward Boyce Road and neighboring Upper St. Clair.

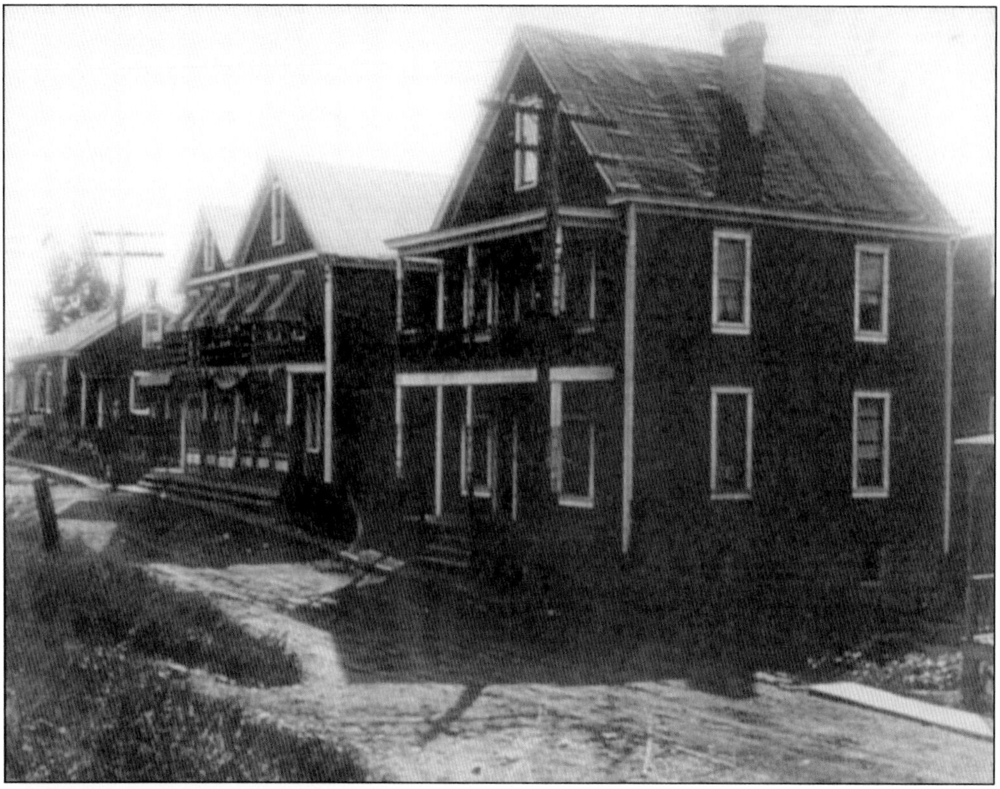

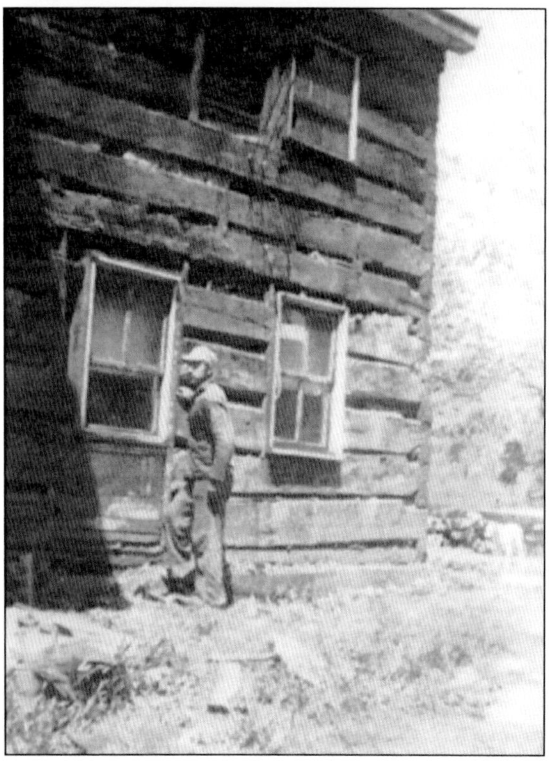

For years, the following three businesses (pictured from left to right) were on Main Street, Sturgeon: Gaston Rank's General Store (now Hunner's Deli), Celine Romaine, and another unidentified store (the latter two became residences). All three structures are still standing and in use today.

This is a picture of the Cardillo log house in 1950 shortly before it was dismantled. German settlers built it in the 1790s. The time period and the nationality of the builders were determined from tool marks left on the wood and some markings on some of the rafters. Most of the logs are currently stored in a shed on the Cardillo farm. Mike and Al Cardillo have donated the log house to the Historical Society of South Fayette Township with the hope that someday it will be rebuilt.

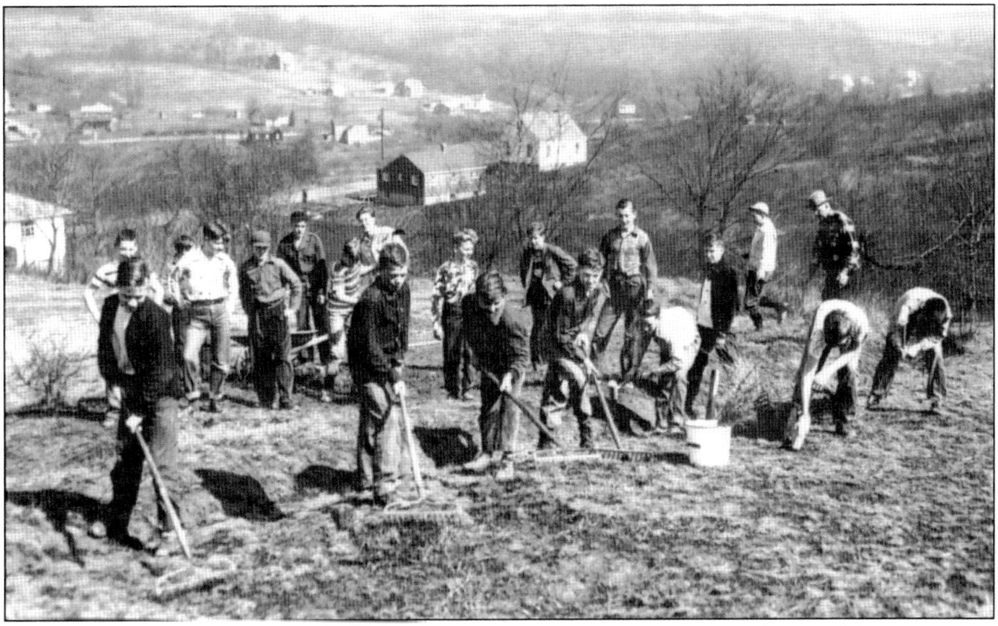

The Boys' Industrial Home of Western Pennsylvania was founded in 1900 by Rev. J.W. Cleland to help the many homeless and neglected boys in the western part of the state. Having initially started in a rented house, the group soon outgrew these quarters and moved into the former Oakdale Academy, South Fayette Township. Over the years, additional land was purchased, expanding the property to 365 acres. The boys went to school, worked on the farm, helped with the laundry and housework, and attended chapel. It operated for 70 years before closing in 1972.

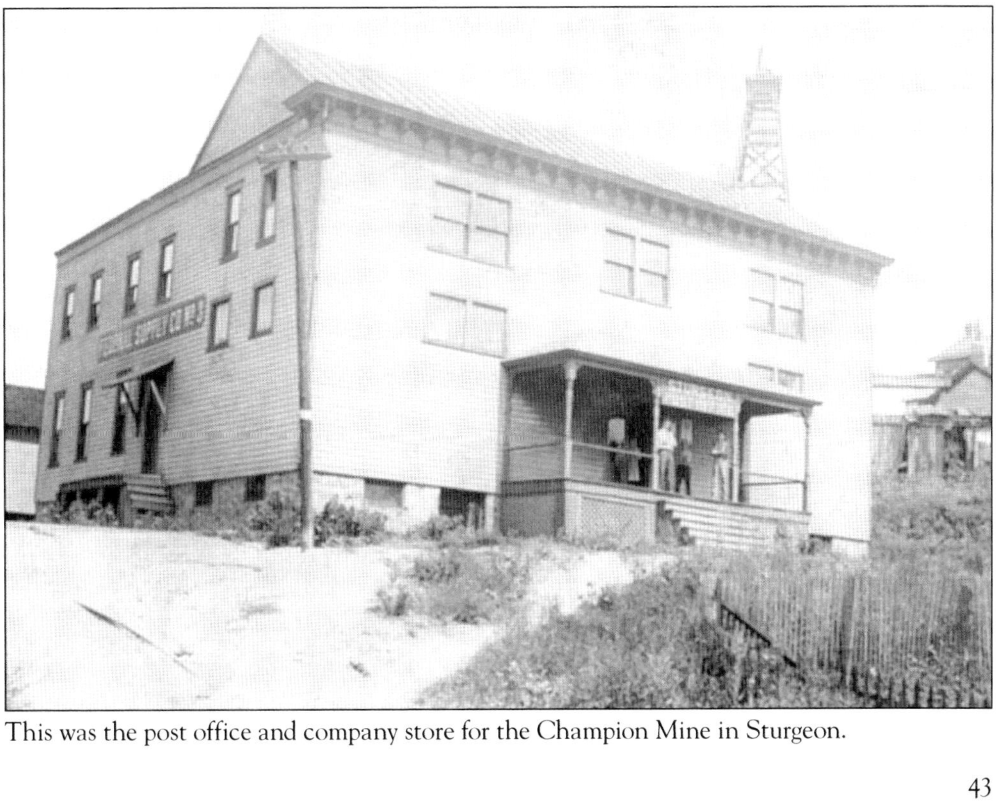

This was the post office and company store for the Champion Mine in Sturgeon.

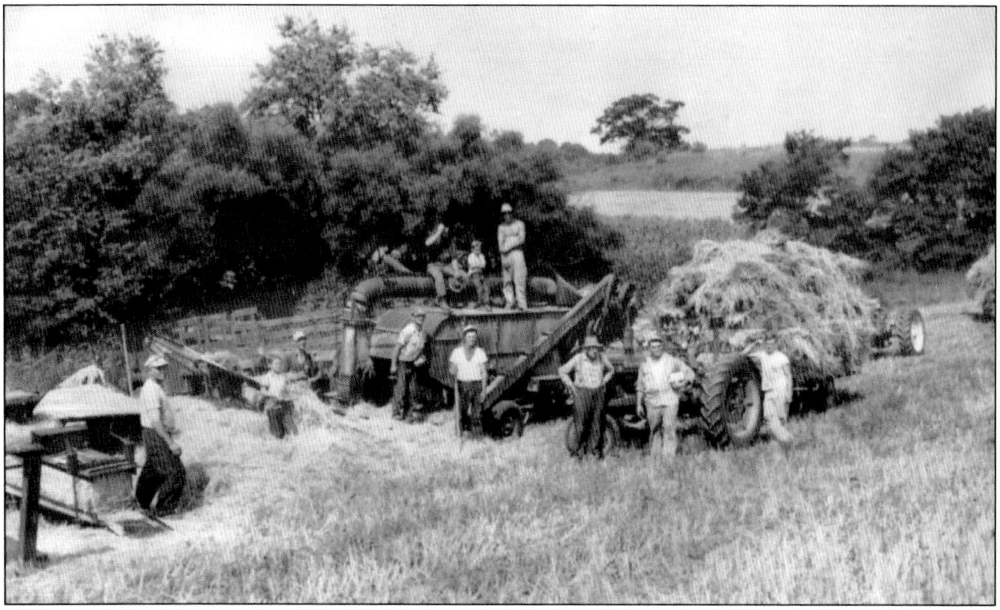

In this 1955 photograph, the thrashing machine and bailer are owned by Stanley Sowinski and are being used on the Delphus property, which used to be part of the 600-acre Bell Farm off Battle Ridge Road. Back then, a thrashing crew would go from farm to farm to thrash the grain, put it into sacks, and bail the straw. All the neighboring farmers joined the work crew at each farm.

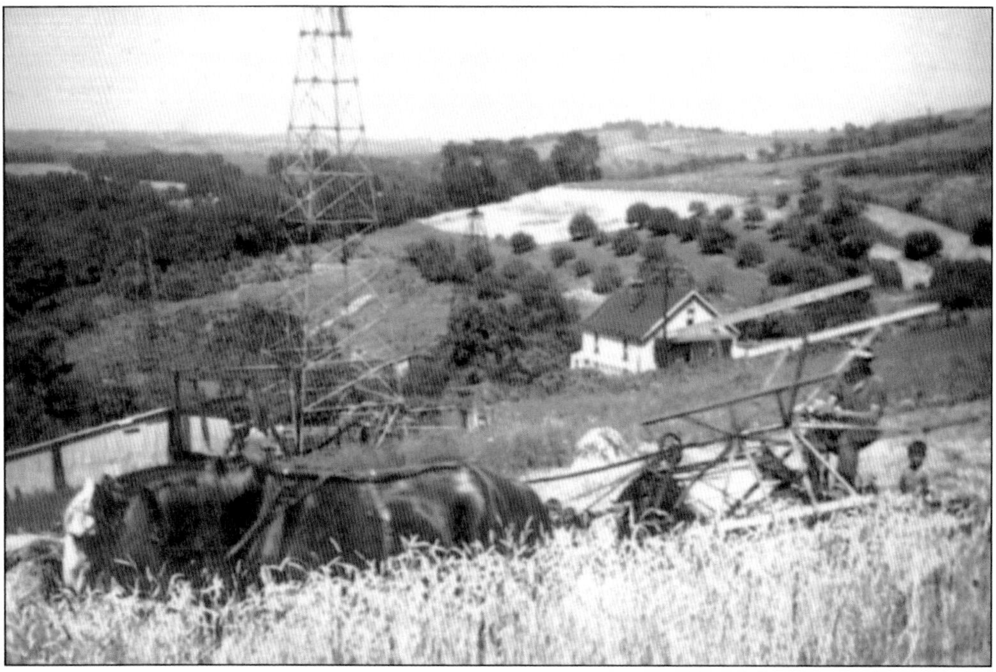

This 1938 photograph shows property off Marshall Road that was farmed by the Cardillo family. Al Cardillo is seen operating the binder, which is being pulled by horses Bob, Dick, and Tom. Brother Mike is riding Tom. Also pictured are brothers John (below the binder) and Julius Cardillo (behind the binder). Early maps show the Cardillo property was previously owned by James Bridge in 1784, Sam Jefferies in 1795, then Andrew Herriott, and J. Waters-Burnes in 1851.

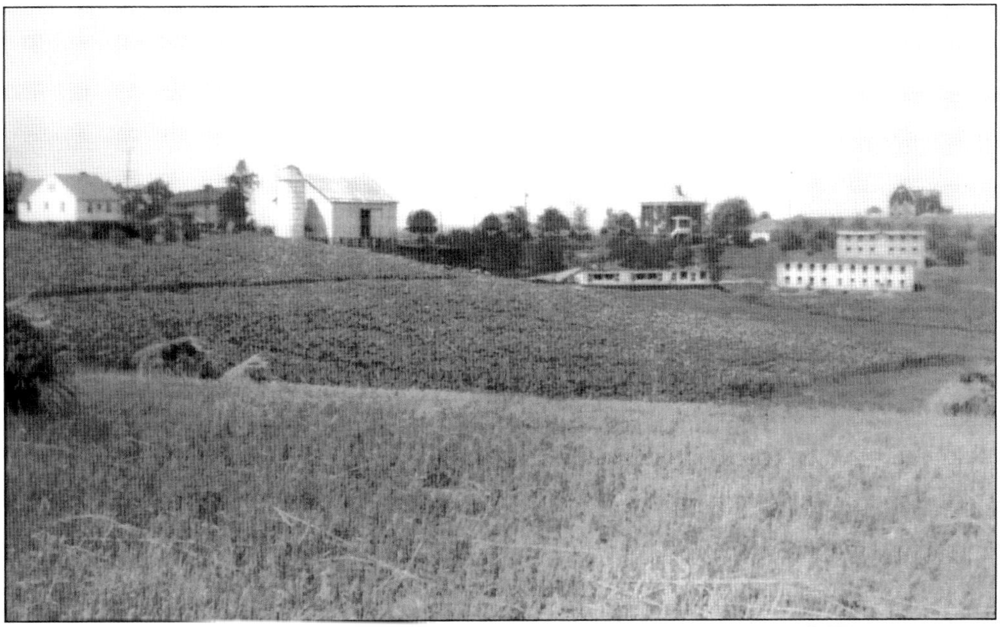

This is the Charles Jacob Schneider Farm at Washington Pike/Alpine Road. The Schneiders are descendants of Christian Lesnett, the first European settler in Fayette Township. Another Schneider owned Tiffany Acres off Lesnett Road, and Jacob Schneider owned Mayview Farms before the City of Pittsburgh appropriated it for housing and taking care of the mentally ill. (See Mayview State Hospital entry on page 61.)

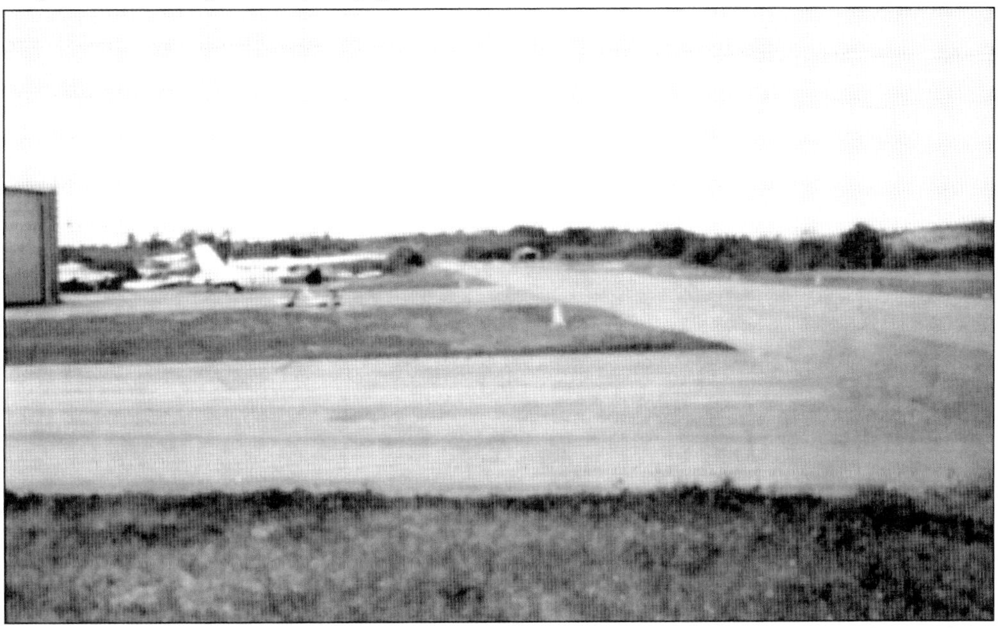

A small municipal airport opened in the early 1950s in the Maude Mine Hollow area along Fishing Run, owned by Charles Campbell Sr. and operated by Charles Campbell Jr. In 1963, it relocated to 700 Millers Run Road (formerly the Mike Dunn farm). A 5,000-foot runway accommodated the many corporate and individually owned planes using the airstrip. Eventually, it became Pittsburgh Metro Airport and closed in 1994.

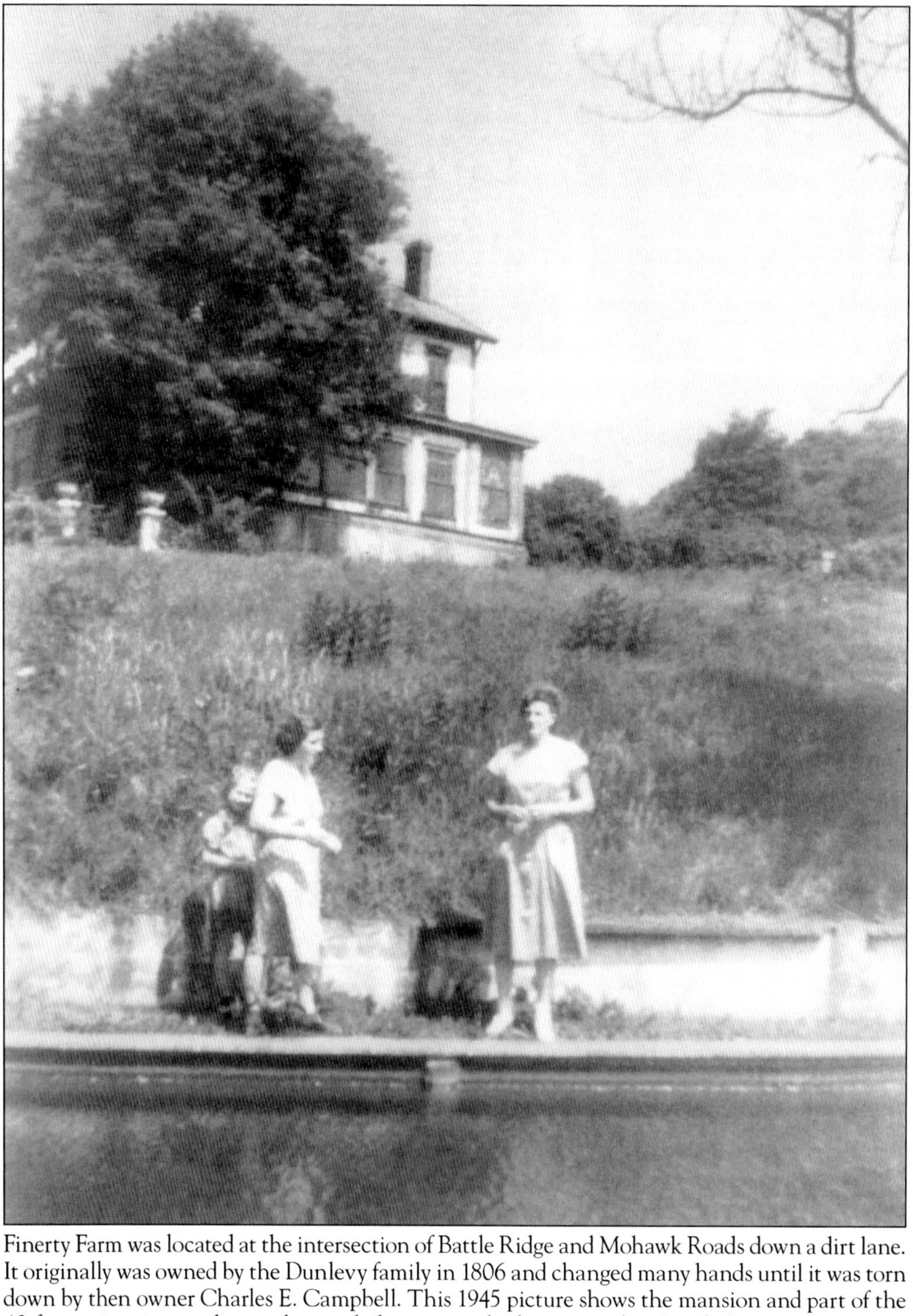

Finerty Farm was located at the intersection of Battle Ridge and Mohawk Roads down a dirt lane. It originally was owned by the Dunlevy family in 1806 and changed many hands until it was torn down by then owner Charles E. Campbell. This 1945 picture shows the mansion and part of the 40-foot swimming pool, complete with fountain—the largest pool in South Fayette.

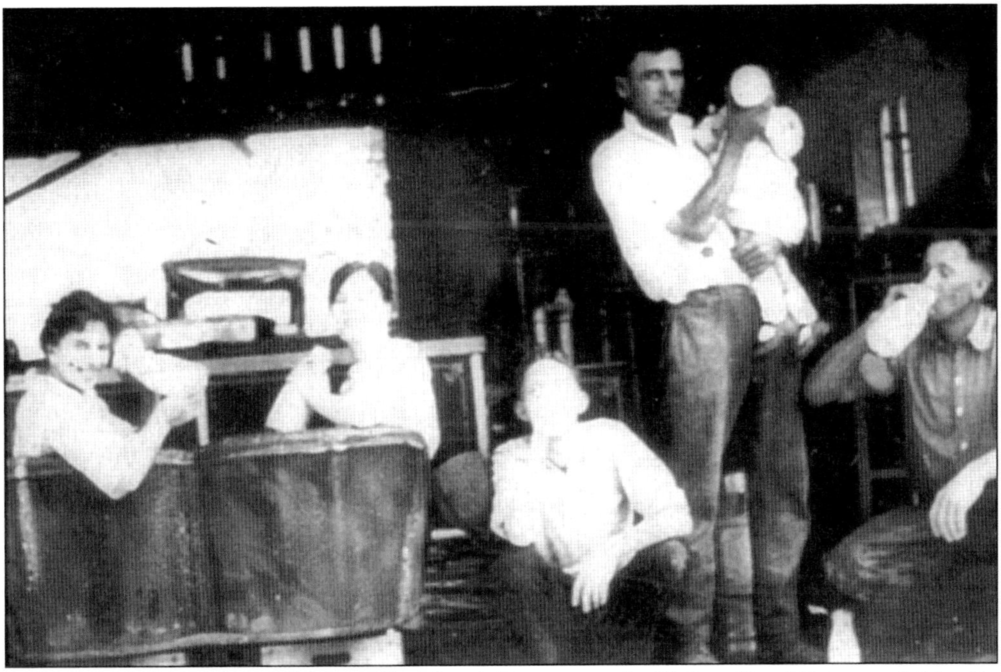

The first dairy to supply and deliver milk in South Fayette was the William Freed Dairy, established in 1922 at Boyce Station and Mayview Road. The family delivered milk to Bridgeville and Canonsburg. The dairy closed in 1934 and equipment was sold to Joseph Portman. Pictured enjoying their milk are, from left to right, Grace Freed Campbell, Marion Freed McCracken, Emmett McCracken, James Campbell (holding Bonnie McCracken), and William Boyce Freed.

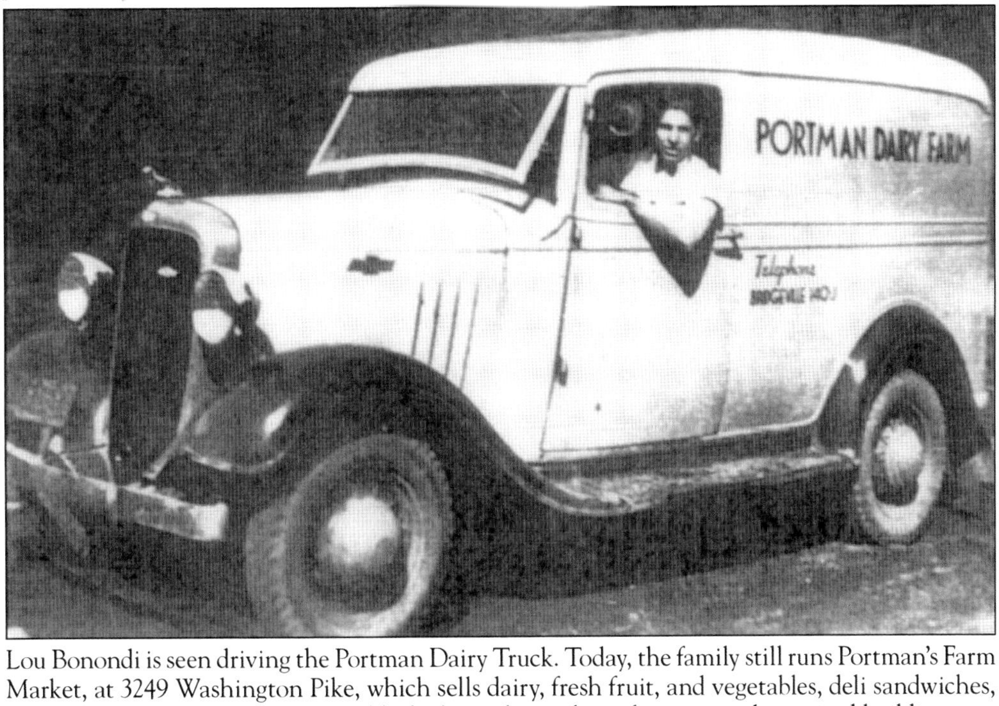

Lou Bonondi is seen driving the Portman Dairy Truck. Today, the family still runs Portman's Farm Market, at 3249 Washington Pike, which sells dairy, fresh fruit, and vegetables, deli sandwiches, and baked goods. The store is notable for being housed in a large green barn-sized building.

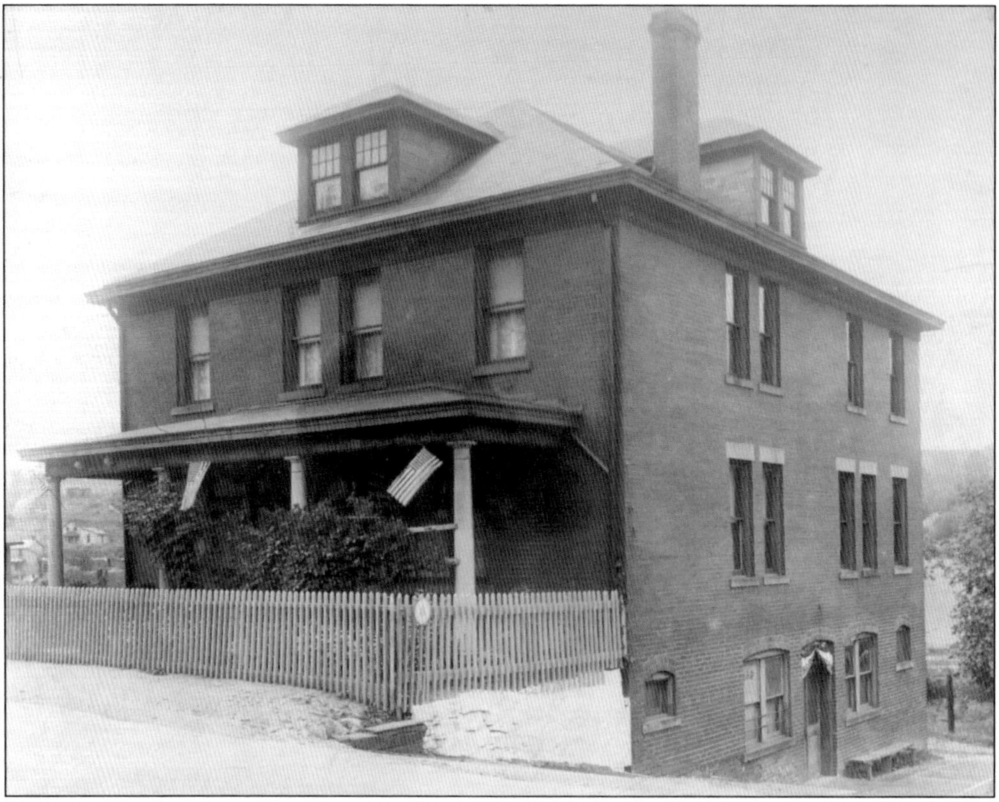

Seen here in the early 1900s, Brown's Hotel, at 572 Millers Run Road, was later known as the Morgan Hotel. The bottom floor was a beer garden operated by the Bioni family. The building is currently in use as the Colonial Apartments with nine rental units.

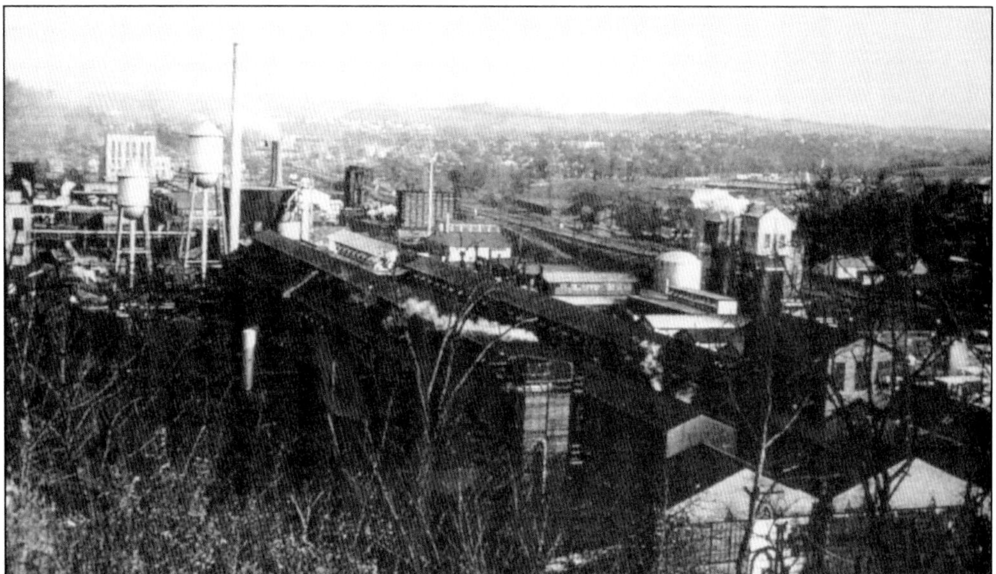

This picture shows the true measure of just how large the American Cyanamid plant was as viewed from Presto-Sygan Road looking toward Bridgeville.

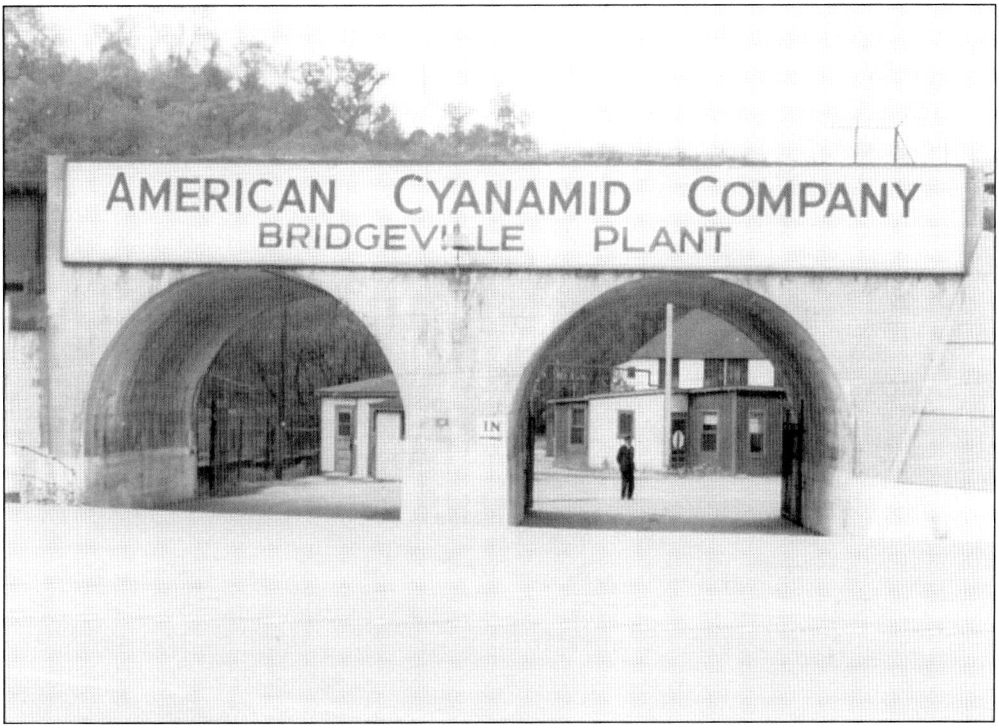

The twin tunnels leading to the American Cyanamid Company were built in the 1930s. The company was first established on the South Side of Pittsburgh to produce chemicals for World War I. It moved to Millers Run when land was purchased from the Pittsburgh & West Virginia Railway. It became the Selden Company, producing synthetic resins; then later, it was known as Koppers and lastly Reichold Chemical, employing more than 500 people. Although the plant was torn down around 2006, the tunnels are still under the present-day Wheeling & Lake Erie Railroad, located along Millers Run Road, adjacent to Limestone Products & Supply. The site is slated to become Newbury Market, a shopping complex.

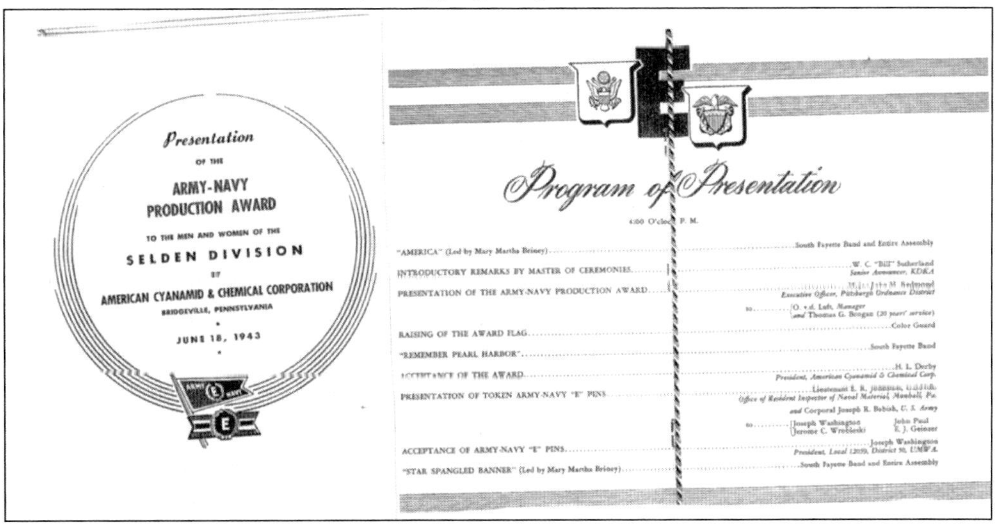

In 1943, a major ceremony was held when a US Army-Navy Production Award was presented to workers at American Cyanamid.

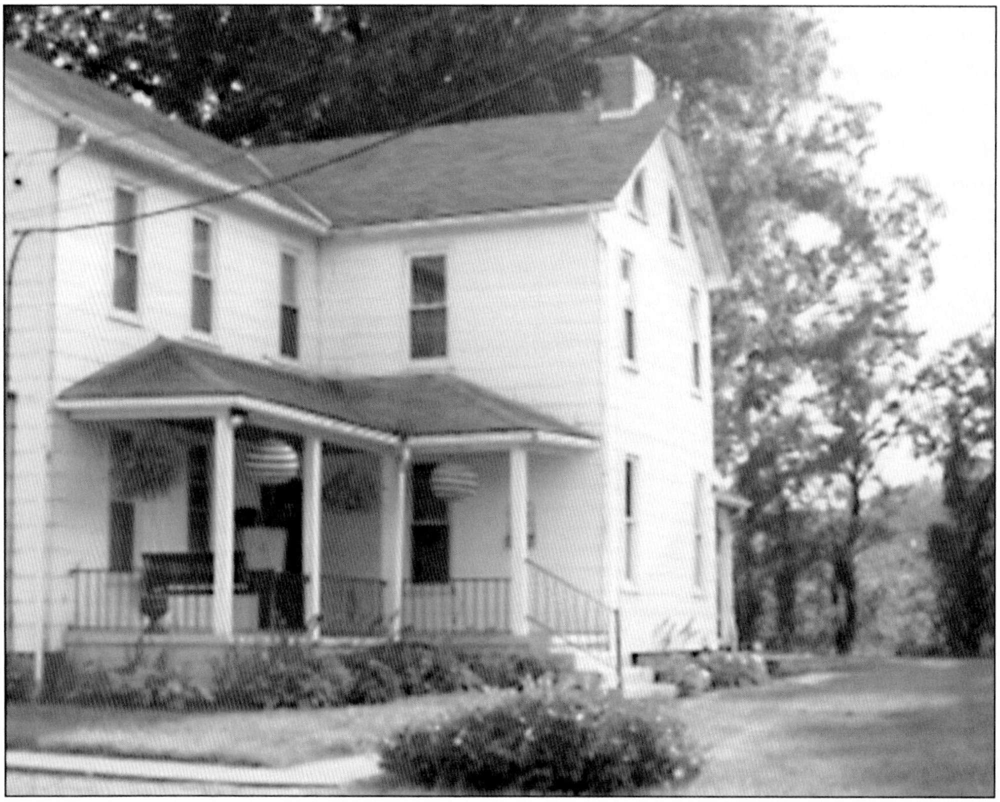

Across from the twin tunnels still stands the Edward Hanna house (now Face to Face Spa). It was an eight-room house owned by the Wabash Railroad to rent rooms to workers and local schoolteachers. The house's foundation was built eight feet aboveground to withstand the occasional flooding of Millers Run. (Courtesy of Linda James.)

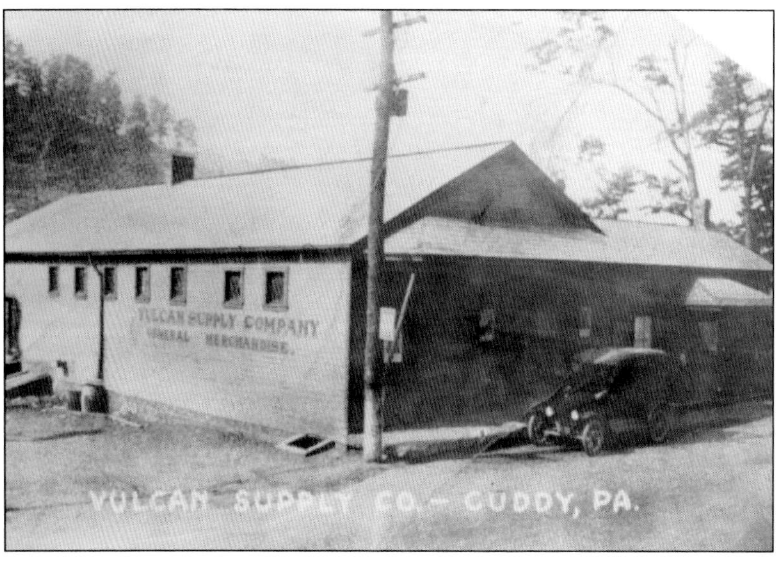

This was the company store for Vulcan Supply Company, owned by Pittsburgh Coal, in 1901. Located on the corner of Millers Run and Battle Ridge Roads, it served as a general merchandise store for local residents. Later, the store was sold to the Santoni family.

Geno and Marie Santoni, shown here on their 50th wedding anniversary, owned the G. Santoni Meat Market and General Merchandise store in Treveskyn (Cuddy). Among its specialty items were furniture, rugs, and stoves. The Santonis, along with Clemente Ferri (confectionary store), Sabatino and Yolanda Fatigati (restaurant), Battista Mittino (shoe store), Emilio Corti (barbershop), and Natlae Tacchino (bakery), helped to form Incremento Colonlale Italiano, with other Italian business owners from Morgan, Cecil, and Hills Station (Lawrence).

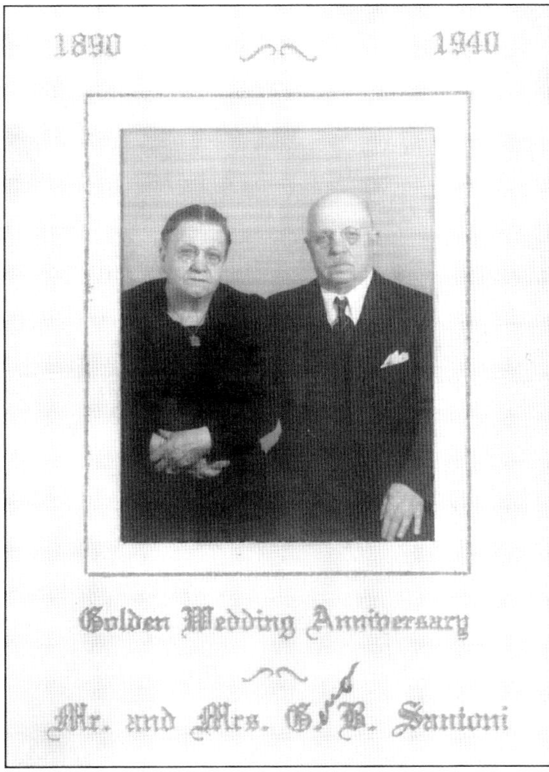

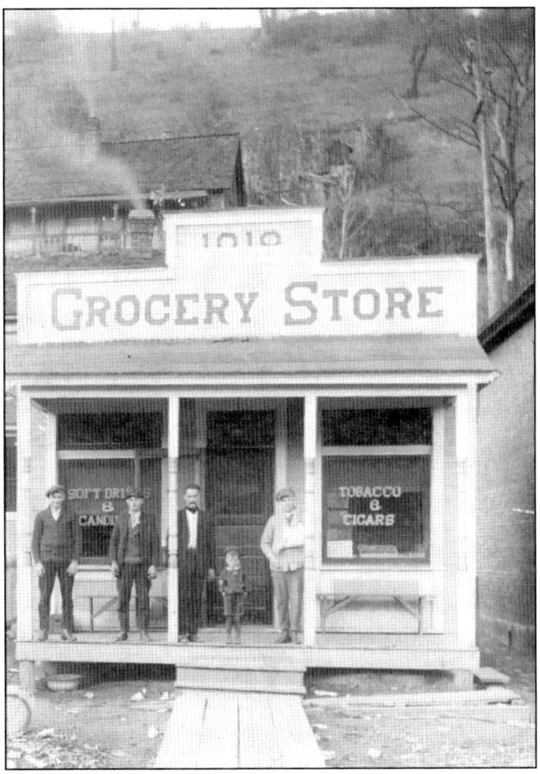

Pictured in 1918 at the Ferri Grocery Store, at 621 Millers Run Road, Treveskyn, are, from left to right, uncle Antonio Ferri; father, Clemente; three-year-old Mondo; uncle Lidokio "Ludwig"; and an unidentified man. The block building on the right was the Dream Theater, today the location of John Kosky Contracting, Inc. Nellie's Bar was located behind the grocery store, operating as a tavern and ice-cream store until the 1950s.

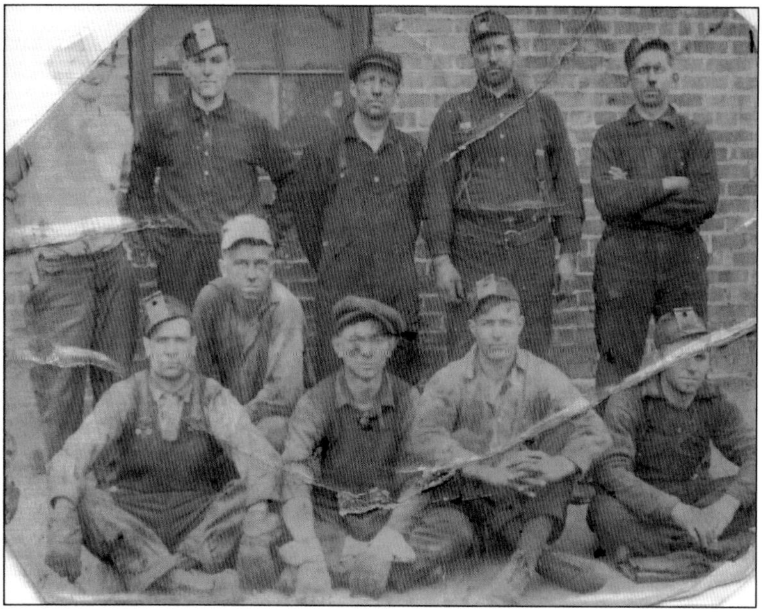

Pictured are several unidentified coal miners from National No. 1 Mine in Morgan.

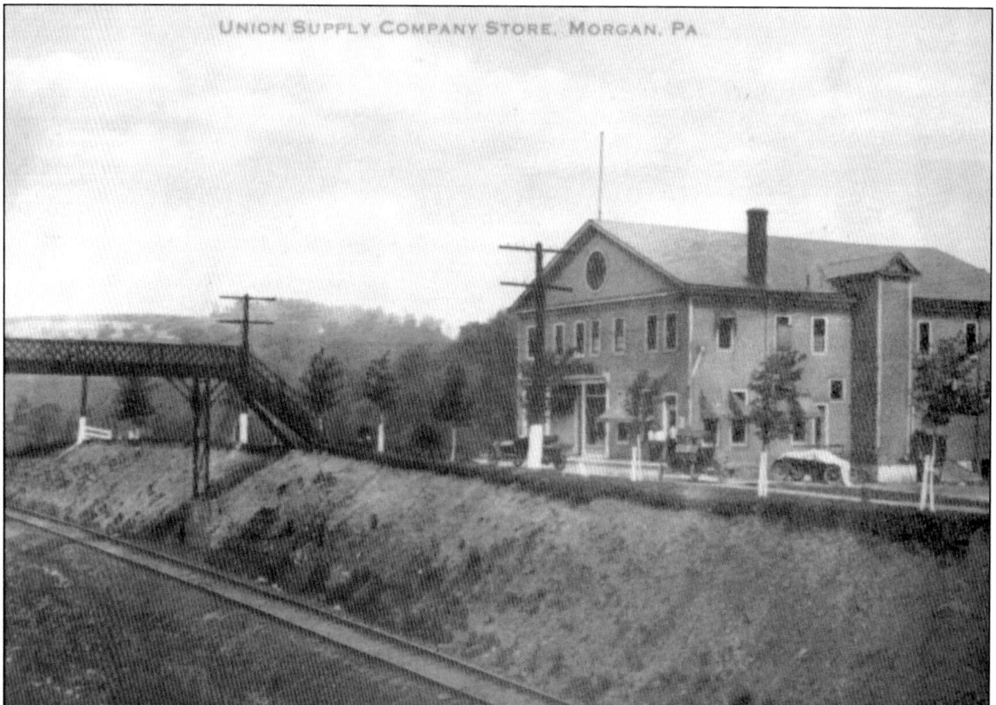

This was the Union Supply Company Store for National No. 1 Mine, located on Central Avenue across from the present-day municipal building and operated by United States Steel (USS). The miners who worked at the mine shopped here and lived in the nearby Morgan Blocks (company houses). It was demolished by fire in the late 1960s.

This is the Union Supply Company Store, National Hill, managed by M.C. Stover. The store served miners and families from National No. 2 Mine. The store closed in 1950. The building is located on Allegheny Avenue and was recently converted into apartments.

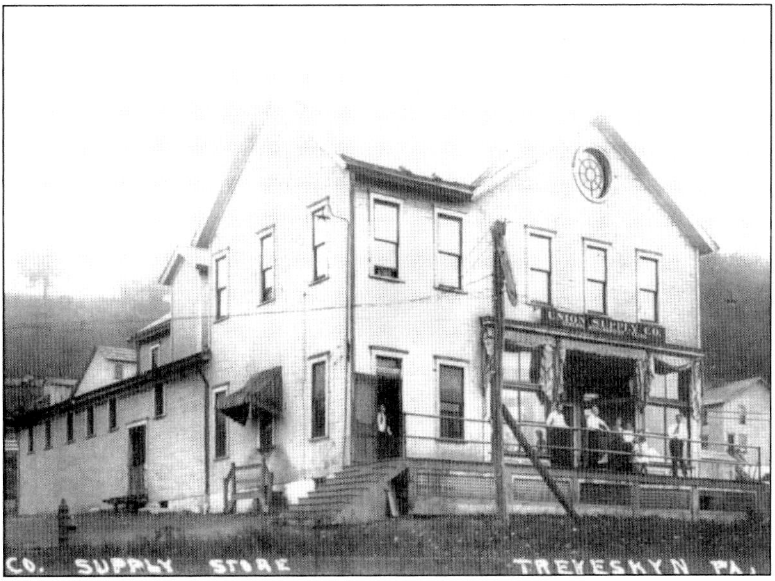

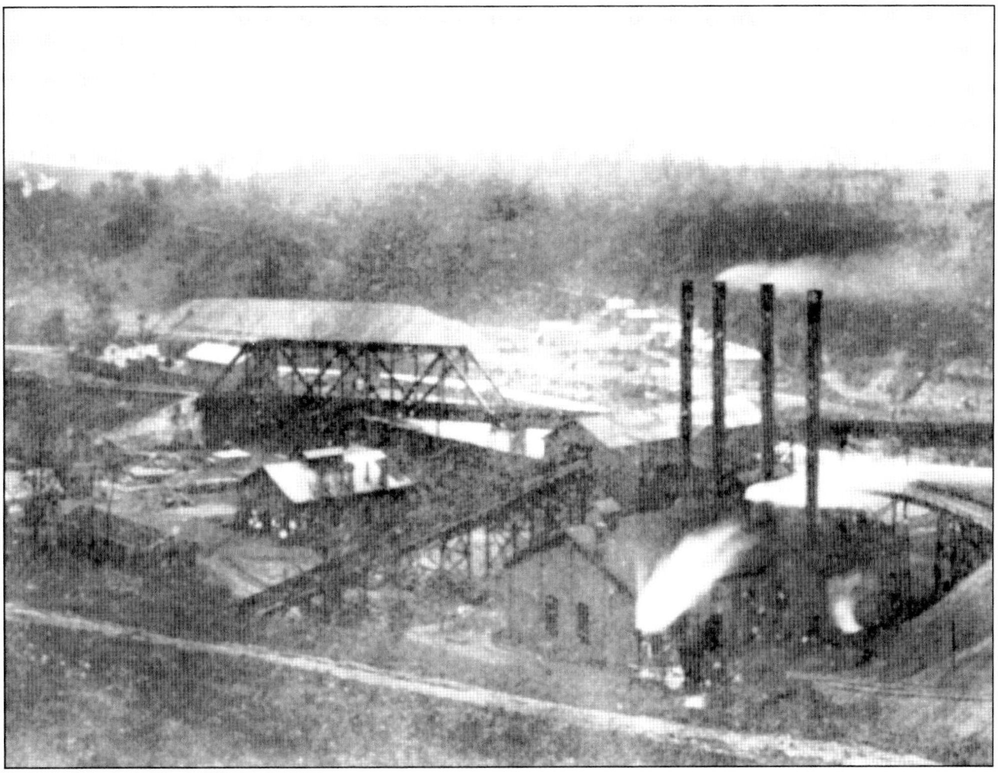

National No. 1 Mine, as pictured in the early 1900s, is along present-day Route 50. In the distance is Blythe. The railroad trestle is still in use today. The mine was operated by United States Steel (USS) and closed in 1953.

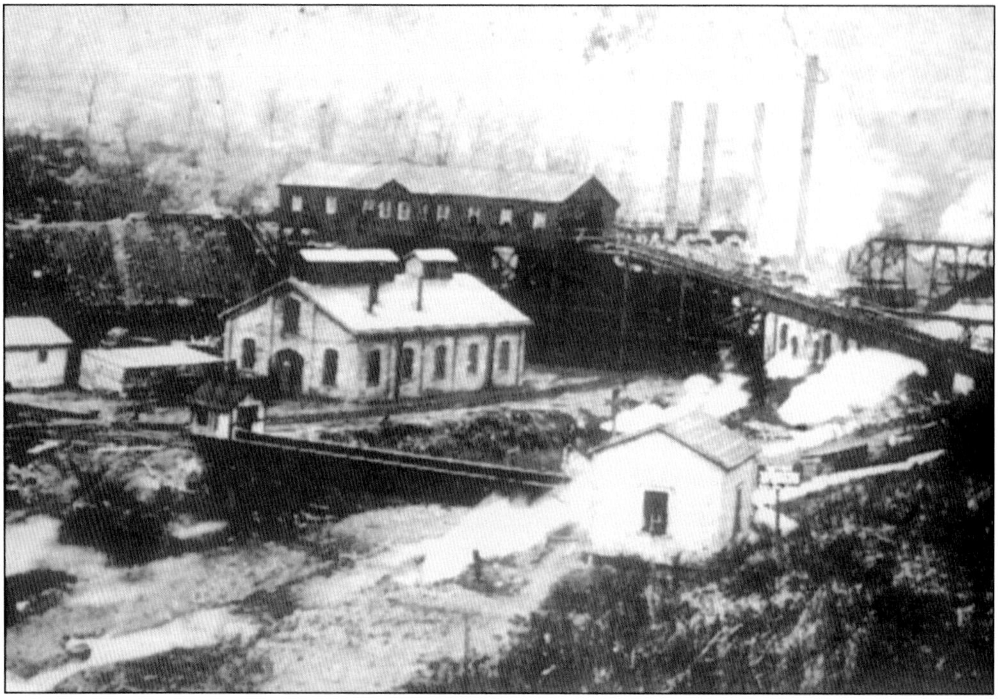

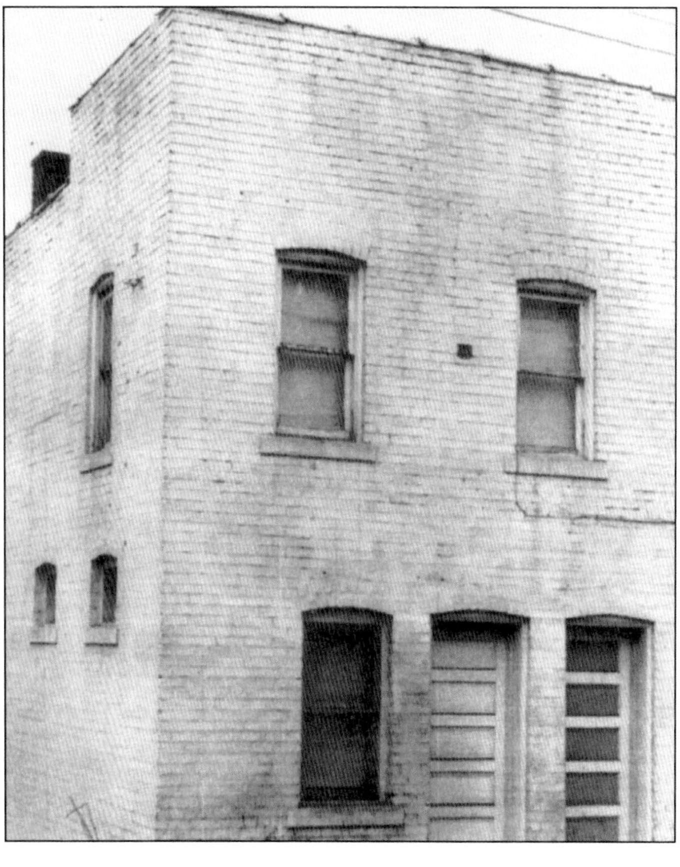

National No. 2 Mine, pictured here, closed in 1936. This is the site of the present-day South Fayette Volunteer Fire Department in Cuddy.

Pictured is the first municipal building for the township, located in Cuddy.

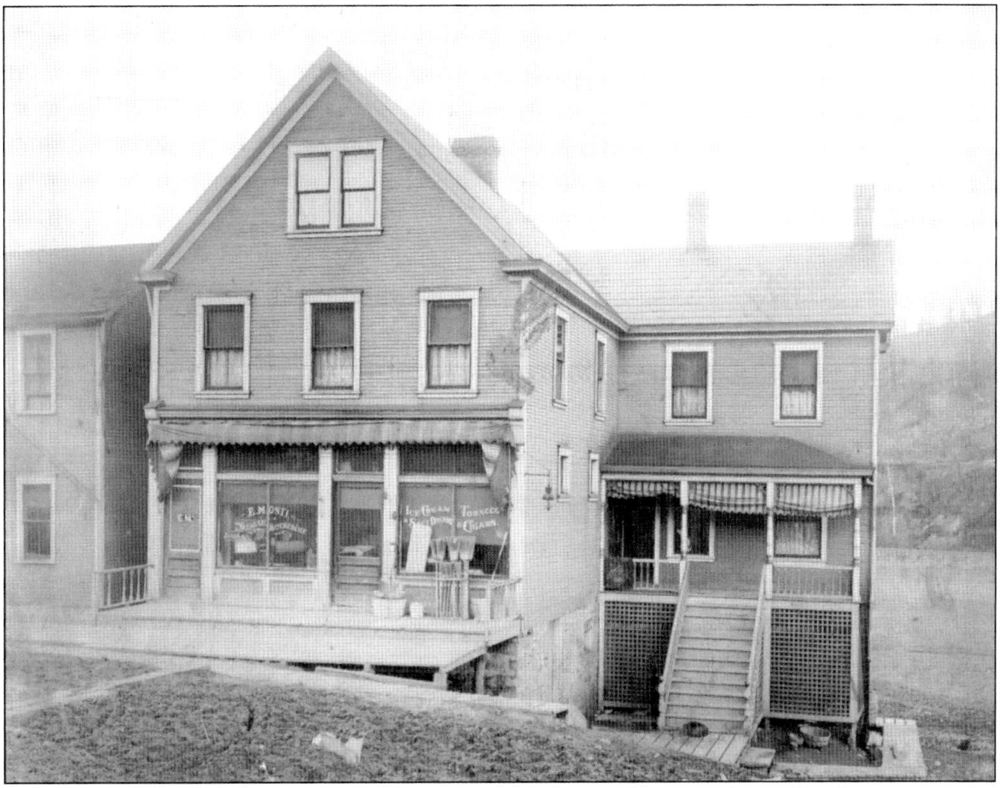

In the 500 block of Millers Run Road, Eugene Mosti operated a general merchandise store in the early 1900s, selling tobacco, cigars, ice cream, and soft drinks along with general grocery items.

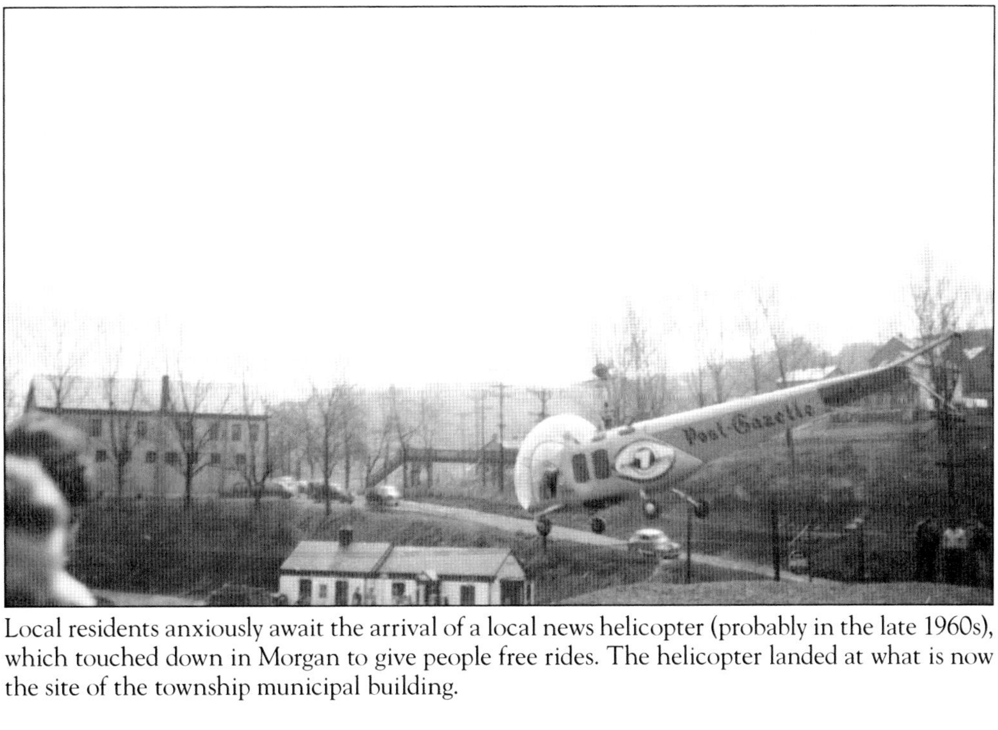

Local residents anxiously await the arrival of a local news helicopter (probably in the late 1960s), which touched down in Morgan to give people free rides. The helicopter landed at what is now the site of the township municipal building.

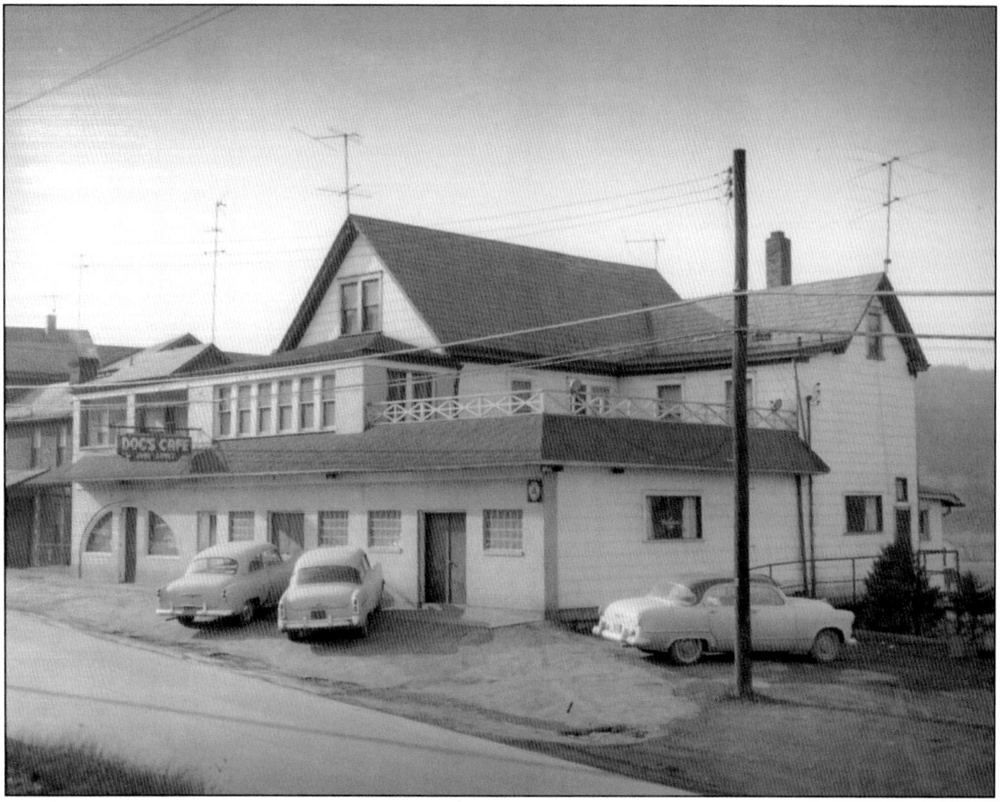

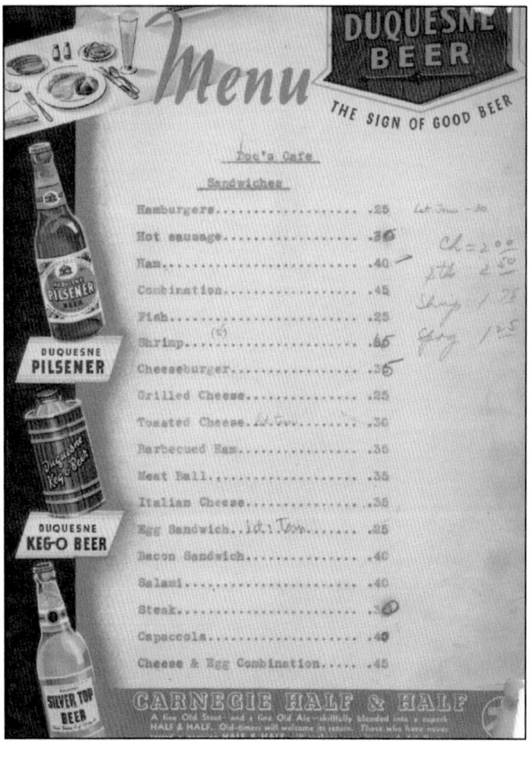

Doc's Cafe

Sandwiches

Hamburgers	.25
Hot sausage	.35
Ham	.40
Combination	.45
Fish	.25
Shrimp	.65
Cheeseburger	.35
Grilled Cheese	.25
Toasted Cheese	.30
Barbecued Ham	.35
Meat Ball	.35
Italian Cheese	.35
Egg Sandwich	.25
Bacon Sandwich	.40
Salami	.40
Steak	.30
Capaccola	.40
Cheese & Egg Combination	.45

Anthony "Doc" Casciola purchased the Mosti Building on August 9, 1946, and made some renovations and opened up Doc's Café Dinner-Dance establishment. The menu included spaghetti and tripe as well as a variety of sandwiches (as seen at left). In later years, the restaurant was known as the Hyd-A-Way Bar. Although no longer a restaurant, the building still stands by Morgan Park.

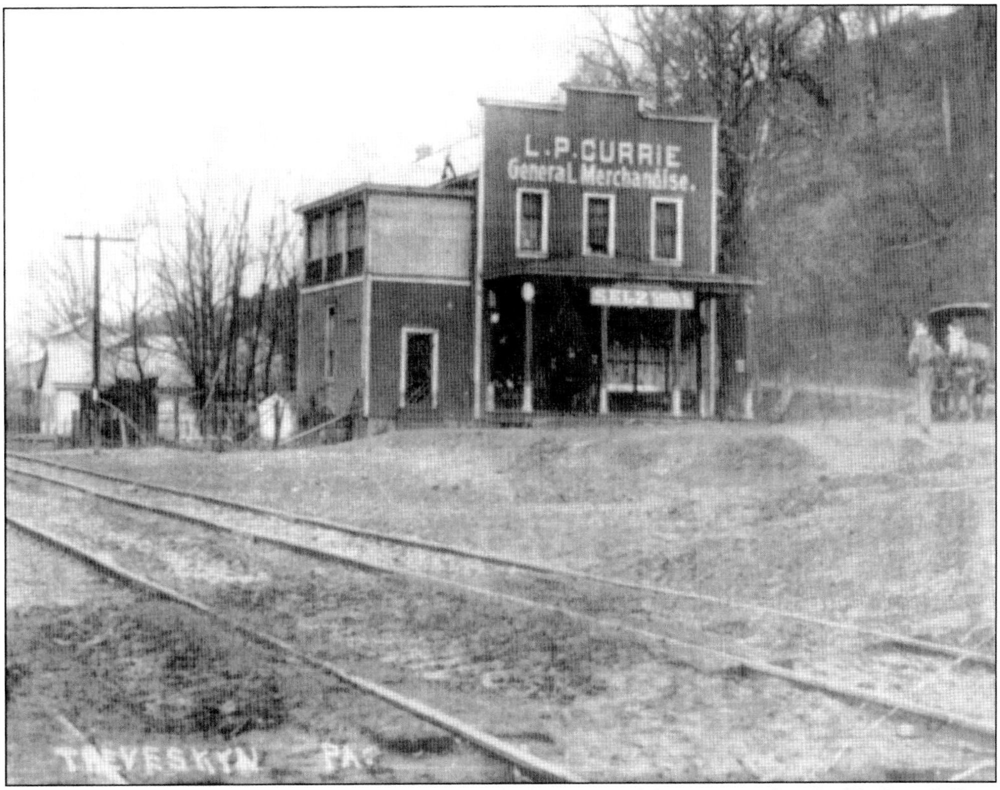

A horse and buggy are traveling eastbound near the location of the present-day Cuddy Post Office. Pictured is the L.P. Currie General Merchandising store in the 1890s. The Treveskyn Train Station can be seen in the background. Veterans of Foreign Wars Post No. 586 currently sits on the site of the former train station, and its parking lot is on the former site of the Fatigati Restaurant.

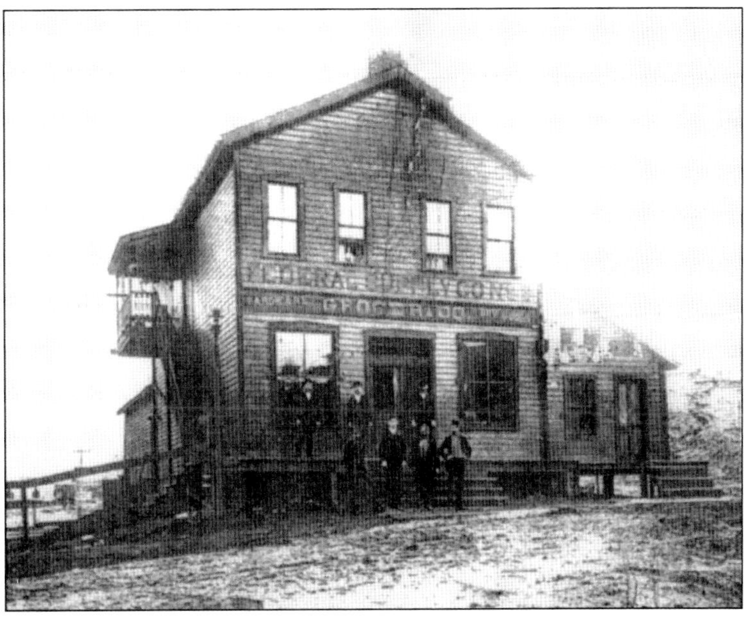

Area residents are seen in front of the Federal Supply Company located on Morgan Hill Road. In the top window is baby Dawson Wright (Sr.) held by his mother. He went on to own and operate Wright Garage Doors.

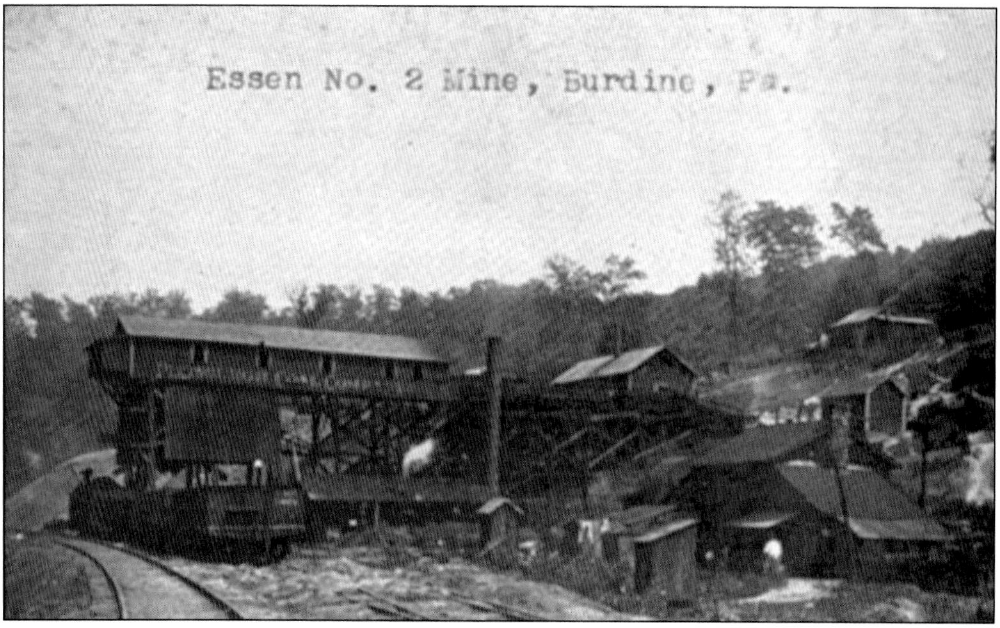

This 1904 picture shows the Essen No. 2 Mine of the Pittsburgh Coal Company in Burdine on Thoms Run Road. Burdine was between Presto and Federal on the South Fayette side of Thoms Run Creek.

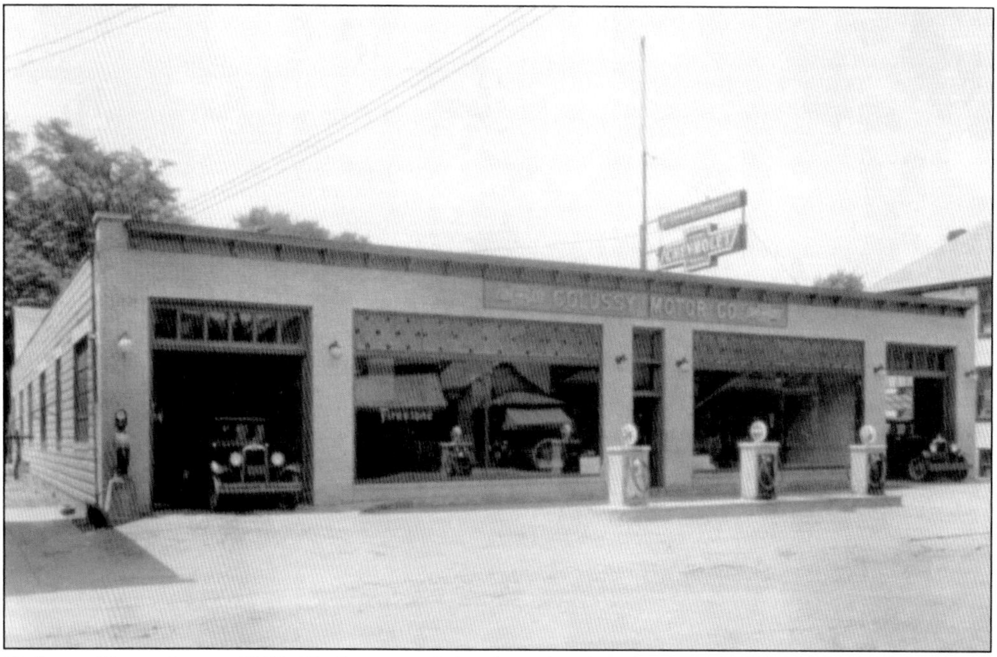

Colussy Chevrolet, at 3073 Washington Pike, has the distinction of being the nation's oldest Chevrolet dealership. The Colussy family members were originally carpenters, who settled in Morgan, farmed, had an ice plant in Bridgeville, and built apartments. Albert Colussy began the dealership in 1918 and was later joined by his two brothers, Gilbert and Arthur. The other three brothers, Ernest, Elmer, and Alfred, joined together to sell Ford cars. Albert's grandsons Tim and Jon Colussy run the dealership today. Pictured is the dealership in 1928.

Pictured in 1905 is the Henry Mickus Horseshoe and General Blacksmith shop in Burdine. The man on the left is Henry Mickus.

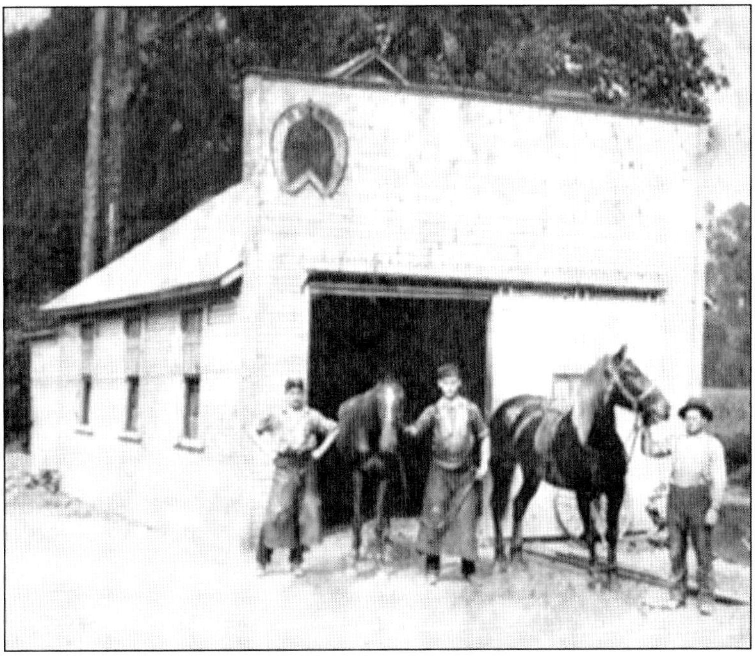

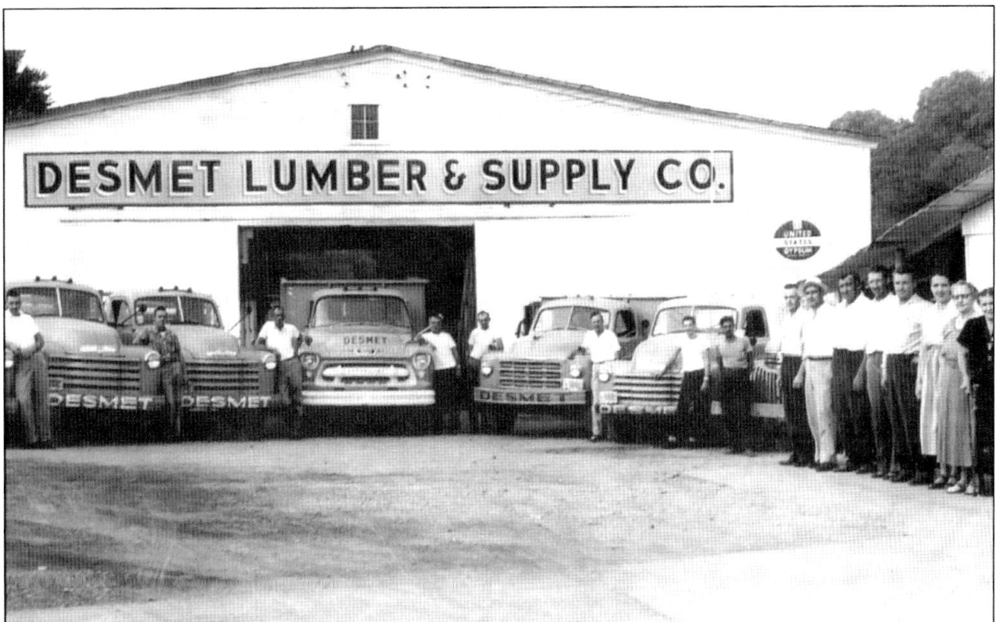

Desmet Lumber began in 1919 on Millers Run Road, selling supplies to professional building contractors. Leonard Desmet, its founder, also served on the school board for many years. His six sons and daughter and their offspring helped run the business until it closed in 2000. Originally, the lumber and building supplies were delivered on a cart pulled by a billy goat. Later, trucks were the main transportation. Pictured in the 1940s in front of their trucks and building are, from left to right, Alfred Desmet Jr., Raymond Wauthier, Charles Carothers, Albert Suhayda, James Havel, Andrew Kristoff, Lenny Desmet, Ed Karmann, John Wauthier, Frank Checca, Alfred Desmet Sr., Leonard Desmet Sr., Oscar Desmet, Rosemarie Seward, Mary Sackett, and Marie Desmet.

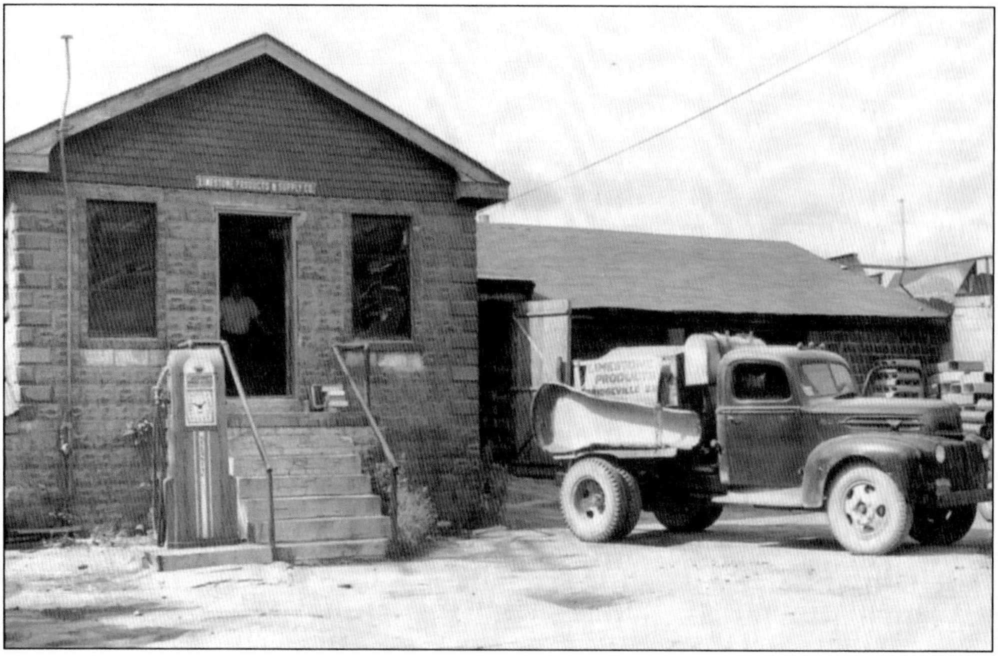

Joseph Hofrichter founded Limestone Products & Supply Co. on Millers Run Road in 1924. The company provides block and ready-mixed concrete to many homes and businesses. Pictured here in the mid-1940s, the business was sold recently and is being operated by 3 Dog Concrete.

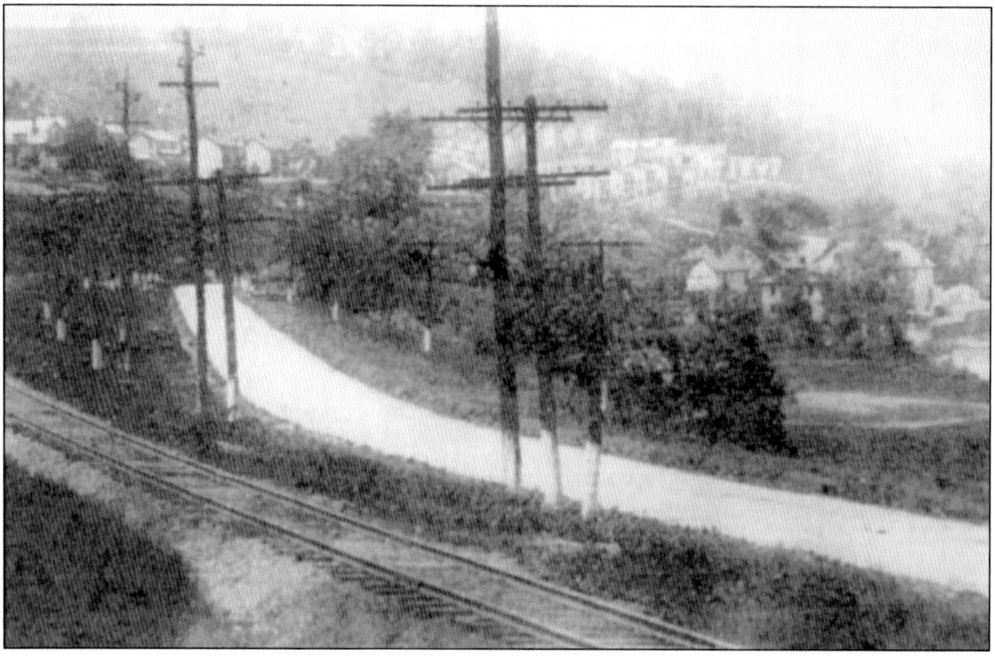

This 1920s picture with a view looking toward Cuddy was taken from the railroad tracks. National Hill is at the top of the picture. Millers Run Creek is on the far left. What seems to be a baseball field is in the foreground. Millers Run Creek has changed locations many times through the years, sometimes because of Mother Nature and other times because of strip mining.

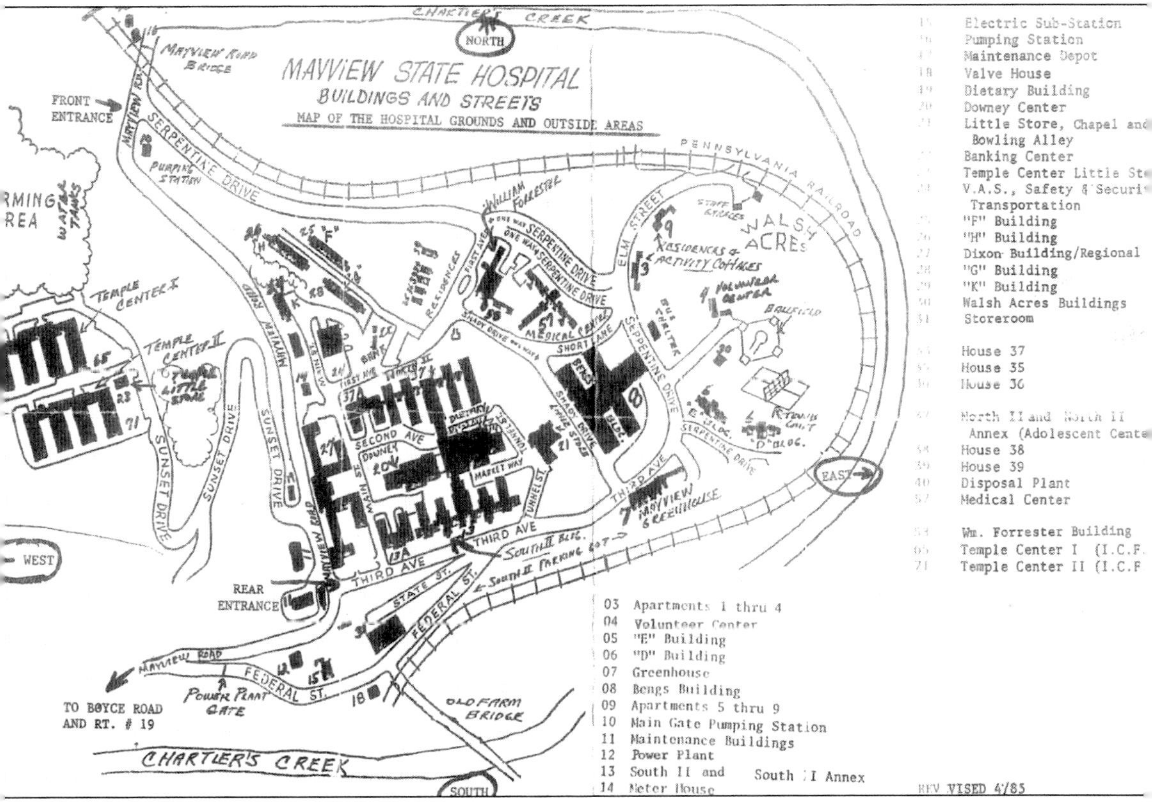

In 1893, Marshalsea, named for the London debtors' prison, was constructed on the Jacob Heiner Schneider Farm to house the mentally ill, the indigent, and unwed pregnant women. Pittsburgh desired to move its former poorhouse (the Pittsburgh City Home and Hospital) that had been built in 1846 along the Monongahela River to the countryside, believing it to be much healthier, and took the land by eminent domain. A 1916 contest was held to choose a less-depressing name for the site, and Mayview was chosen. During the early years, there was a coal mine that fueled a power plant and a farm. It was very self-sufficient. At its height in 1934, Mayview housed more than 4,000 patients, 450 employees, and 80 buildings. An observation unit was established in 1946 to provide treatment for those in the criminal justice system, evolving into a forensic center in 1974. On December 29, 2008, Mayview State Hospital closed for good, relocating its 37 remaining patients. The buildings have since been demolished.

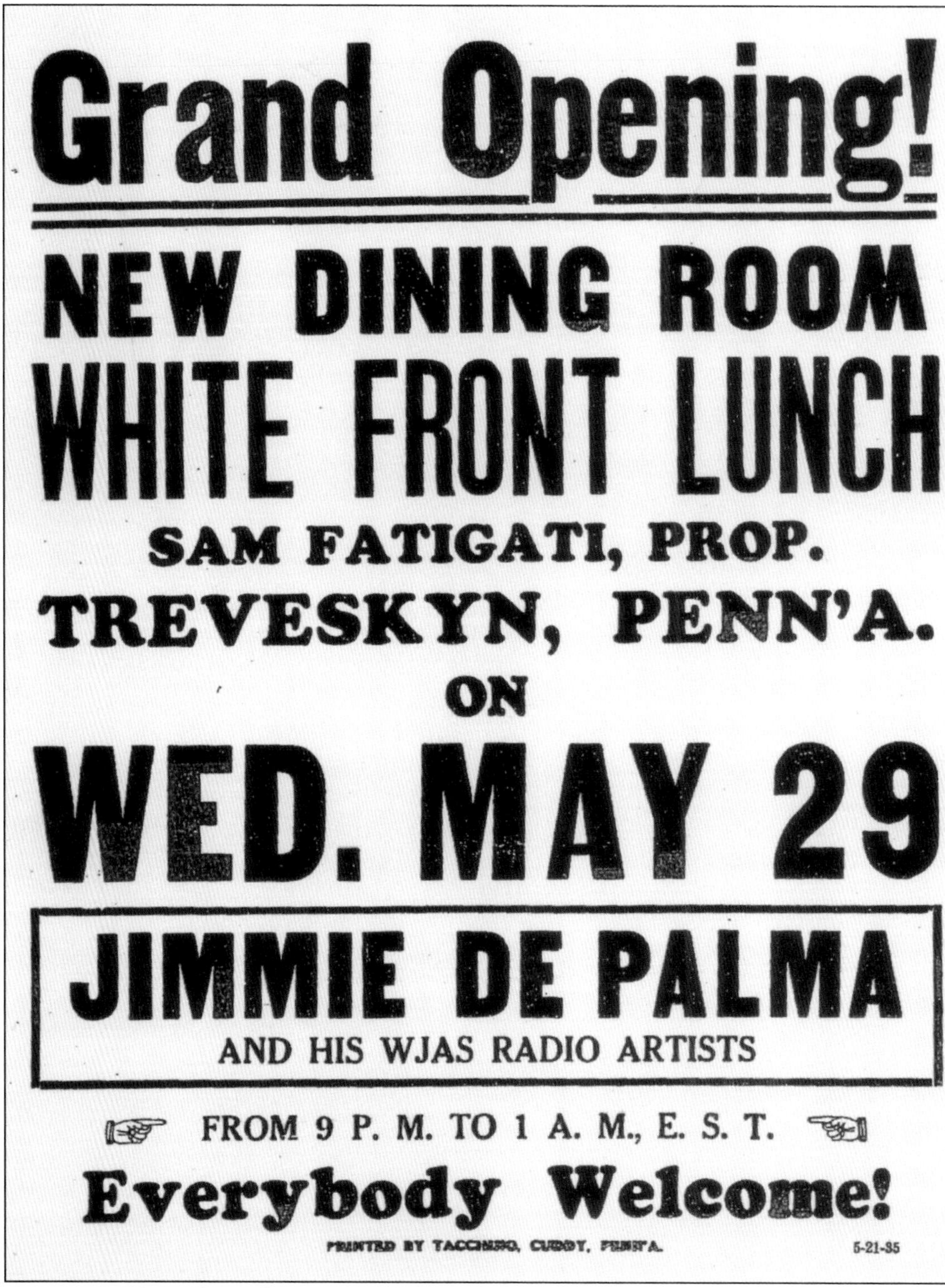

In operation from the early 1920s until 1992, Fatigati's Italian Restaurant was Cuddy's claim to fame. People traveled from all over the tristate area to partake of the cuisine and the famous New York strip steak. It began with Sabatino and Yolanda Fatigati buying a small storefront grocery store with Yolanda selling soup to the local coal miners at lunchtime. She soon added large dishes of pasta. The basement of the store became a speakeasy at night, with Yolanda supplying food to the gentlemen who came to play cards and drink the wine made by Sabatino in the style of his father in L'Aquila, Italy. The store was converted into a small restaurant known as the White Front Restaurant. Shown is the advertisement for the restaurant's grand opening.

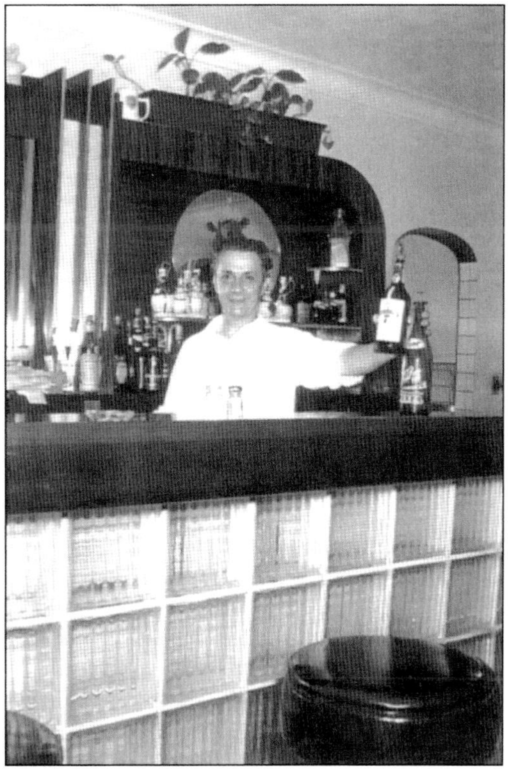

Ivo Fatigati, Sabatino's son, graduated from the University of Notre Dame and worked for the State Department. He later worked at the family restaurant, then owned by Sam Fatigati, and helped it evolve into the White Front Bar and Grill and finally Fatigati's. In 1992, new owners changed its name and reopened it as a club and dance hall; it burned down in 2001. The Veteran of Foreign Wars Post No. 586 parking lot sits on the property today. Pictured are the bar in 1923 and the cover of Fatigati's menu.

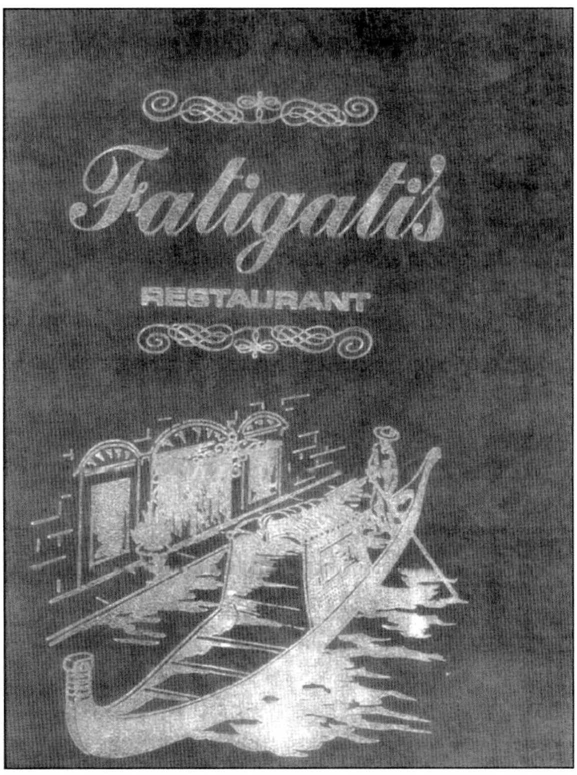

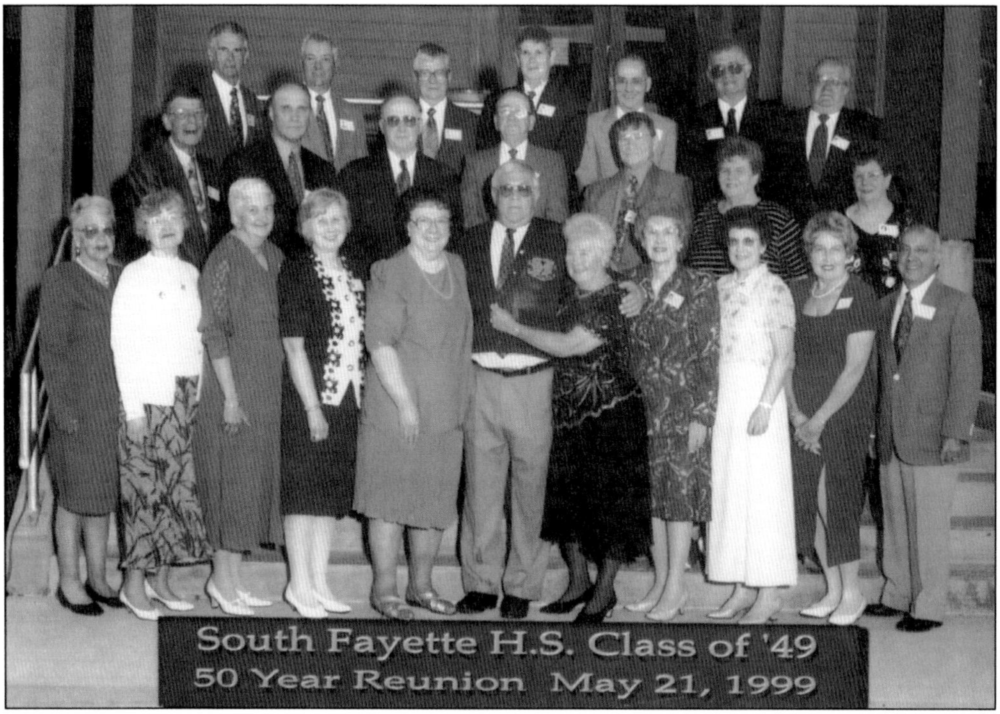

The class of 1949 is pictured at its 50th reunion. Many of these graduates stayed in the community to open businesses and raise families, and some became the founding members of the Historical Society of South Fayette Township.

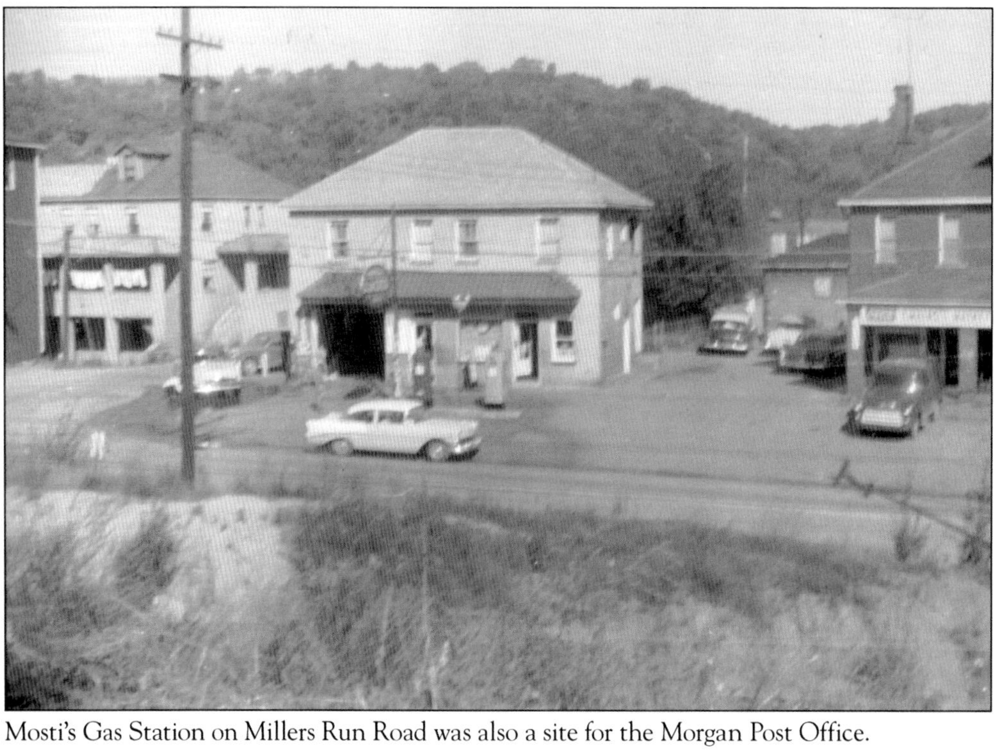

Mosti's Gas Station on Millers Run Road was also a site for the Morgan Post Office.

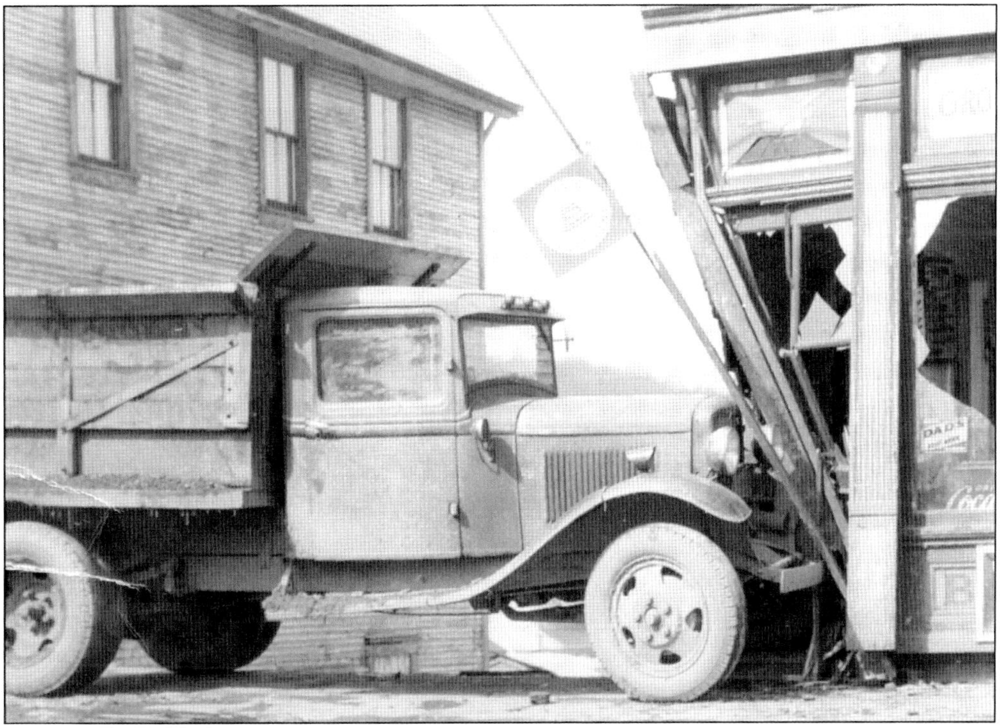

One year, a local dump truck crashed into Mosti's Grocery Store on Millers Run Road. Local roads were mostly dirt and slag throughout the township.

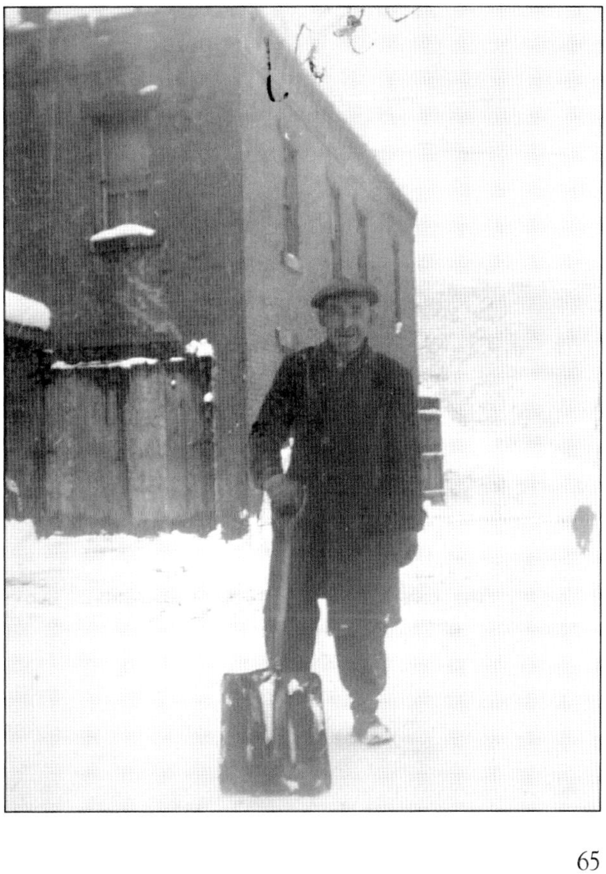

Joseph Beitle is shown shoveling snow with a no. 4 coal shovel. His grandson operated John Kosky Coal, which has evolved into John Kosky Contracting.

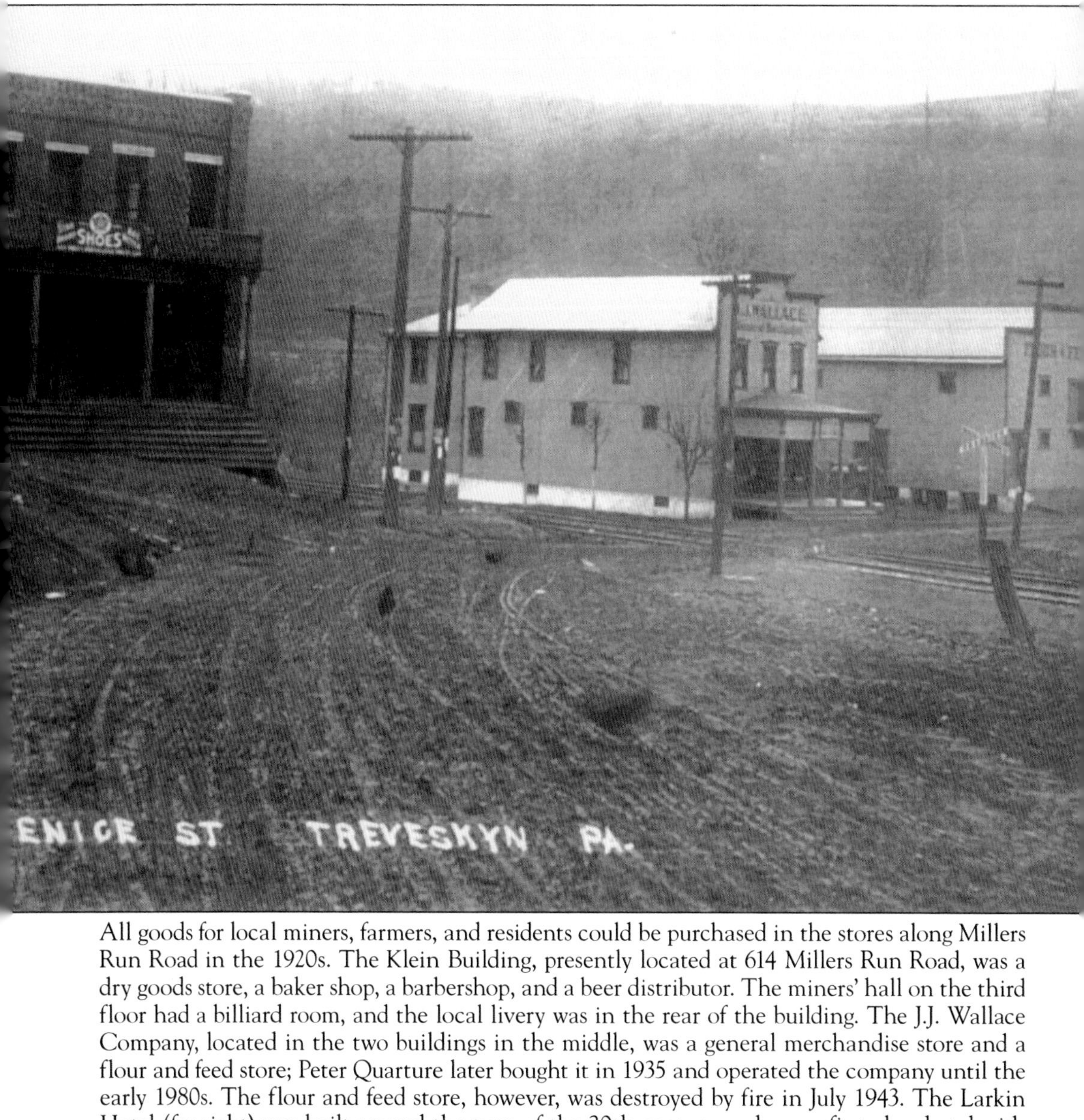

All goods for local miners, farmers, and residents could be purchased in the stores along Millers Run Road in the 1920s. The Klein Building, presently located at 614 Millers Run Road, was a dry goods store, a baker shop, a barbershop, and a beer distributor. The miners' hall on the third floor had a billiard room, and the local livery was in the rear of the building. The J.J. Wallace Company, located in the two buildings in the middle, was a general merchandise store and a flour and feed store; Peter Quarture later bought it in 1935 and operated the company until the early 1980s. The flour and feed store, however, was destroyed by fire in July 1943. The Larkin Hotel (far right) was built around the turn of the 20th century and was a first-class hotel with bar, restaurant, and rooms above. Many of the clientele came from the Wabash Railroad, which is still in service today as the Wheeling & Lake Erie Railroad. The Klein Building and Larkin Hotel still exist along Millers Run Road. The J.J. Wallace Building was demolished in 2007 to create Cuddy Lane.

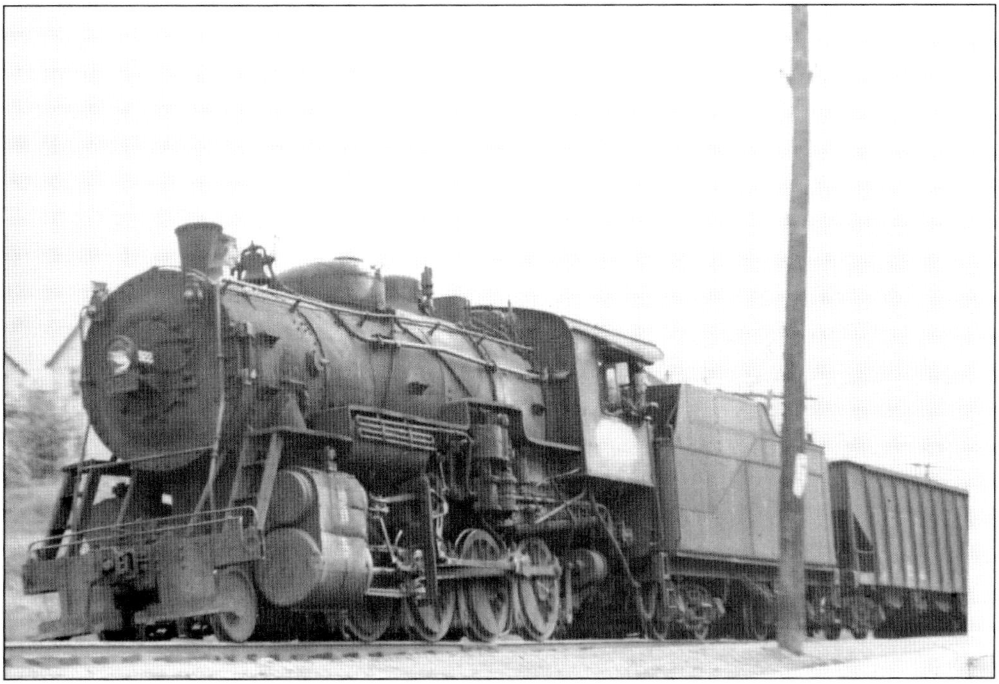

This is the Wabash train passing through Morgan. Trains passed through South Fayette and other local towns on a daily basis, carrying coal and various commodities. This railroad still serves the local gas, oil, and coke industries.

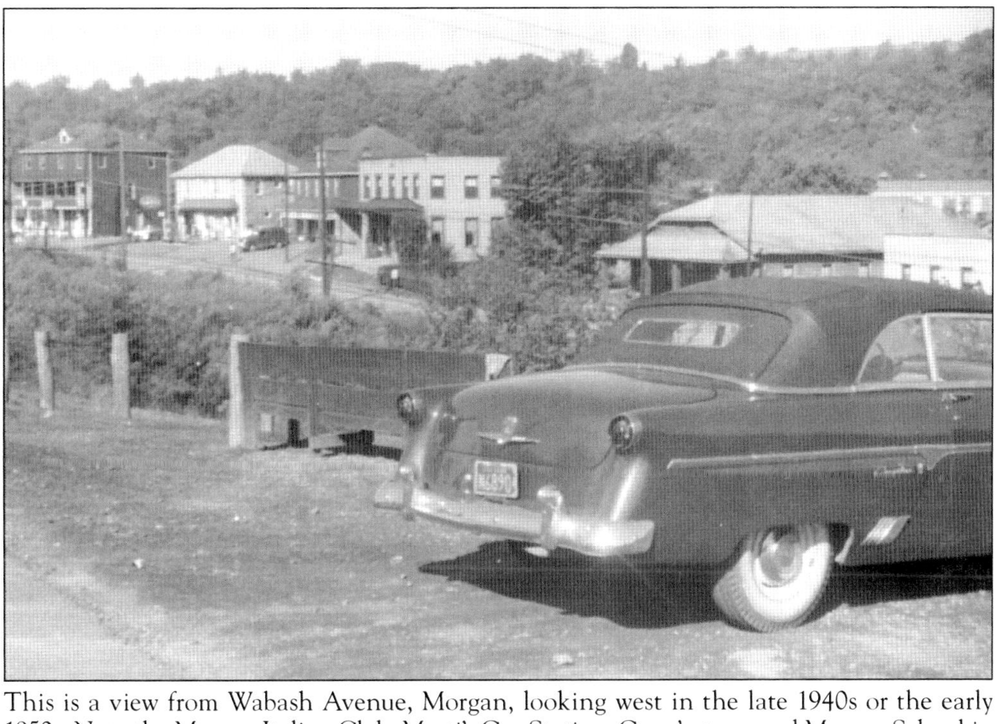

This is a view from Wabash Avenue, Morgan, looking west in the late 1940s or the early 1950s. Note the Morgan Italian Club, Mosti's Gas Station, Gross's store, and Morgan School in the background.

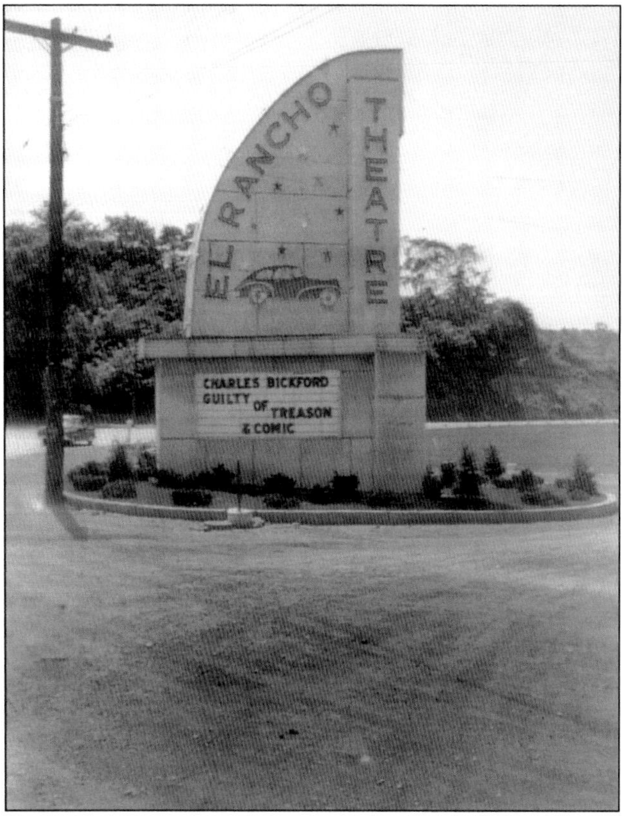

El Rancho Drive-In had two "lives." The picture at left shows the entrance from 1949 to 1964 at the corner of Washington Pike and today's Route 50 (where Burgunder Dodge, and now Gillece Plumbing, is located). Because of the Interstate 79 property acquisition, El Rancho moved a mile away to Hickory Grade Road and was open from 1971 to 1984. The photograph below shows the big screen where many local families enjoyed an evening under stars watching a cartoon, coming attractions, and the feature presentation. South Fayette soccer fields were later on this site, which will now be home to the Watson Institute.

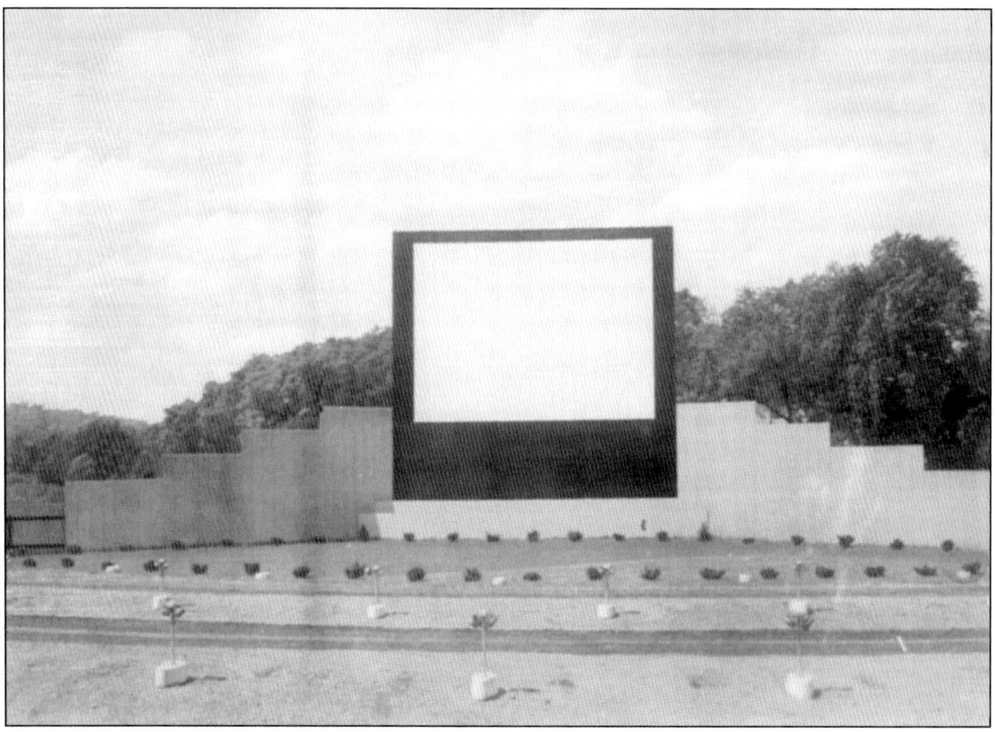

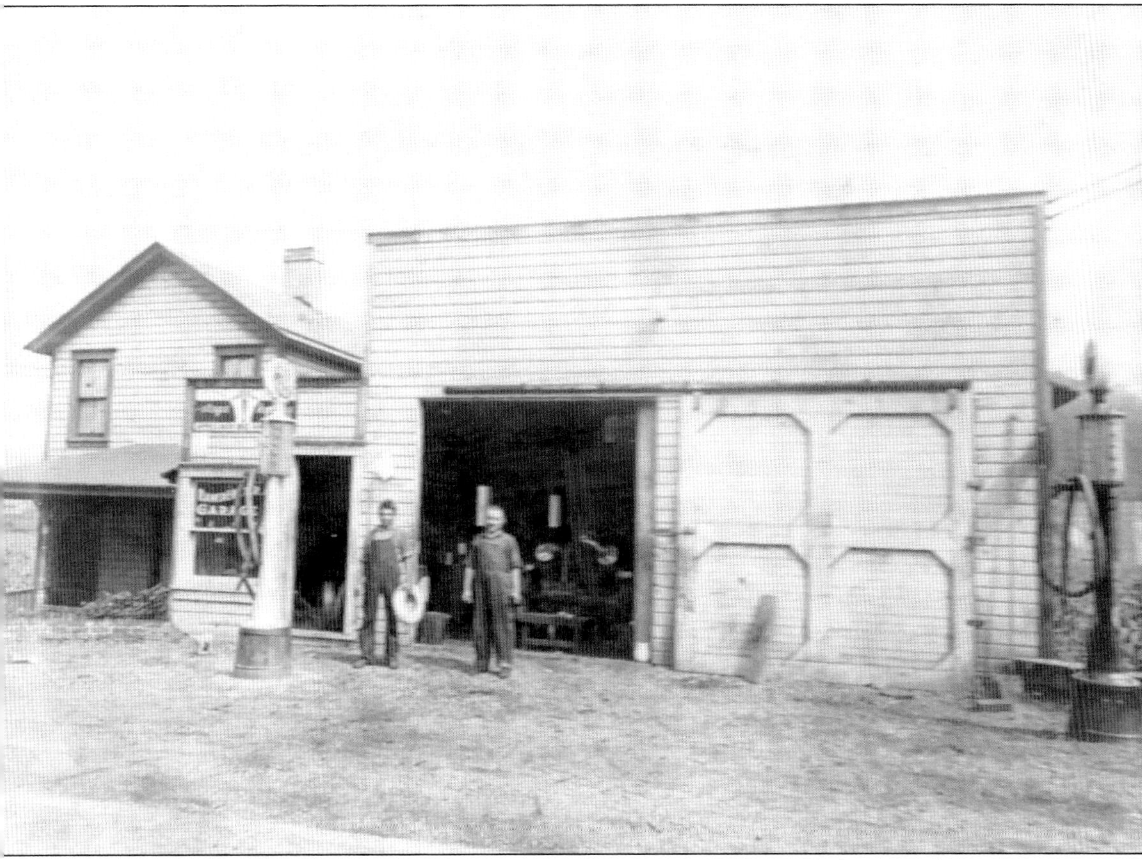

Rainier's Garage, 697 Millers Run Road, in the 1920s had a hand pump with dispenser for pumping up to five gallons of gas at a time. Presently, Bell Container Company and Howard Concrete Pumping are on this site. Note the train trestle at the far right, which is still in use today by the Wheeling & Lake Erie Railroad.

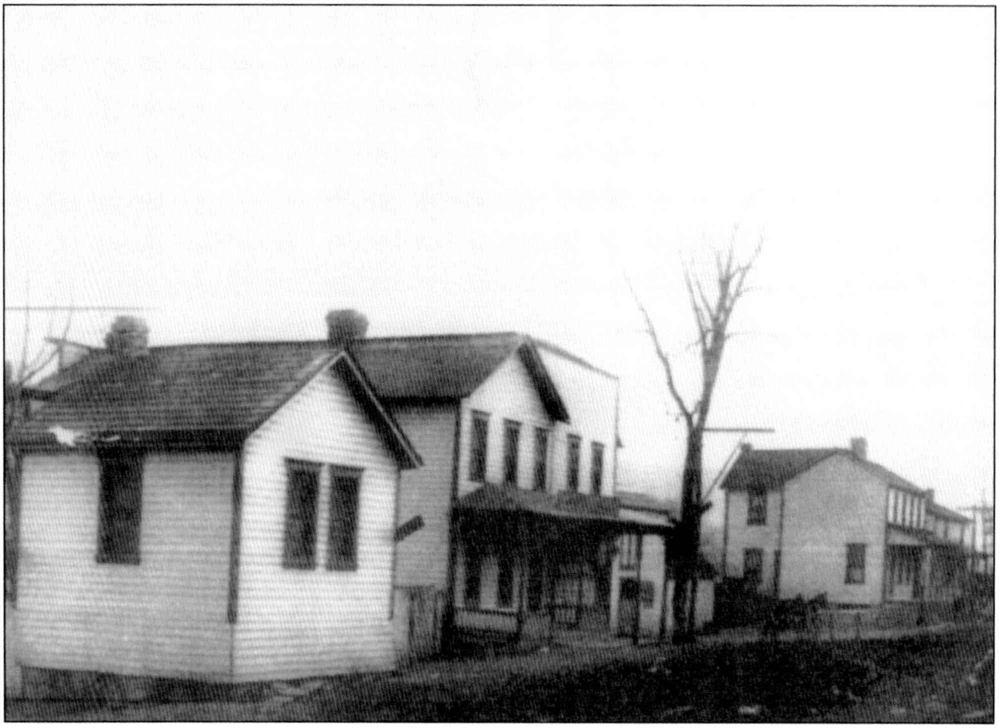

The Cecil Hotel, Millers Run Road, Gladden, was located near the entrance of Cecil-Sturgeon Road and the former Desmet Lumber Company.

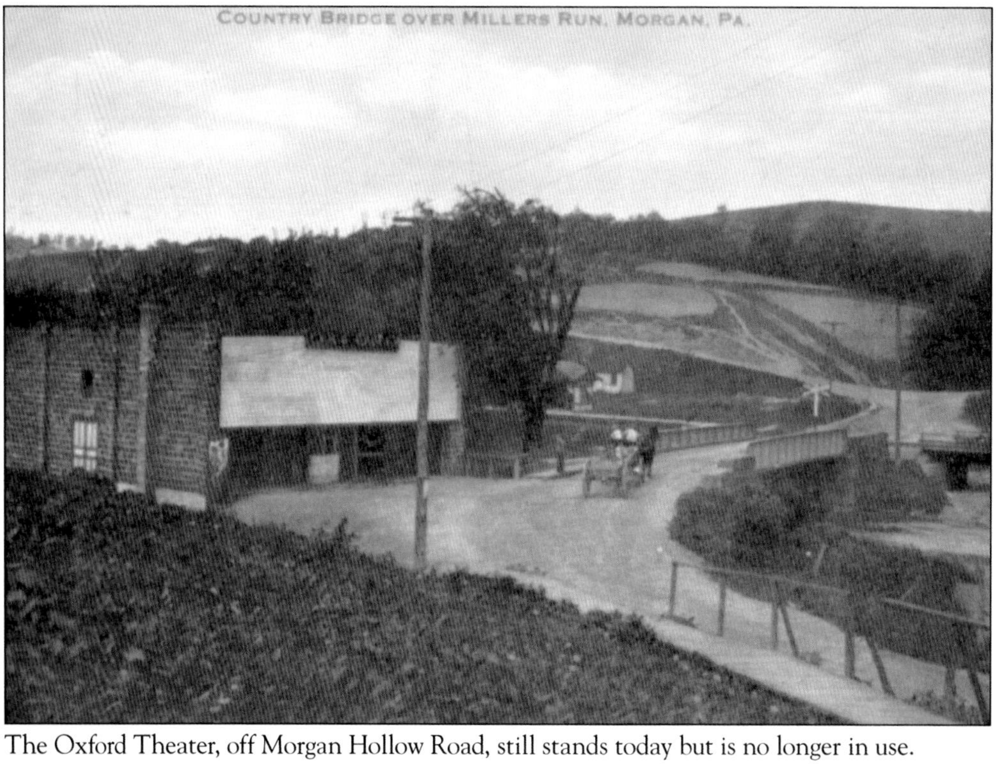

The Oxford Theater, off Morgan Hollow Road, still stands today but is no longer in use.

These are tools used by the local barber and are representative of the time period around the beginning of the 20th century. (Courtesy of Matthew Shuck.)

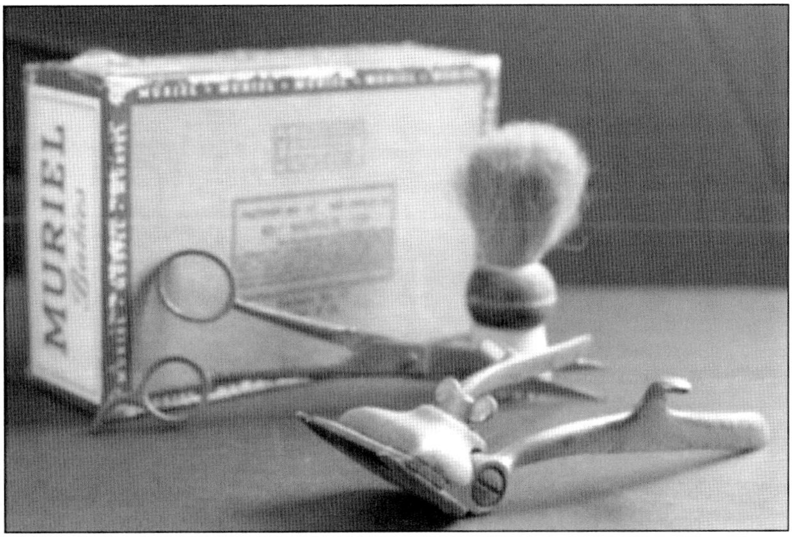

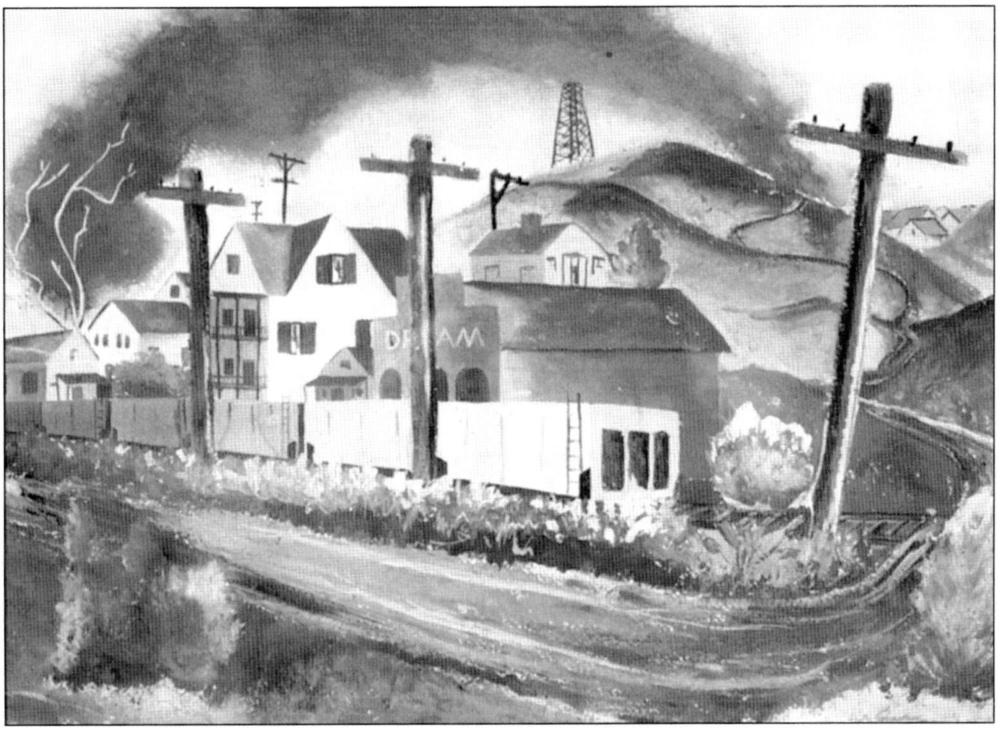

This is a painting by Mildred Quarture; it depicts the Dream Theater as viewed from the window of her home. The Dream Theater was located at 619 Millers Run Road and was started in the early 1900s by the Tearpok family, operating through the late 1930s. It showed silent movies. In the 1950s, the fire department relocated to the theater with the school district adding its bus garage to the firehouse before the fire department eventually moved to its present location in 1967. (Courtesy of Matthew Shuck.)

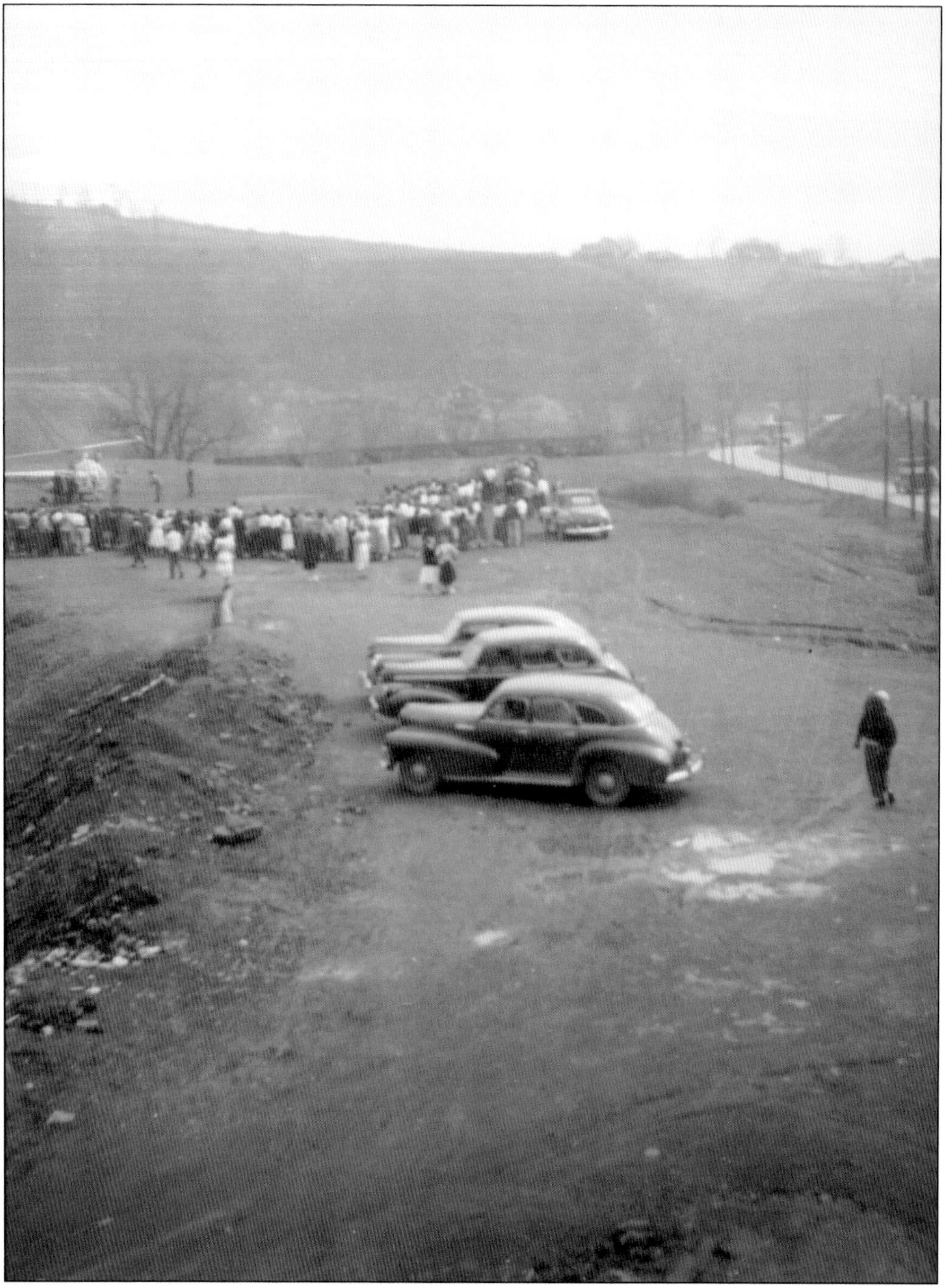

This was taken from Doc's Café, with a view looking east toward Bridgeville. This is the present-day location of the South Fayette Township Municipal Complex. Sygan Hill is in the background; Millers Run Road is on the right.

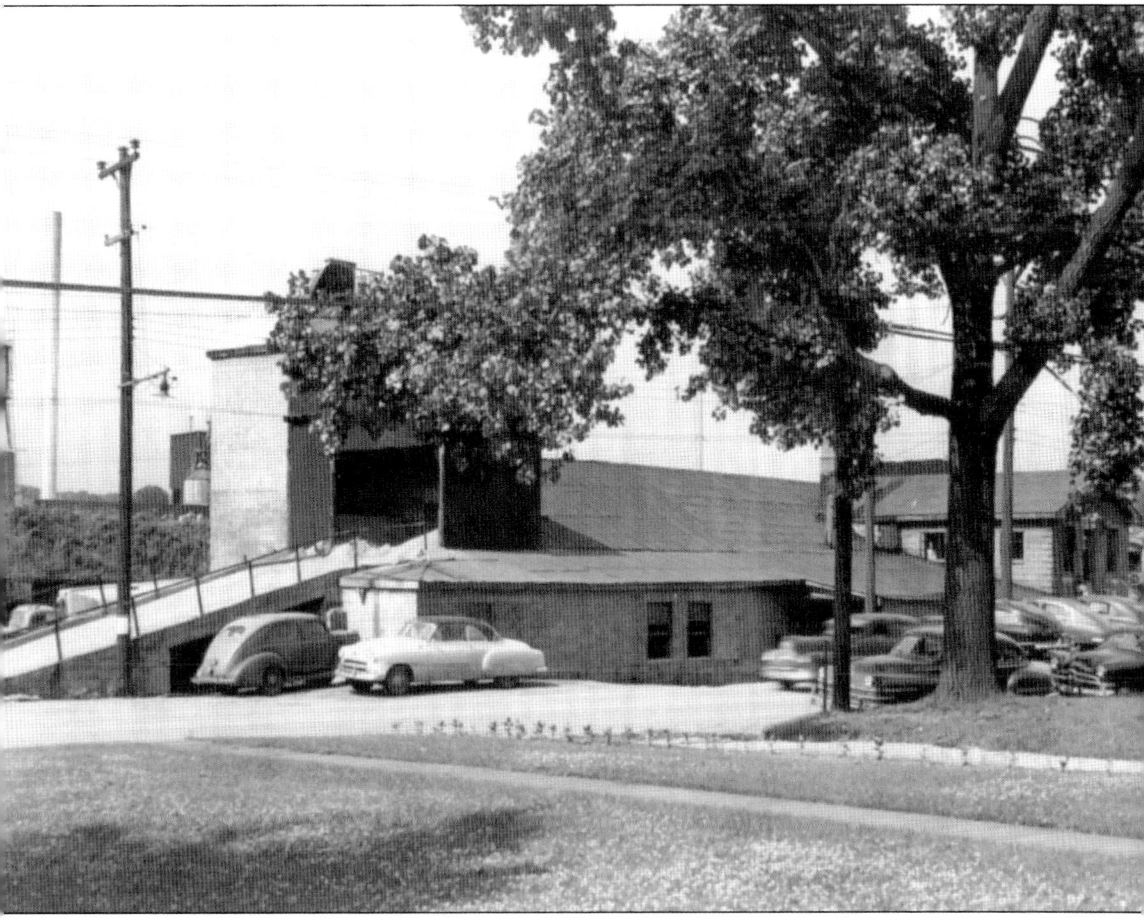

This was taken along Millers Run Road in the yard across from what is now Limestone Products. The main road to Bridgeville ran directly in front of the building. This yard is now under what is present-day Route 50. Note Reichold (American Cyanamid) toward the left.

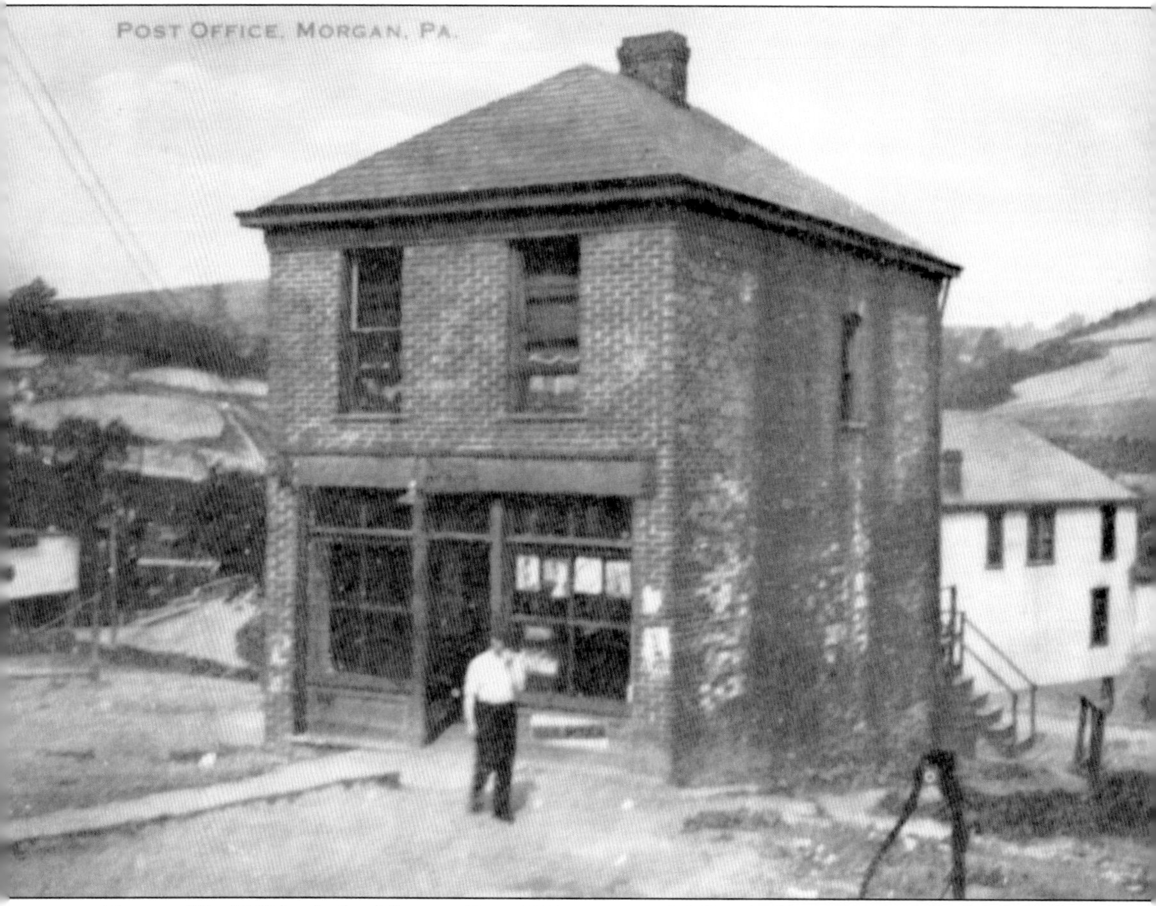

During World War I, the Morgan Post Office was in Malbos's Grocery Store. Eugene Malbos was the postmaster, and 17-year-old Alice McKean was the assistant. When Malbos died in 1926, McKean became the postmistress, and the office was moved into a building at the corner of Millers Run and Old Oakdale Roads. In 1932, it moved again to 570 Millers Run Road next to the Morgan Hotel, and then in 1944, it moved to the Lisi house and to a gasoline station run by Theodore Mosti. The 570 Millers Run building is currently a residential apartment. Today's Morgan Post Office is in its own building at 514 Millers Run Road next to the current municipal building. The Cuddy Post Office was established in 1899 with Arthur E. Orr serving as the first postmaster. Later, Josephine Levi ran it from her house until the new post office was built.

Four

Fire Departments and Clubs

South Fayette is served not only by its own police department, but also by four volunteer fire departments. Once they began, the residents did not have to rely on nearby Bridgeville or other communities to come to their aid.

Several social clubs, mostly tied to nationalities and benevolent needs, began during the 1920s, and some of them are still in business today.

THE HISTORICAL SOCIETY OF SOUTH FAYETTE TOWNSHIP

Dedicated to the preservation of the history of South Fayette Township
Volume #2 - April 2004 *Sue Caffrey - Editor*

Domenick Invernezzi (1915-2003)
Founding Member
South Fayette Fire Department

"We were all green horns. We didn't know nothing about fighting fire. We went everywhere. We helped everybody."

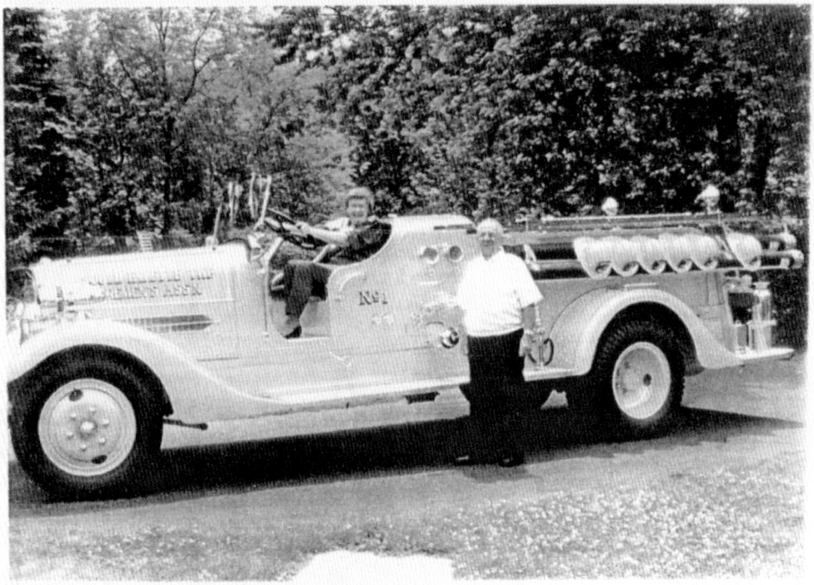

Dom and Elizabeth Invernezzi
1937 Ahrens Fox Pumper
South Fayette Volunteer Fire Department

December 16, 1945 (11:00 p.m.). Domenick Invernezzi arrived home from Navy service two years to the hour of his enlistment date. Working as part of a LST561 team (a land/ship/tank vehicle), Dom brought medical staff and supplies into Italy during WWII and German prisoners out of France. The rest of his tour was spent in Saipan, serving as a Master at Arms and preparing servicemen for their return home.

Lunch at Fatigati's in 1937 resulted in the birth of South Fayette's first volunteer fire department. Bridgeville and Oakdale used to cover the fires in the area. After the announcement that a South Fayette company was beginning, 200 men signed up, paying 10¢-a-month dues. Coverage included Gladden, Maude Mine, Cuddy, Morgan, and Sygan. The first truck purchased was a 1937 Arhens-Fox triple combination pumper and booster with hose carrier and a chemical tank, painted yellow with gold pinstriping. This was very innovative for the times since all other fire vehicles were traditionally red. The department's current location—since 1967—is 661 Millers Run Road on the former site of a mountain of mine residue known as the "smelly slate dump." Domenick Invernezzi, pictured here, was one of the first firemen. He was also instrumental in reviving Veterans of Foreign Wars Post No. 586 in Cuddy.

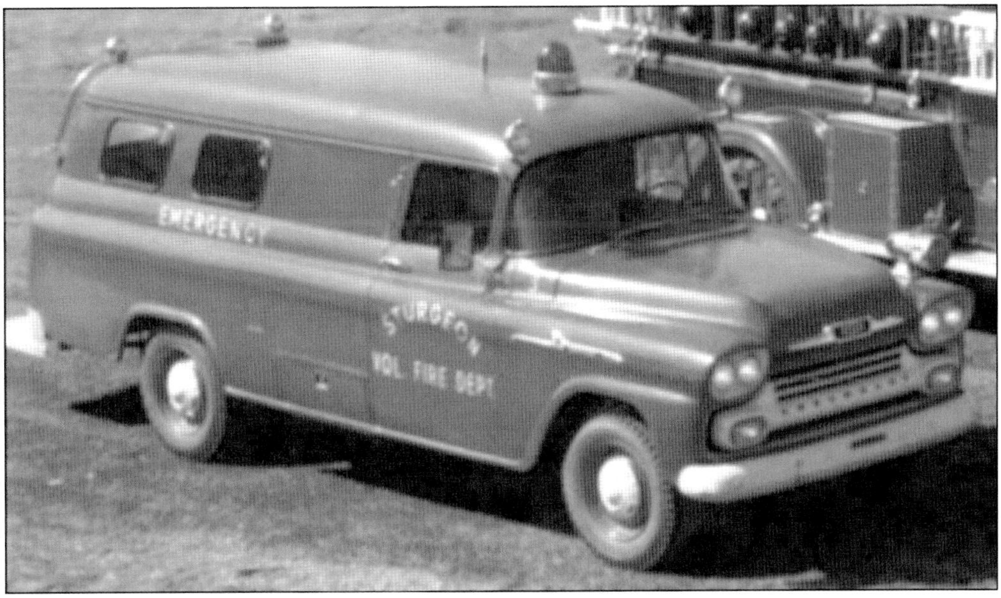

In 1943, a toddler playing with matches caused a fire at the Sturgeon Hotel on Main Street. Departments from four other communities responded, but an entire block burned down and 35 people were left homeless. By 1946, a group of men had formed the Sturgeon Volunteer Fire Department. In 1947, the department built a new garage. In 1958, a squad Chevrolet Apache panel truck was bought (pictured). In 1964, a social hall was added onto the garage.

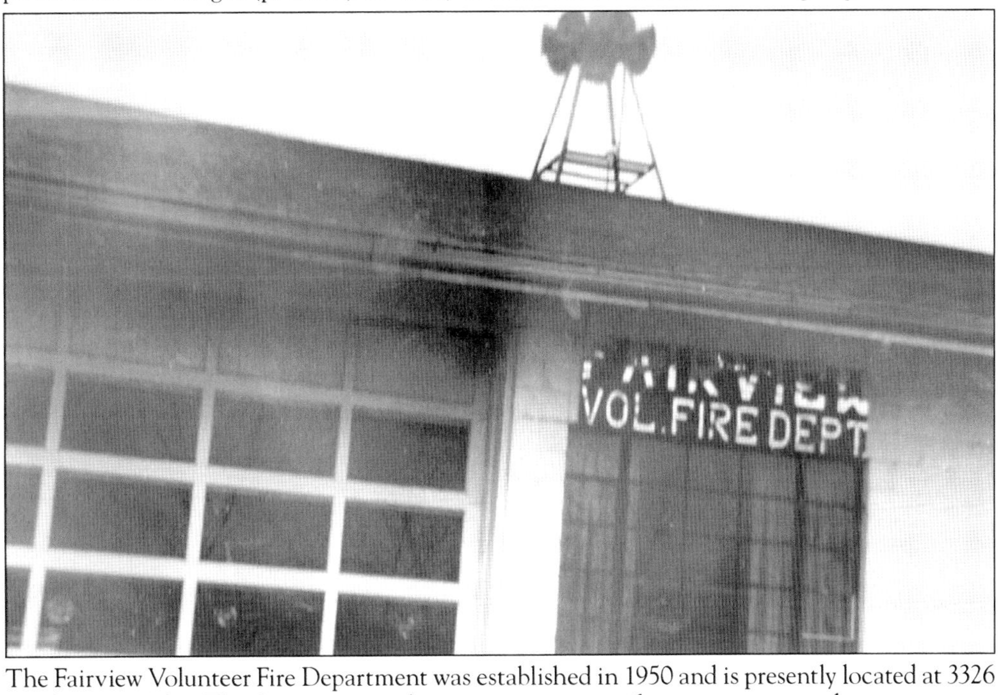

The Fairview Volunteer Fire Department was established in 1950 and is presently located at 3326 Washington Pike. The firemen specialize in ice rescue, swift water rescue, and rope rescue as well as all kinds of fires. Attached to the fire station is the Sunset Room, a large banquet facility that is the site of many graduation parties, wedding receptions, and local dinners. Pictured is the alarm equipment on the roof of the original station.

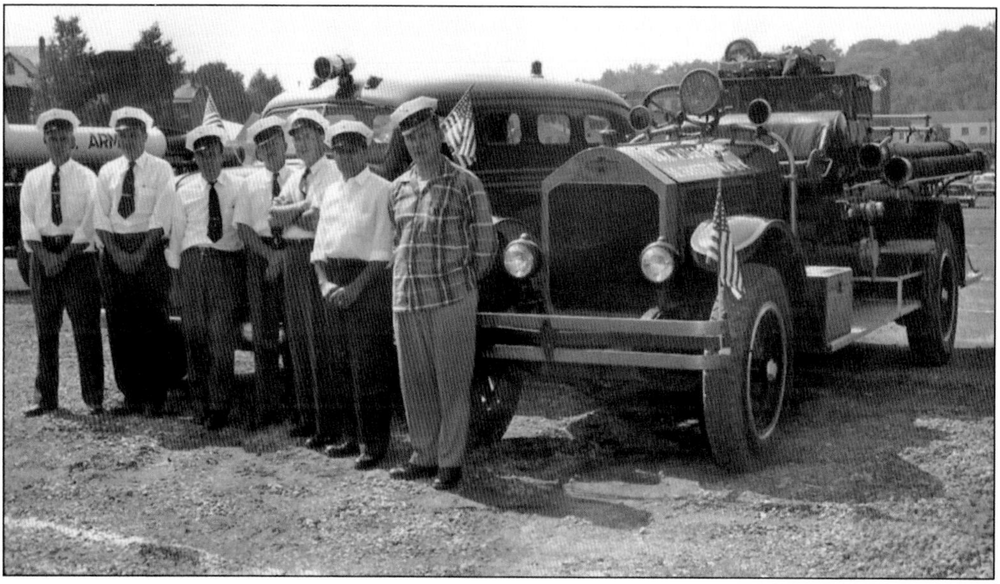

In January 1956, a small group of residents met to lay the groundwork for the Oak Ridge Volunteer Fire Department. A ladies auxiliary was formed that July, helping to fundraise for the next 38 years with Monday night bingo, fish fries, and card parties. The members helped build the fire station, constructed on land purchased from Henrietta Meyer and completed in 1961, with additions made in 1977 and 1986. Standing in front of Oak Ridge Volunteer Fire Department's American LaFrance 1929 truck and 1941 Chevrolet squad car are, from left to right, Tom Robinson, Joe Ballo, Andy Sasfai, Jim Hormel, Bill Taylor, Mario Martino, and John Ballo.

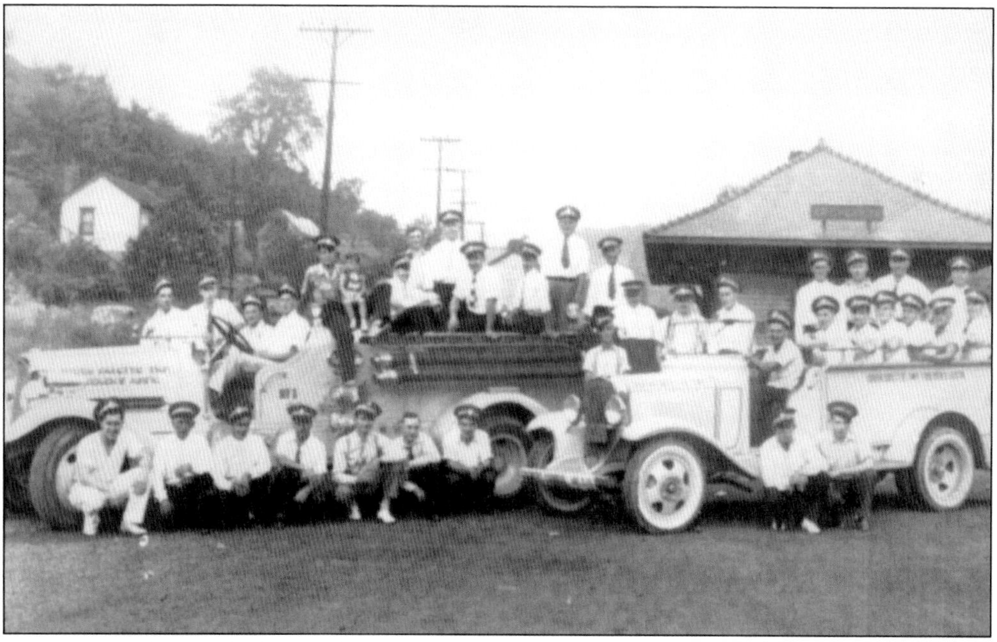

Members of the South Fayette Fireman's Association gather in front of the Treveskyn Train Station. Some members identified include Joseph Teyssier, Frank Hollman, Lou Guerra, John Gardner, Domenick Invernezzi, George Usnick, Joe Kamovich, Harry Saussol, Waldo Mencarelli, Henry Bourg, Guy Petrillo, and Sam Fatigati.

The Franco-Belgian Club was founded in 1908 in Sturgeon as a beneficial society for insurance and camaraderie among area French and Belgian immigrants. Previously, the three-story brick building housed a reading room, which still contains hundreds of books written in French and English, and a ballroom and stage, which hosted many dances and holiday performances. The tavern on the first floor remains functional, and a framed letter of congratulations from the Belgian embassy on the club's 100th anniversary is proudly displayed inside.

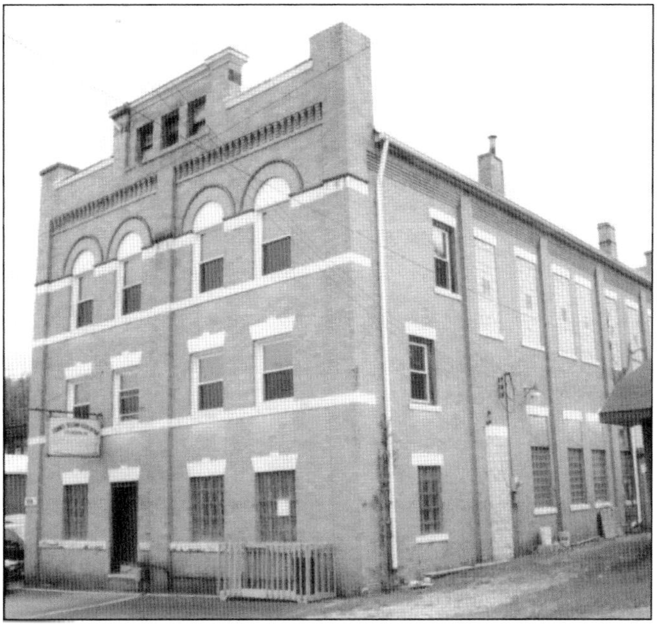

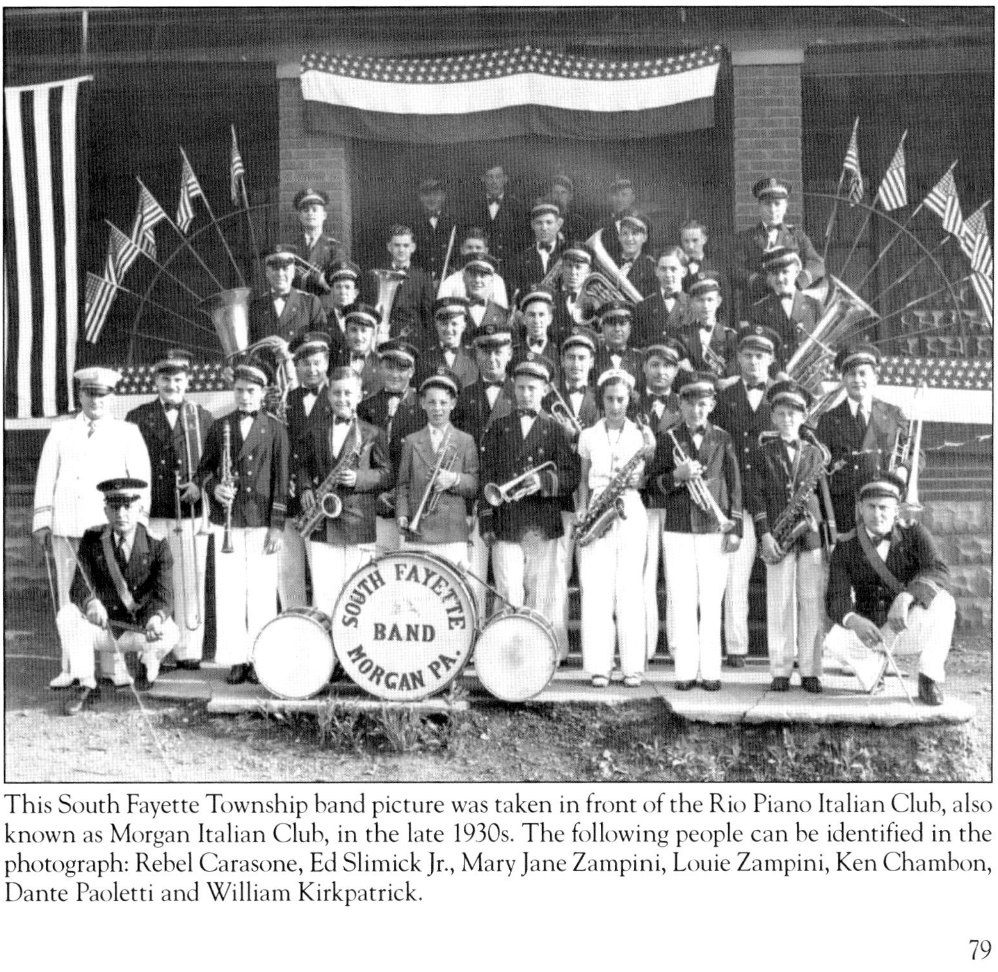

This South Fayette Township band picture was taken in front of the Rio Piano Italian Club, also known as Morgan Italian Club, in the late 1930s. The following people can be identified in the photograph: Rebel Carasone, Ed Slimick Jr., Mary Jane Zampini, Louie Zampini, Ken Chambon, Dante Paoletti and William Kirkpatrick.

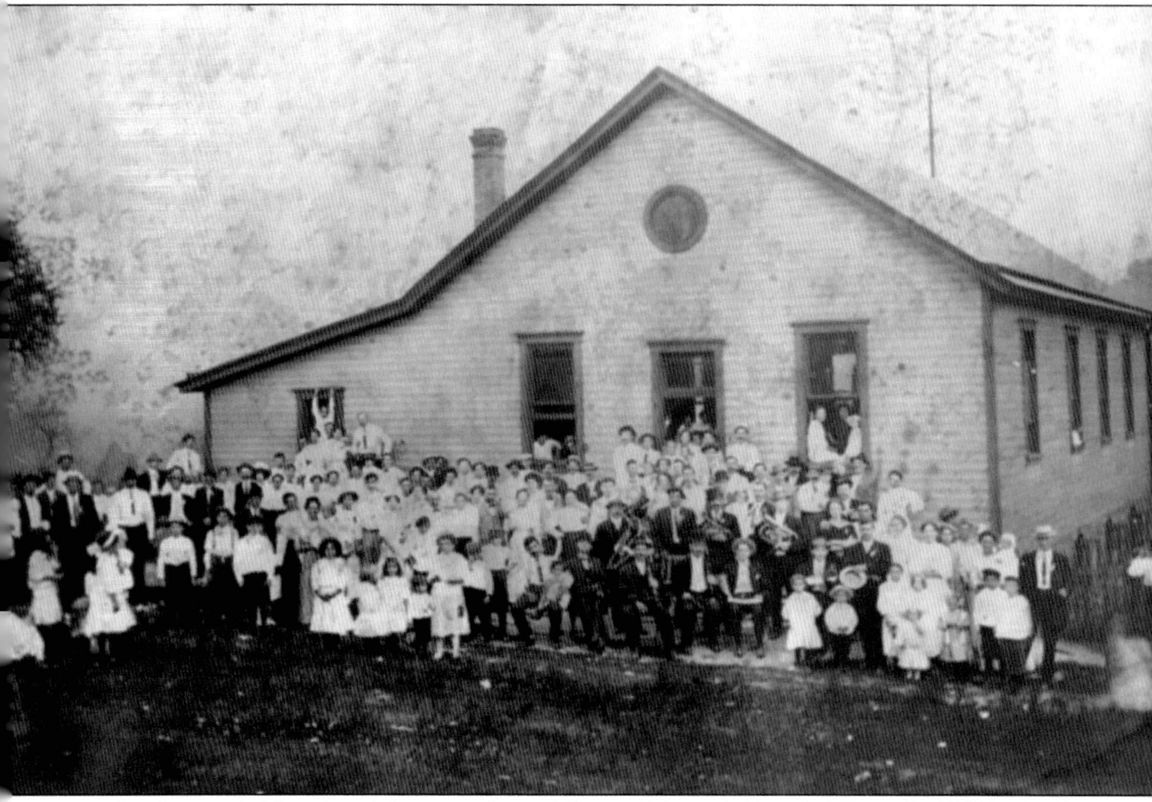

The Slovenska Narodna Podporna Jednota (Slovene National Benefit Society [SNPJ]) Lodge No. 6 opened on Hook Street (540 Third Avenue) in 1911, seven years after the organization was founded in Chicago in 1904. The SNPJ lodge burned down on April 8, 1982, and was rebuilt on the same site in 1984. The lodge is known for its polka dances and maintains a large library of hundreds of Slovenian/Cleveland-style polka recordings. It offers a bowling alley, 300-seat banquet room, social and cultural opportunities, a youth division, college scholarships, and community service projects. Pictured is the lodge as it looked in the 1920s.

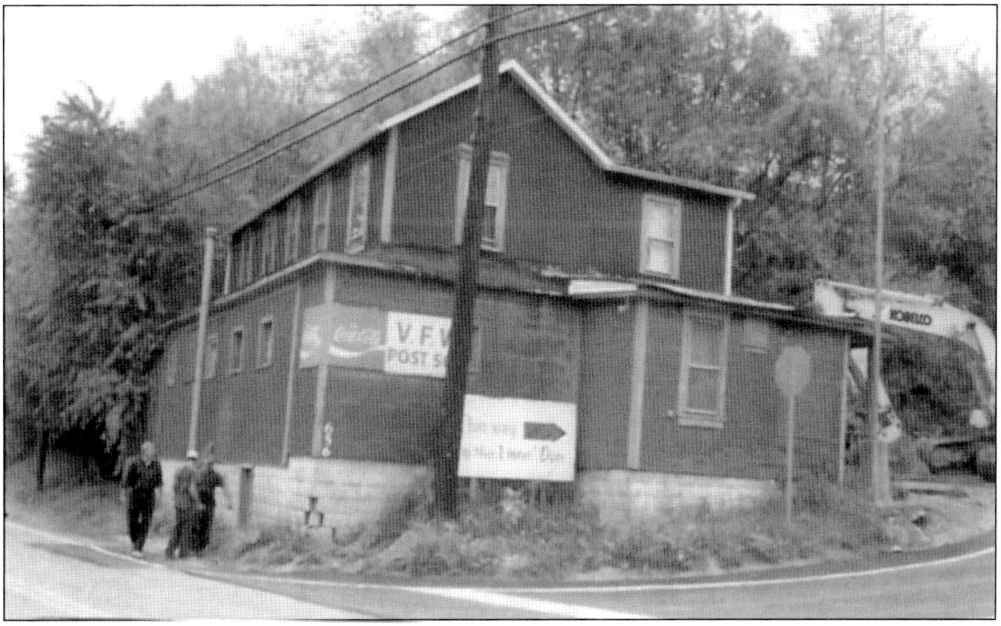

The James F. McClusky Veterans of Foreign Wars Post No. 586, pictured here on the corner of Old Oakdale and Millers Run Roads, was formed in 1943 to help and support the returning veterans from war. Eleven of the thirteen founding members were World War II veterans, and the other two were Spanish-American War veterans. In 2005, this building was torn down and the post moved to new quarters at 637 Millers Run Road, Cuddy.

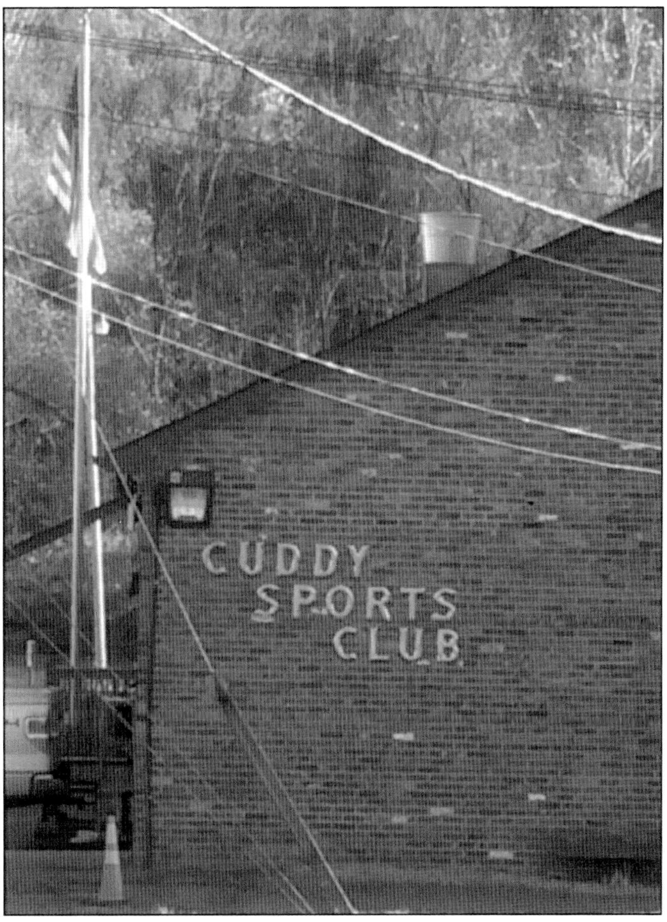

Established in 1936 when the township was primarily a coal mining community, the Cuddy Sports Club, at 61 South Fayette Street, is a vestige of "old" South Fayette in a rapidly changing present. It has been noted that "from businessmen and the rich to the very poor, everybody gets along here."

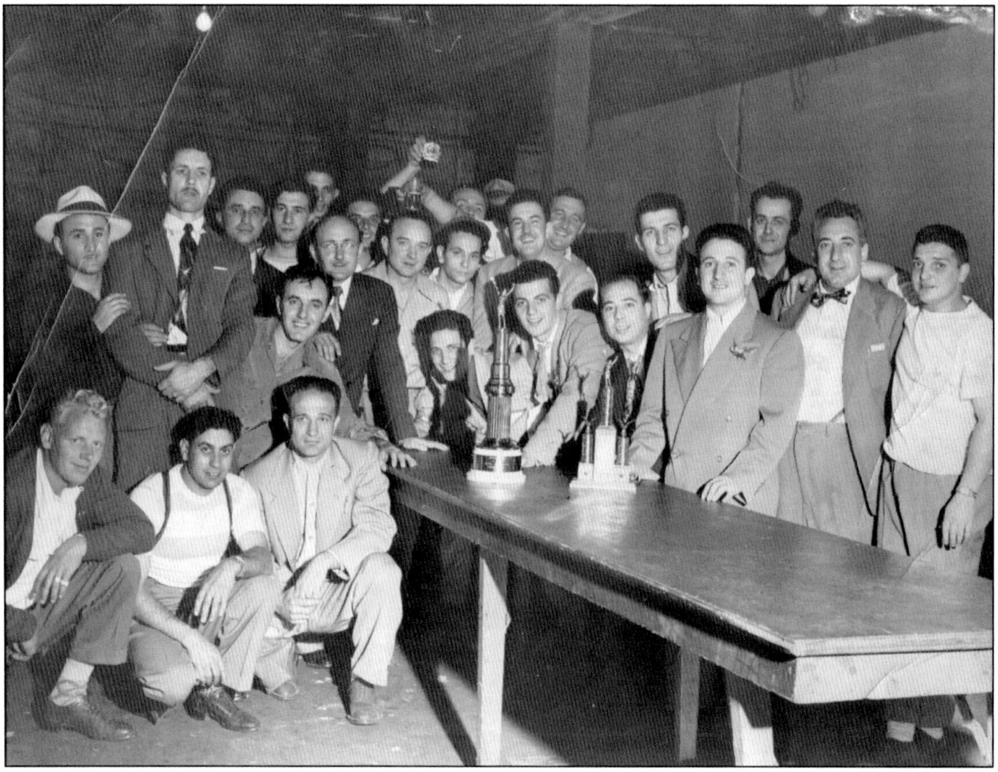

Members of the Morgan Italian Club have gathered for a photograph.

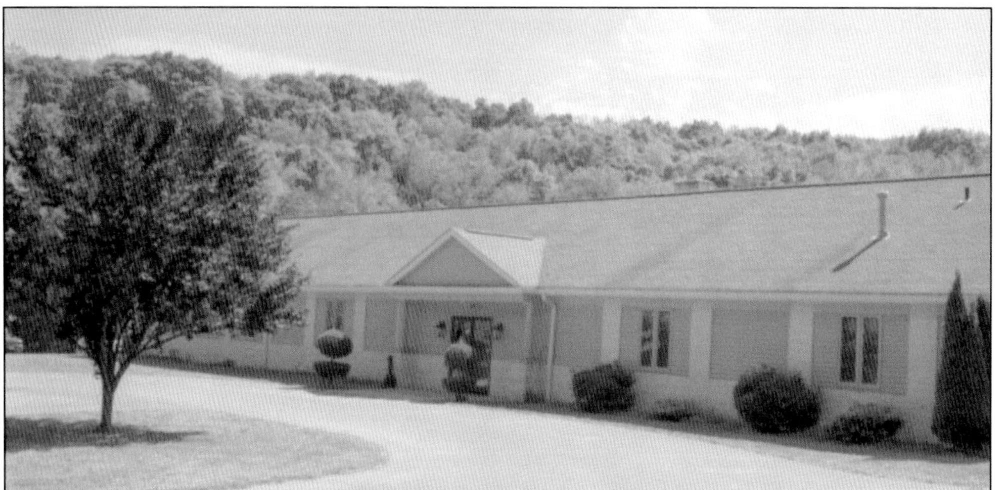

The Alpine Hunting and Fishing Club, headquartered at 220 Alpine Road, was founded in 1946 by Italian immigrants from Tuscany who had become successful family-oriented businessmen and restaurant owners in the Pittsburgh area. The clubhouse was completely destroyed in 2002 by a bolt of lightning and fire, resulting in a reconstruction of the facilities, which now include a rebuilt clubhouse, a bocce court, a stocked pond, an outdoor shooting range, an archery range, bird pens, a dog kennel, a springhouse, a picnic pavilion, a club garden, and improved fields for the propagation of wildlife. The club limits itself to 200 members and is a licensed shooting preserve on 143 acres. (Courtesy of Linda James.)

Five

Soccer, Baseball, and More

The Morgan Strasser soccer team competed in the National Amateur Cup many times, making it to the championship game four times and winning twice. The Morgan Soccer Club was the best amateur team in the entire United States in 1940 and 1943. It also competed in the National Open Cup many times, reaching the championship three times and winning once, in 1949.

The North American Professional Soccer League consisted of the Chicago Maroons, Chicago Vikings, Detroit Wolverines, Toronto Greenbacks, and the Pittsburgh Indians in 1946. After finishing fourth in the 1946 season, the Indians won the league championship easily the following year. Prior to 1946, the Indians had been the Morgan Strasser team, a powerful amateur team that dominated the Western Pennsylvania Keystone League. Pete Strasser, who was inducted into the Western Pennsylvania Chapter Hall of Fame in 1977, owned the Morgan Strasser team and the Pittsburgh Indians. The manager was Anthony "Doc" Casciola. The Morgan Strasser team was the Keystone champion in 1939–1940.

Morgan High School (the predecessor to South Fayette Township High School) owns the record for the most WPIAL soccer championships at 14 (1945, 1936, 1938, a 10-year run from 1943 to 1952, and 1959). The South Fayette Township Soccer Association continues to this day, and in 2014, it was training more than 600 children to compete in-house and on travel teams affiliated with Pennsylvania West Soccer.

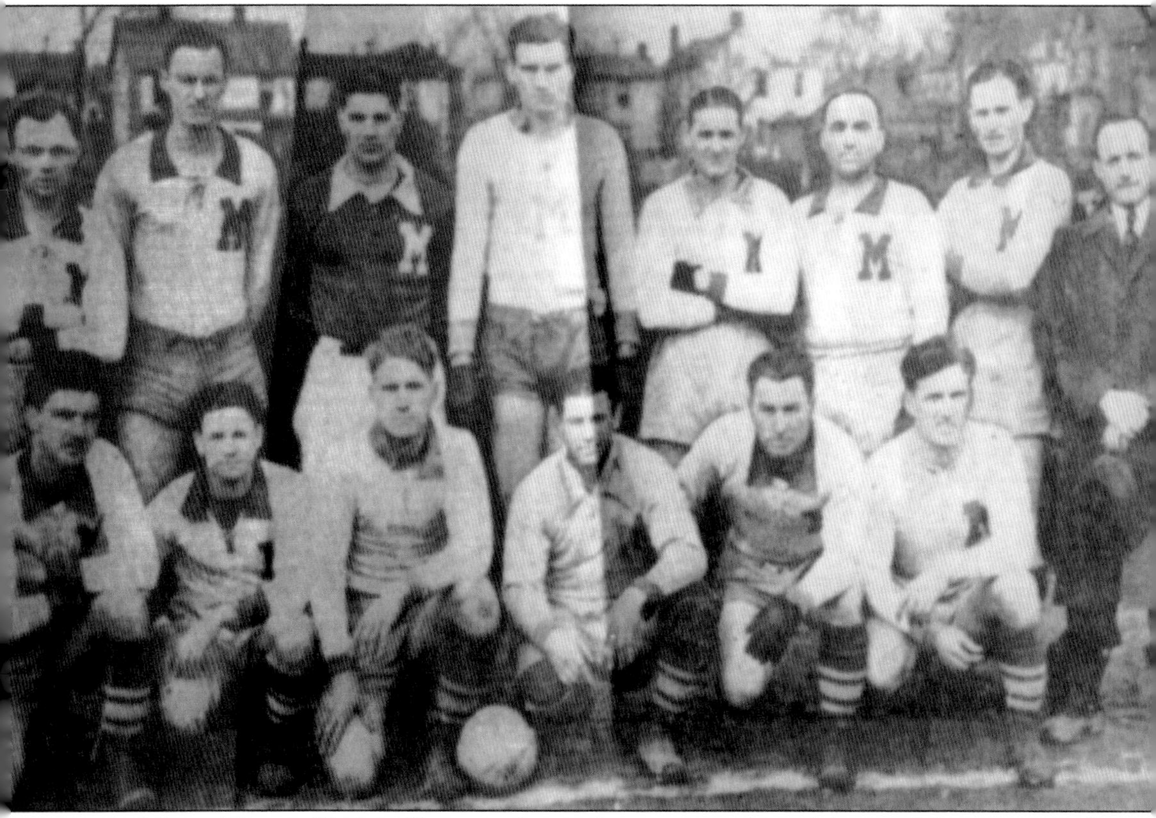

Paul "Doots" Danilo (1919–2013), pictured in the first row, second from left, scored the winning goal for Morgan Strasser in the 1940 National Amateur Cup final and played for the Pittsburgh Indians professional soccer team. He held positions as secretary and then president of the Pennsylvania West Soccer Association, commissioner for the National Cup Games and the National Amateur Cup, and was inducted into the National Soccer Hall of Fame in 1997. Retiring from play in 1952, Danilo managed the Morgan Soccer Club from 1953 to 1957. He worked for Koppers Co. polyester resins plant for 44 years. He was the son-in-law of Daniel Zampini, also a member of the National Soccer Hall of Fame, inducted in 1963.

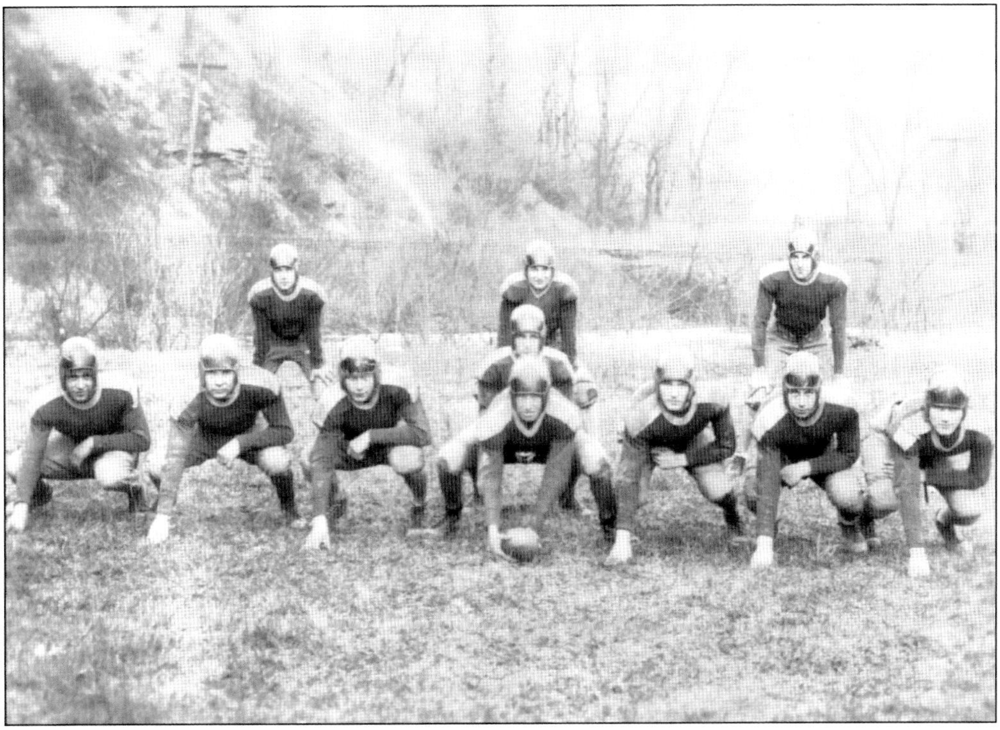

Players came from the coal mining towns of Cuddy and Morgan to form South Fayette's first football team in 1930. They practiced (with Millers Run Creek in the background) on land where the current municipal building is located. From left to right are (first row) Ralph Spalveri, George Simpson, Mike Matesia, Armando Ferri, Jake Berman, Louis Kremer, and Tony Kockosky, (second row) Earl Bushmire, Harry Pletersek, Joe Fornella, and Marshall Marianna.

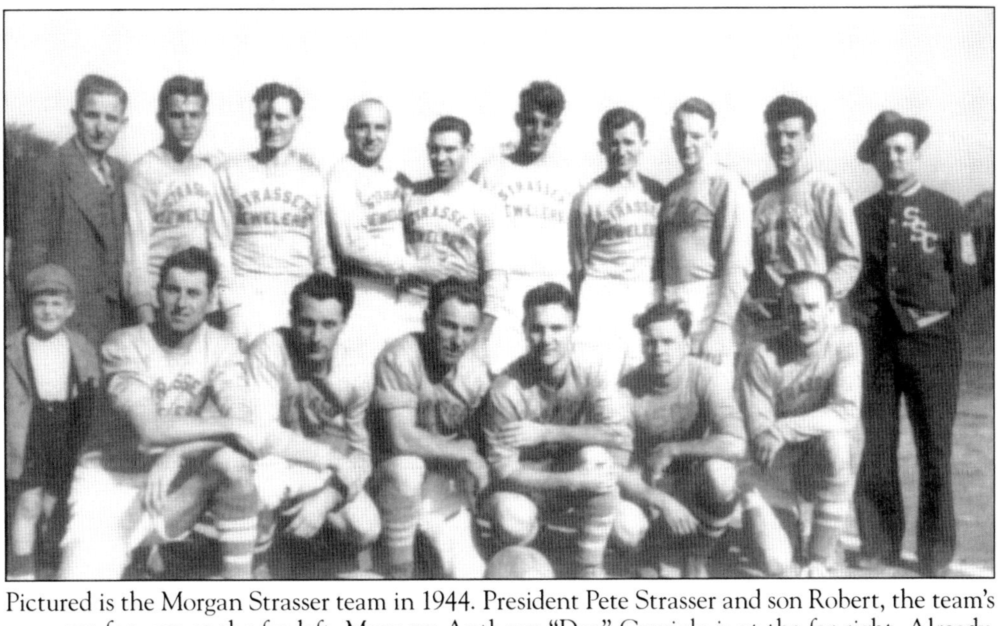

Pictured is the Morgan Strasser team in 1944. President Pete Strasser and son Robert, the team's youngest fan, are at the far left. Manager Anthony "Doc" Casciola is at the far right. Already, the team had been state champions three times and the US champion twice.

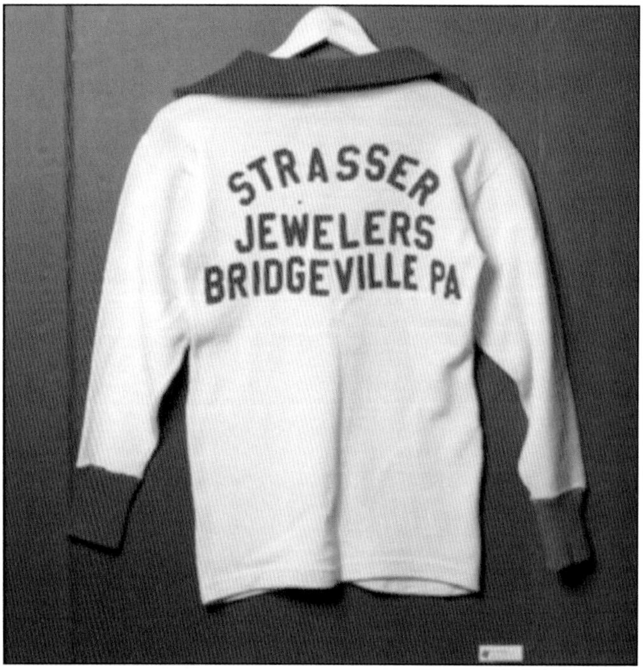

This is a Morgan Strasser soccer uniform. The Strasser Jewelry name is on the back. (Courtesy of Matthew Shuck.)

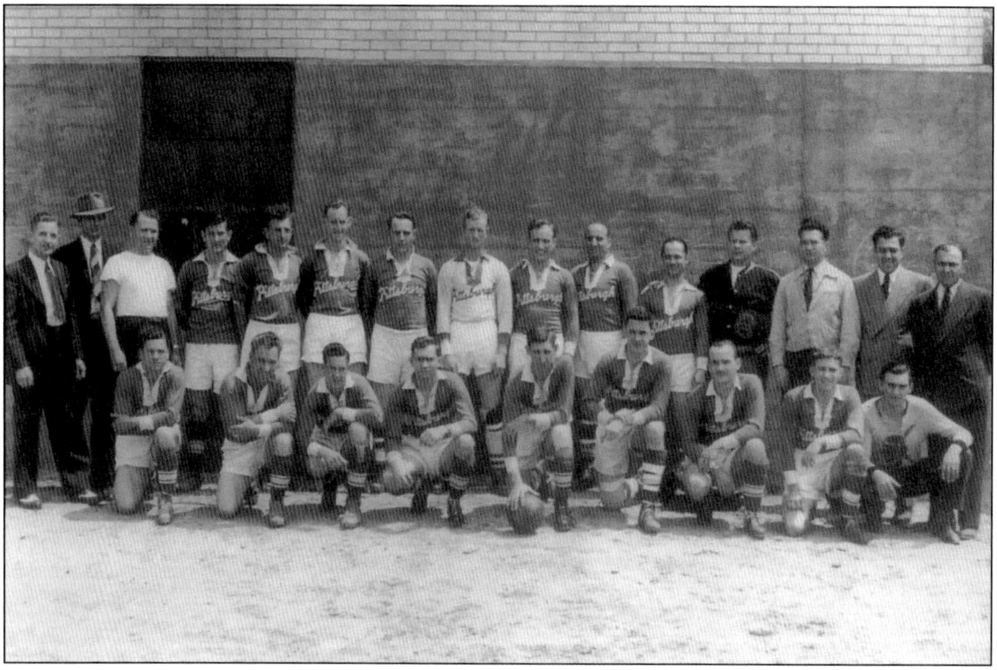

Members of the Pittsburgh Indians soccer team in 1947 are pictured. They are, from left to right, (standing) Pres. Peter Strasser, Alex Deblander (president of Keystone League), George Blake (property manager), players Romeo Vezzi, Richard Gossic, Dick Heart, Dan Gossett, George Kachurik, Tony Monaco, Fred Donelli, and Lefty Pletersek, Dick Dirs (trainer), Eugene Hillen (manager), Joseph Abraham (vice president), and Mike Abraham (secretary); (kneeling) Paul Danilo, Felix Mitchell, Merle Utchell, August Behling, Harry Pitchok, Bud Utchell, Pete Pawlik, John Bodonsky, and John Farkus (trainer). George Ross (treasurer) was absent.

Pictured is an official program from the Pittsburgh Indians 1945–1946 season.

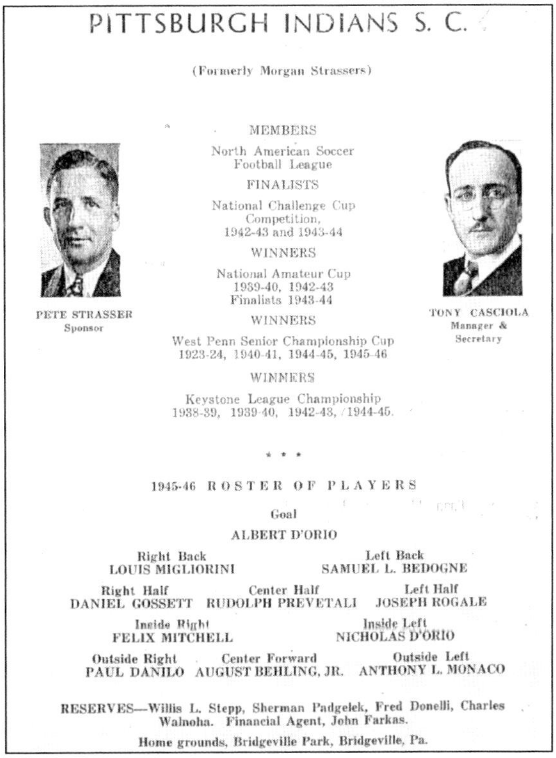

PITTSBURGH INDIANS S. C.

(Formerly Morgan Strassers)

MEMBERS
North American Soccer Football League

FINALISTS
National Challenge Cup Competition, 1942-43 and 1943-44

WINNERS
National Amateur Cup 1939-40, 1942-43
Finalists 1943-44

WINNERS
West Penn Senior Championship Cup 1923-24, 1940-41, 1944-45, 1945-46

WINNERS
Keystone League Championship 1938-39, 1939-40, 1942-43, 1944-45.

PETE STRASSER
Sponsor

TONY CASCIOLA
Manager & Secretary

* * *

1945-46 ROSTER OF PLAYERS

Goal
ALBERT D'ORIO

Right Back
LOUIS MIGLIORINI

Left Back
SAMUEL L. BEDOGNE

Right Half
DANIEL GOSSETT

Center Half
RUDOLPH PREVETALI

Left Half
JOSEPH ROGALE

Inside Right
FELIX MITCHELL

Inside Left
NICHOLAS D'ORIO

Outside Right
PAUL DANILO

Center Forward
AUGUST BEHLING, JR.

Outside Left
ANTHONY L. MONACO

RESERVES—Willis L. Stepp, Sherman Padgelek, Fred Donelli, Charles Walnoha. Financial Agent, John Farkas.

Home grounds, Bridgeville Park, Bridgeville, Pa.

Pictured is the local Cuddy soccer team, with its trophy, in the 1930s. Members are, from left to right, (first row) Charles Bourg, Chelso Donelli, and Pat Greer; (second row) T. Ludevic, Dino Castelli, Berk Jones, James Kirby, and Fred Donelli; (third row) August Mitchel, Jim Gardner, Dan Zampini, Ed Slimick, Homer Canal, Phil Dolguda, and John Townsend, manager.

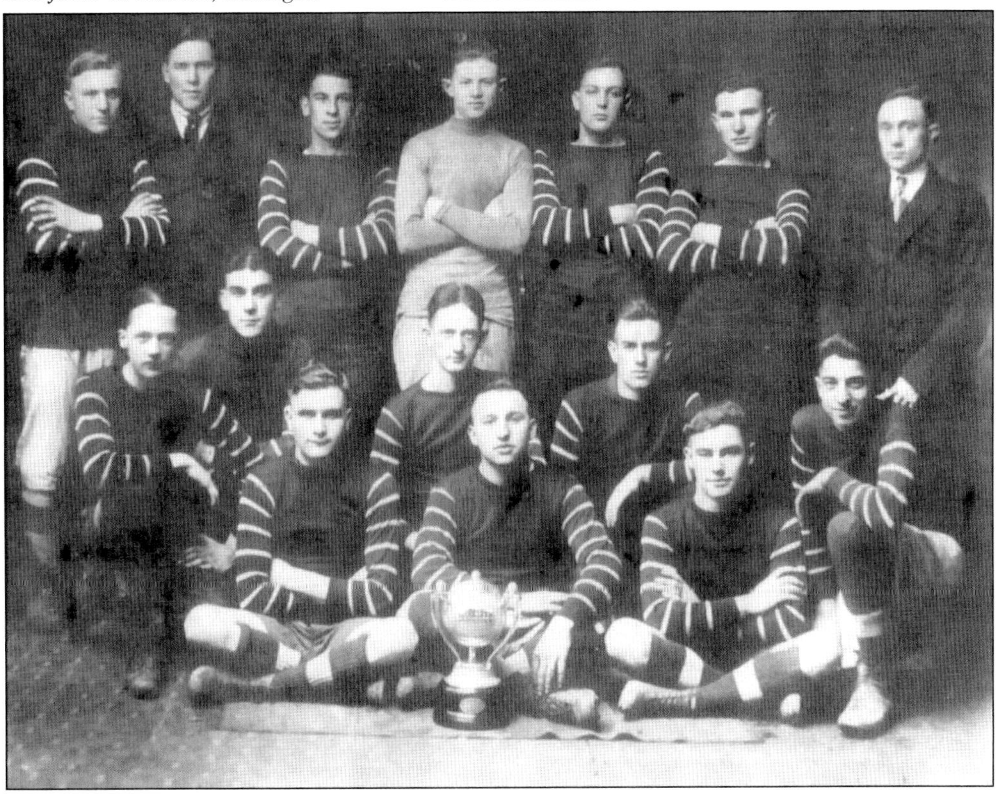

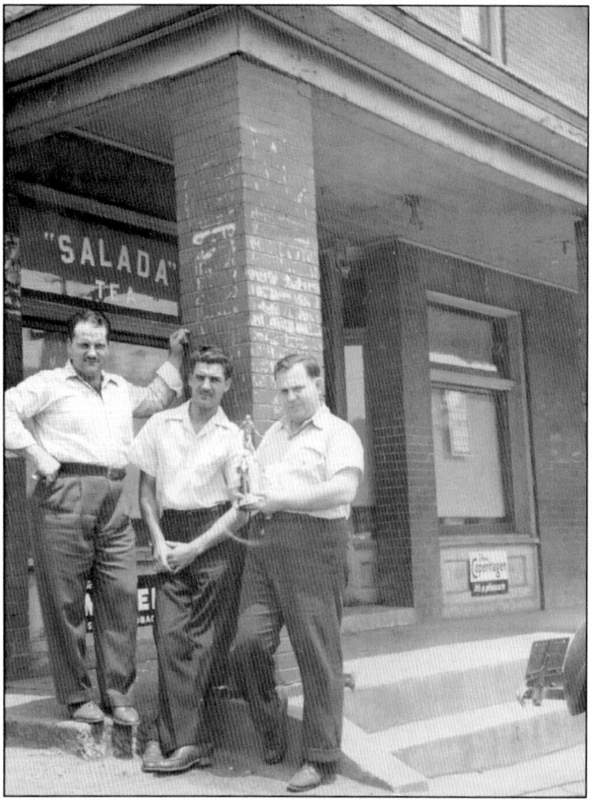

From left to right, Rebel Carasone, Al "Blackie" DiOrio, and Eugene "Singer" Malbos are proudly displaying their team's soccer trophy.

The 1947–1948 championship-winning Morgan Soccer Club is shown here. Pictured are, from left to right, (first row) Thomas Mannering, Louis Berceli, Francis "Fritz" Tkach, Frank De Caesar, Donald Bourg, William Duchess, and William Aliesky; (second row) Sam Simone (coach), Mario Battistone, Ralph Gumpf, Steve Pucker, Francis "Christy" O'Donnell, Ernest "Mack" Hodge, Ralph Berquist, and John Franjione (manager).

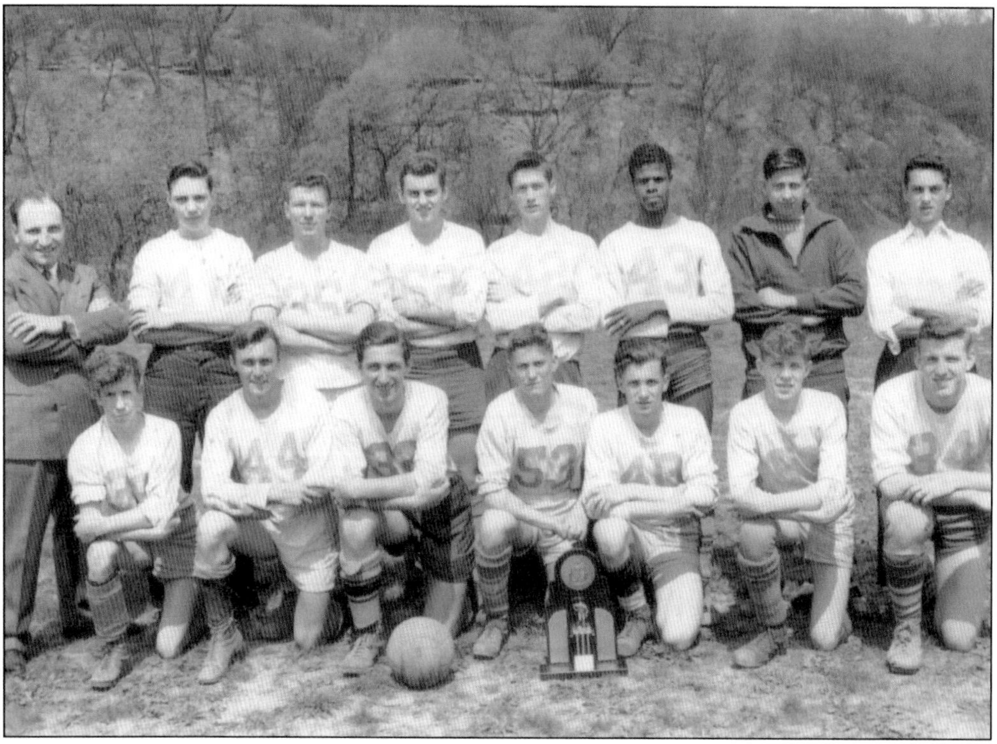

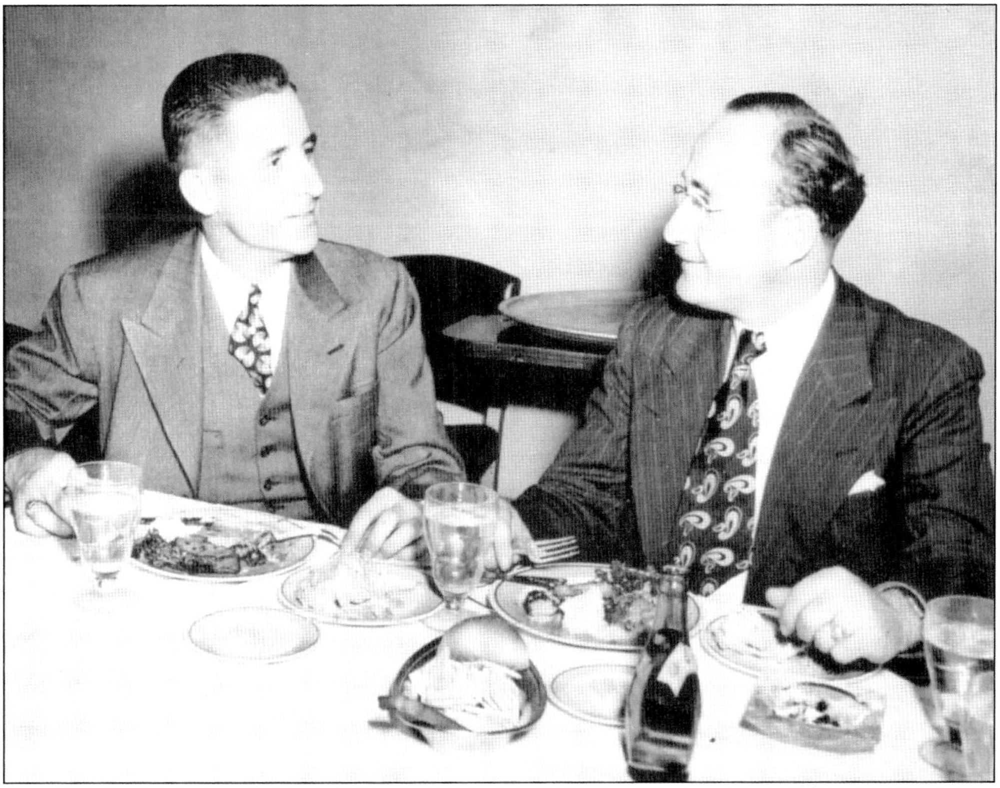

From left to right, Pete Strasser and "Doc" Casciola are celebrating one of their many soccer victories. Strasser was the sponsor of the team, and Casciola was the manager and secretary.

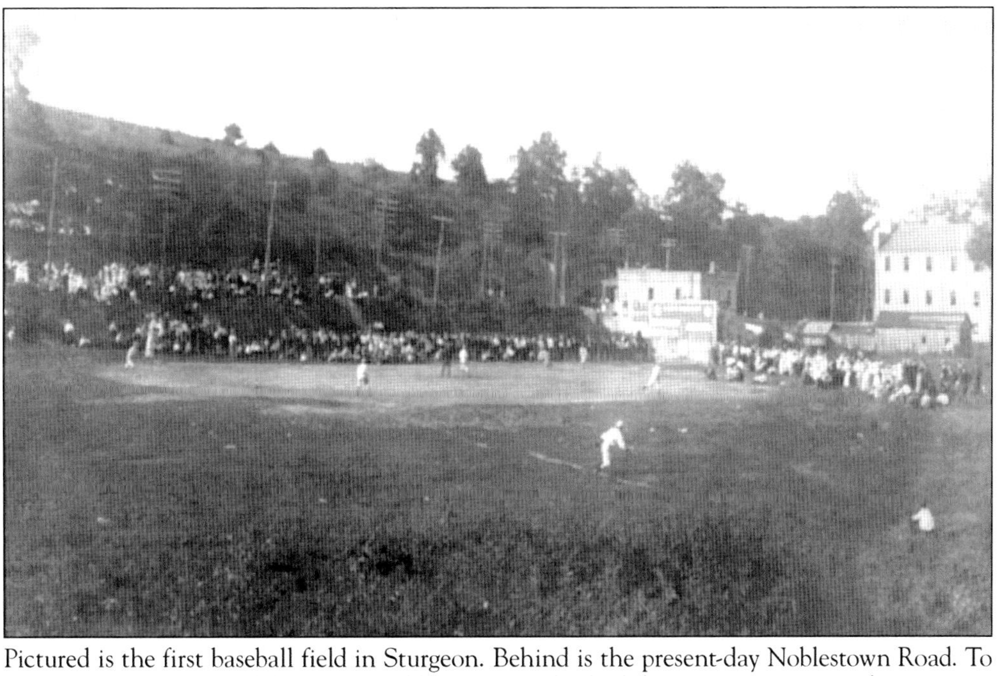

Pictured is the first baseball field in Sturgeon. Behind is the present-day Noblestown Road. To the right is the Eagles Club at 7621 Noblestown Road, which houses apartments today.

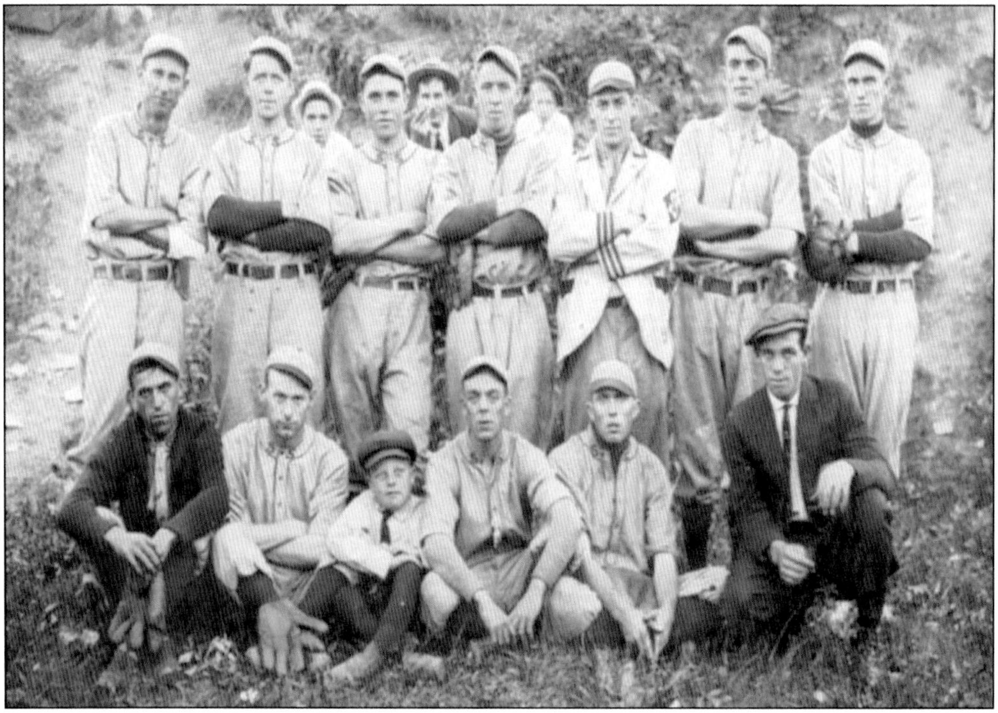

This was one of the many baseball teams in Sturgeon. Many of the players were miners and farmers.

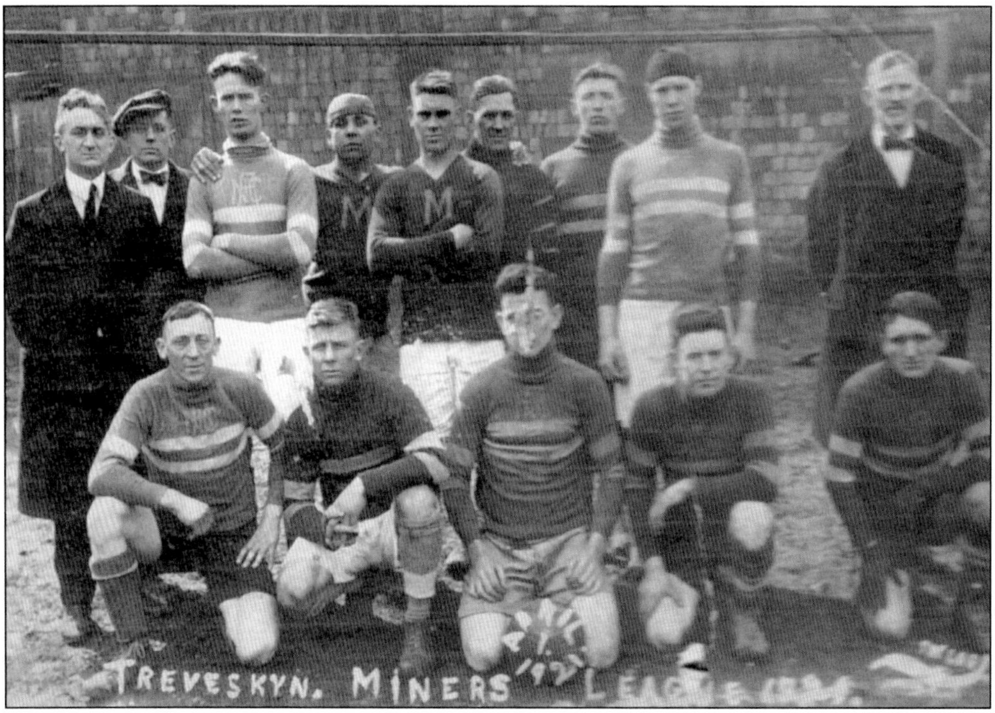

Although the names are not known, this picture is of a soccer team in the Treveskyn Miners League in South Fayette.

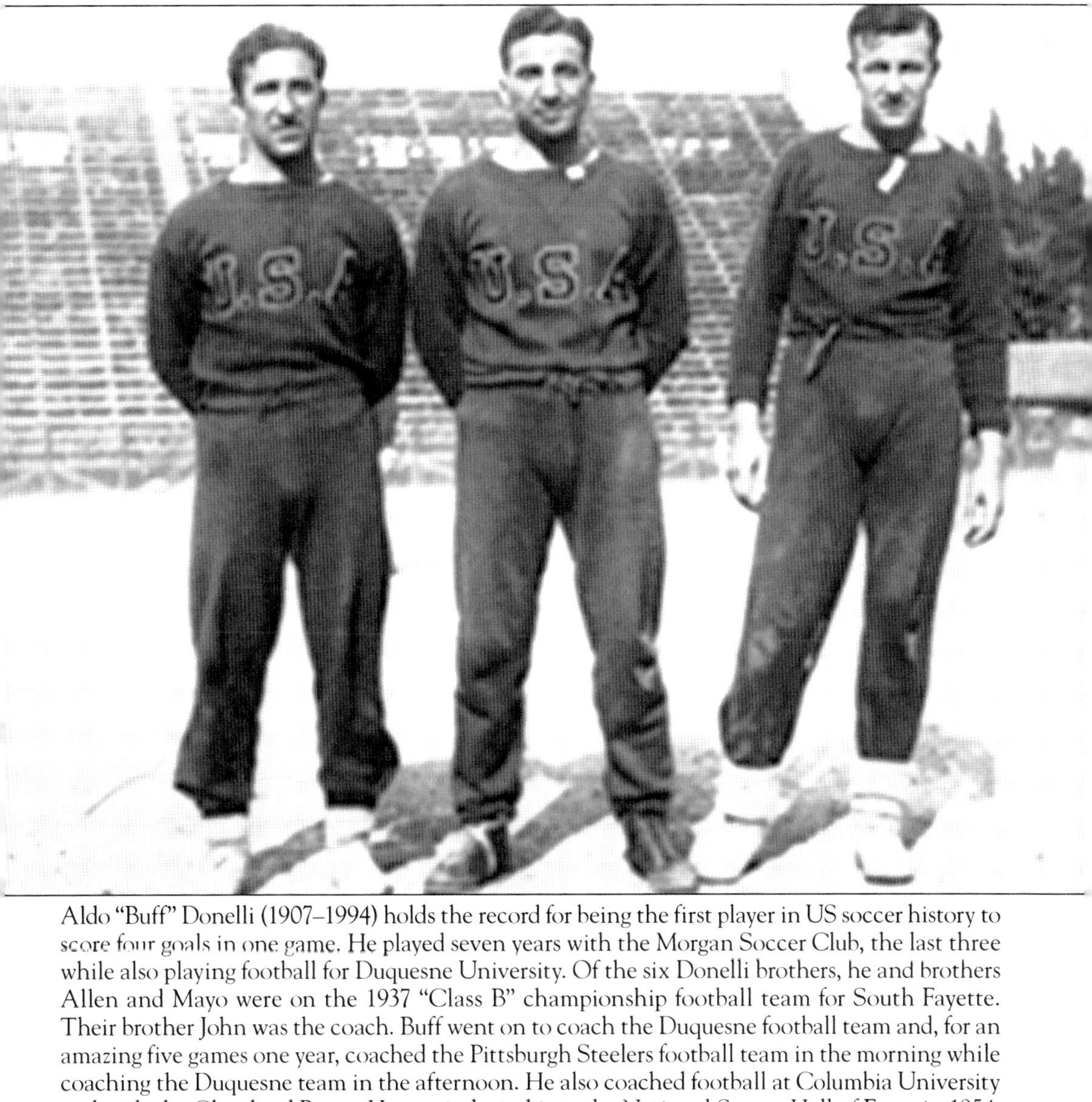

Aldo "Buff" Donelli (1907–1994) holds the record for being the first player in US soccer history to score four goals in one game. He played seven years with the Morgan Soccer Club, the last three while also playing football for Duquesne University. Of the six Donelli brothers, he and brothers Allen and Mayo were on the 1937 "Class B" championship football team for South Fayette. Their brother John was the coach. Buff went on to coach the Duquesne football team and, for an amazing five games one year, coached the Pittsburgh Steelers football team in the morning while coaching the Duquesne team in the afternoon. He also coached football at Columbia University and with the Cleveland Rams. He was inducted into the National Soccer Hall of Fame in 1954. Pictured are, from left to right, Tom Florie, Buff, and Joe Martinelli as members of the 1934 US World Cup team. (Courtesy of National Soccer Hall of Fame Archives.)

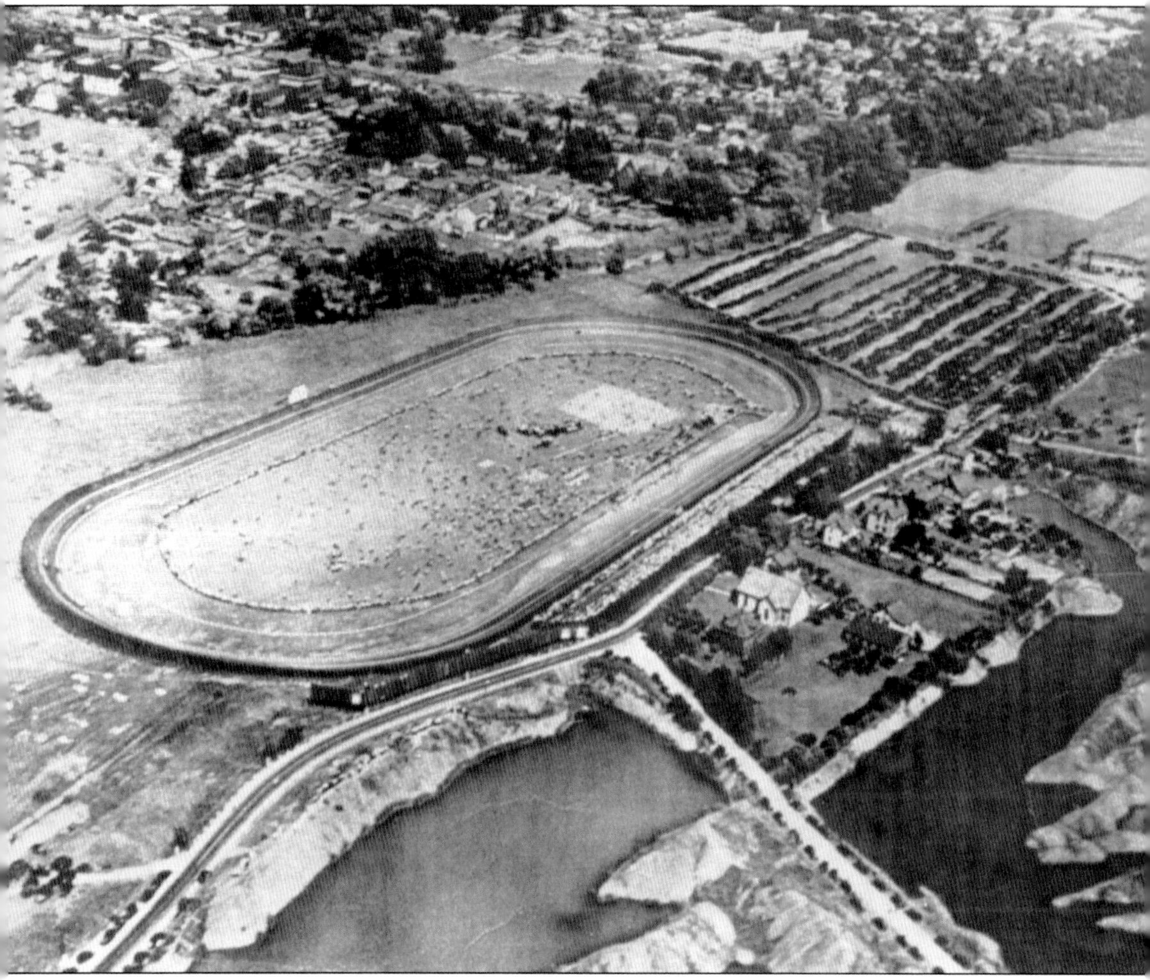

The Bridgeville Pittsburgh Speedway, begun in 1927, is pictured before it closed down in the early 1930s. In the foreground is present-day Hickory Grade Road. The pond on the left is the present-day site of the former Star City Cinema and the newly built University of Pittsburgh Medical Center (UPMC) Children's Hospital. The pond on the right presently is the site of the Knights Inn and Abele Business Park. The church in the center was the former St. Anthony's Church, which was torn down in 2012. After the speedway closed, the property served as a location for Bridgeville/South Fayette Sports Stadium, El Rancho Drive-In, the Fruit Bowl, Putt-Putt Golf, and Champ's Pizza. It now is part of Interstate 79 and the Bridgeville Interchange.

Six

Floods and Natural Disasters

Many floods have occurred throughout the township over the last 200 years. In June 1904, a cloudburst caused a flash flood in the Oakdale section, backing up the junction of Robinson Creek. Another flood, in the mid-1960s, swept through Cuddy. The worst and latest was in 2004 after Hurricane Ivan.

In 1943, a B-17 airplane was on a routine flight from Bradley Field, Connecticut, to Patterson Field, Ohio, when three of the engines quit and the pilot made the decision to land. As the plane approached from the northeast, it hit the top of the ridge off Sygan Hill Road, bounced into the air, came down on the other side, hit an elm tree, then an oak tree, and finally came to rest on the hillside above the home of Joe and Mary Hohn at the corner of Oak Ridge Road. The four crew members who rode the plane to the ground were not hurt and were ordered to stand guard over the wreckage for a week until it was removed. Four others bailed out, with one breaking his left foot. All were taken to Woodville County Home Hospital in nearby Collier Township to be examined. The men slept in a car in the Hohns' front yard, and Mary fed them until the investigation was completed.

The Nike Missile Site was controlled in Oakdale. A missile silo was located at the military facility that borders the school campus. The Missile Maters, developed by the US Army Signal Corps, were placed strategically in 10 key industrial population centers for protection. South Fayette, with its proximity to Pittsburgh's steelmaking companies, was the location for one of these installations. The Bell light system, which provided warnings in the case of a bomb threat, was located in the civil defense headquarters in the township's municipal building in Morgan. In the late 1960s, these missiles were removed.

Many residents remember the "green snow" of February 1978 when an area the size of four football fields on Presto-Sygan Road was covered with 25,000 pounds of vanadium pentoxide and sand because an industrial pipe burst at the chemical plant of the Koppers Company. No serious injuries were reported. It took several days to shovel everything into barrels for disposal while an investigation continued.

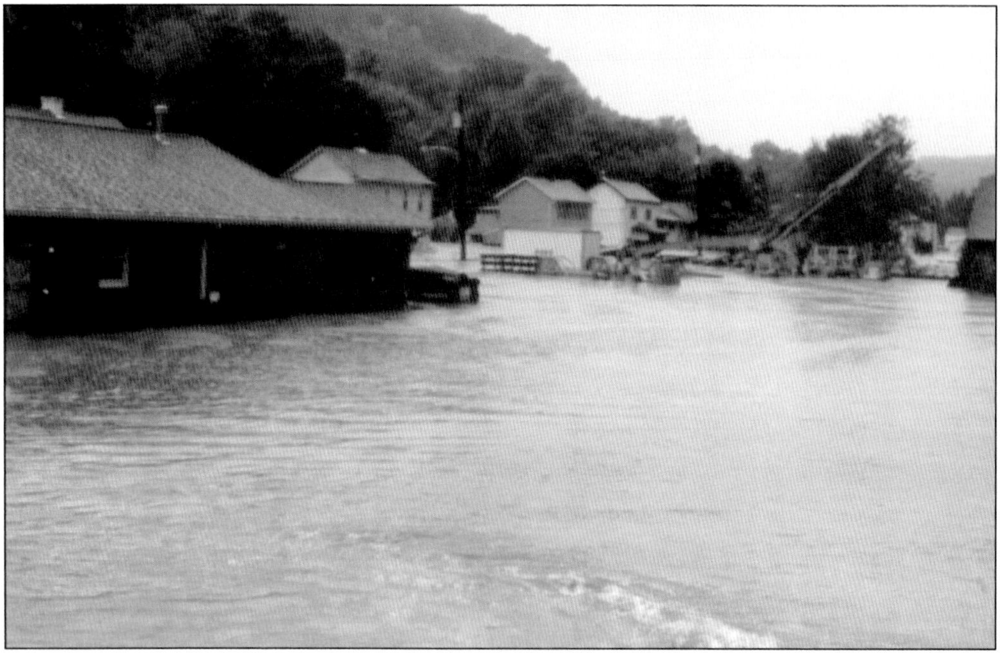

Flood damage on September 17, 2004, from Hurricane Ivan and the week's prior Hurricane Frances, spread out over the entire 20.95 square miles of the township. More than 65 homes and businesses bore the brunt of the storm. The cost of infrastructure repairs and improvements to local parks, particularly Morgan Park, which was completely submerged, reached more than $700,000. Cleanup went on for several months. Pictured is part of Sturgeon under water.

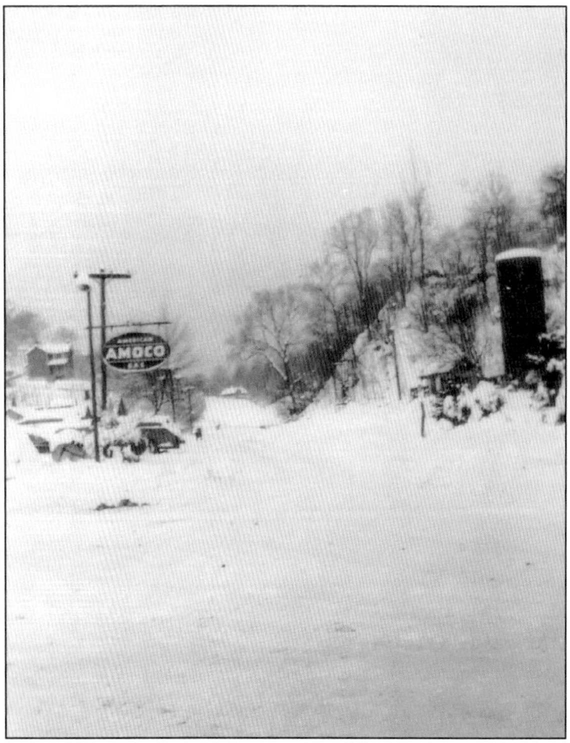

This photograph was taken in 1942 at the intersection of Battle Ridge and Millers Run Roads during a very large snowstorm. The schools were closed for many days. The roads were cleared with the help of local coal stripper, Don McCuene, and his D-7 dozer. Note the dozer tracks in the snow.

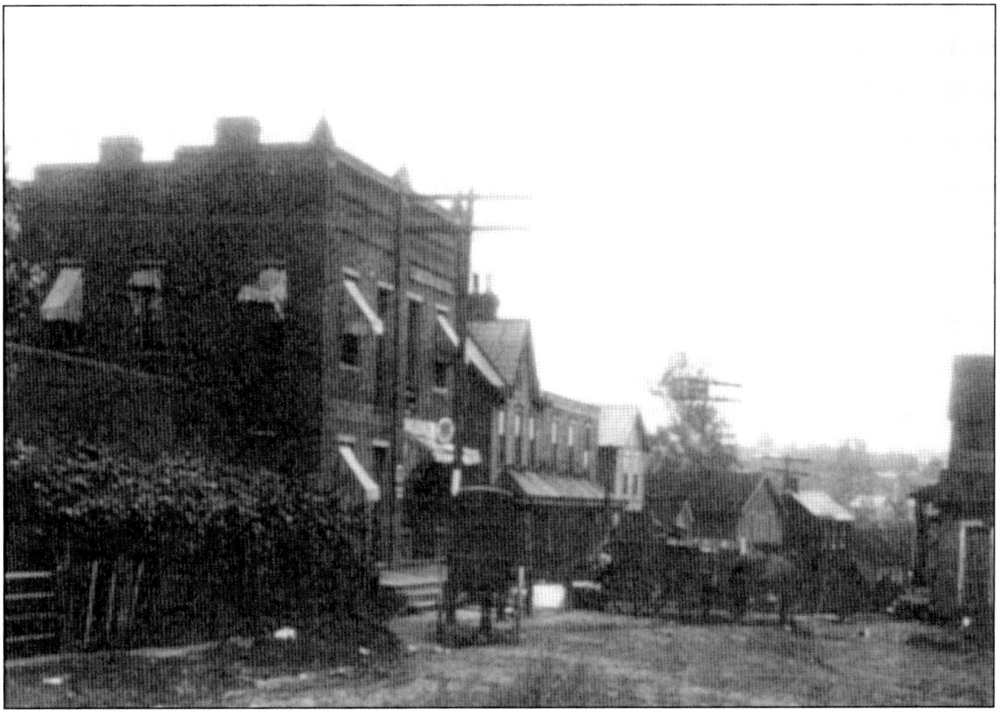

All the buildings in the picture above were razed after the 1943 Sturgeon fire, which ruined several blocks of the community. The picture at right shows the Sturgeon Hotel before the fire.

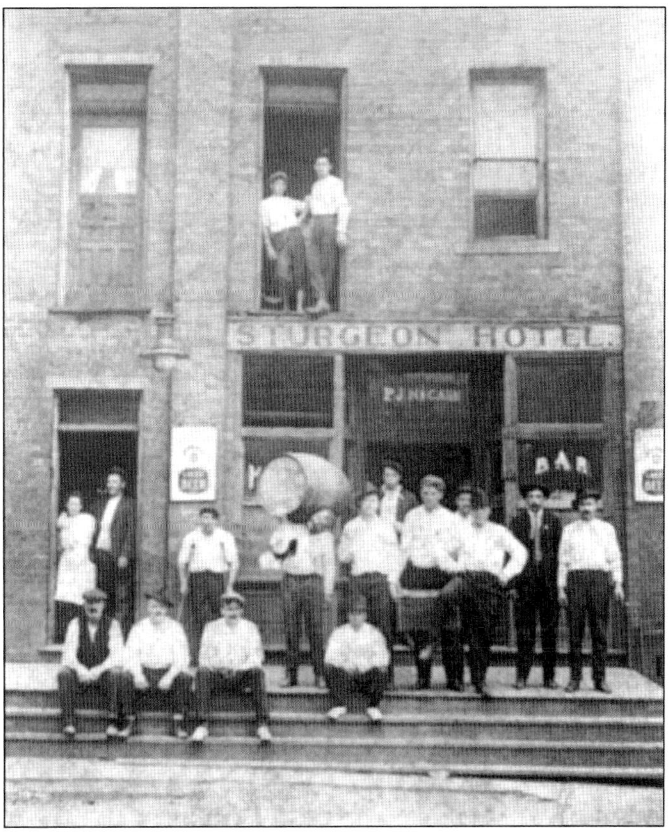

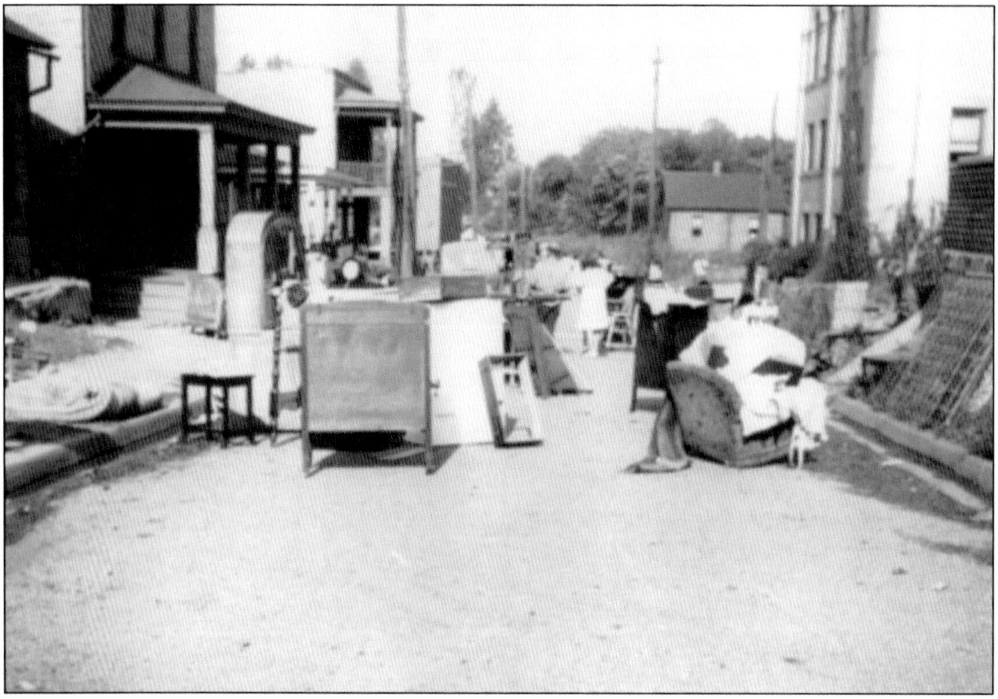

Shown is part of the immense cleanup that occurred after the 1943 Sturgeon fire.

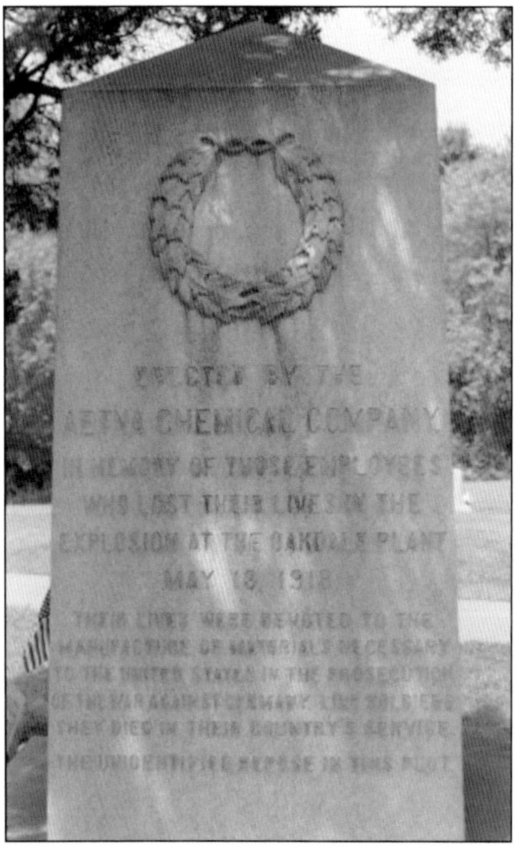

Aetna Chemical Co., a subsidiary of New York City–based Aetna Explosives Co., was under contract during World War I to produce explosives for trench warfare. The company had a 15-acre manufacturing plant in Oakdale, South Fayette Township, which employed about 450 workers to produce TNT. An explosion occurred on May 18, 1918, hurling debris a mile away. The area's population temporarily swelled from 2,000 to 50,000 because of onlookers, volunteers, reporters, and those looking for loved ones. About 200 people died. The remnants of the plant ruins are south of Oakdale along the Panhandle Trail, formerly a busy railroad line. The monument at the Oakdale Cemetery stands as a tribute to the workers' heroism and patriotism.

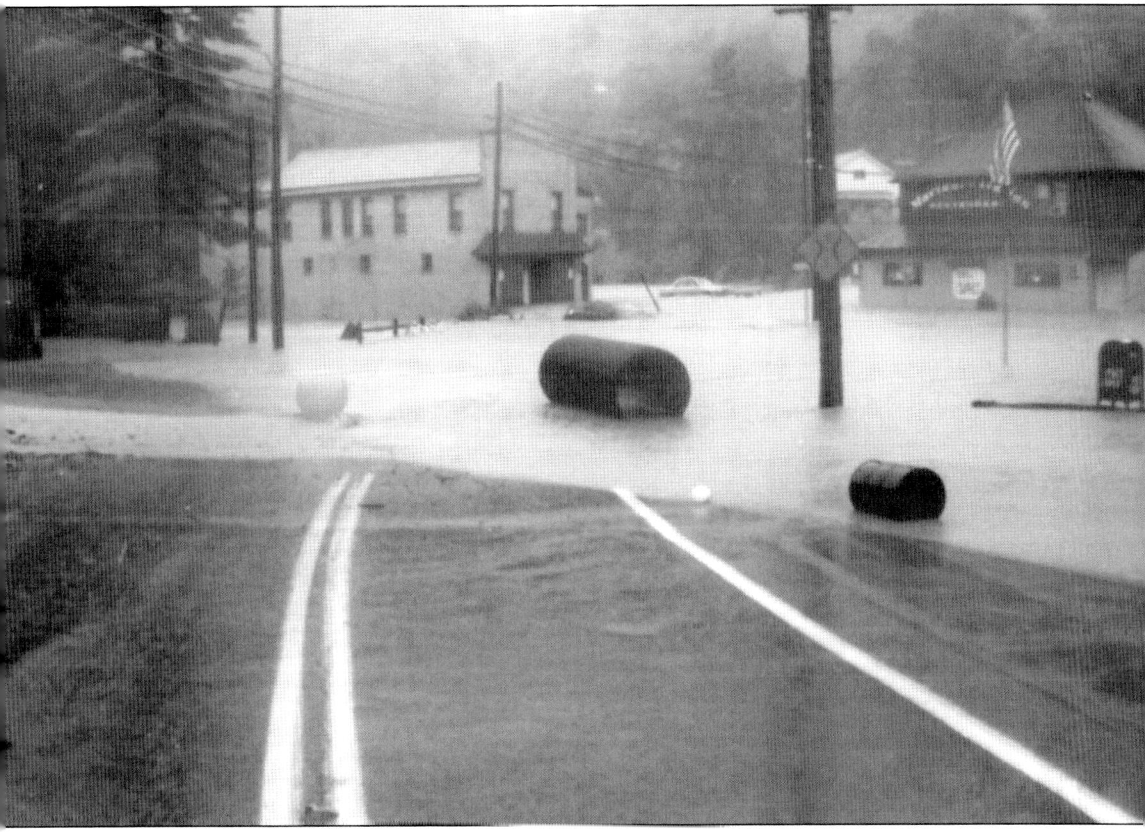

September 17, 2004, started out with light showers that soon became very heavy. By 1:00 p.m., it became evident that Millers Run Creek would soon leave its banks. School was let out early, only to have the buses find alternate routes around the flooded Millers Run Road. This is a photograph of Millers Run Road in the 600 block. Cars, pipes, drums, and more were floating by. South Fayette Volunteer Fire Department was surrounded by water, but the firemen were still able to help the many residents in need, along with the other three township volunteer fire departments.

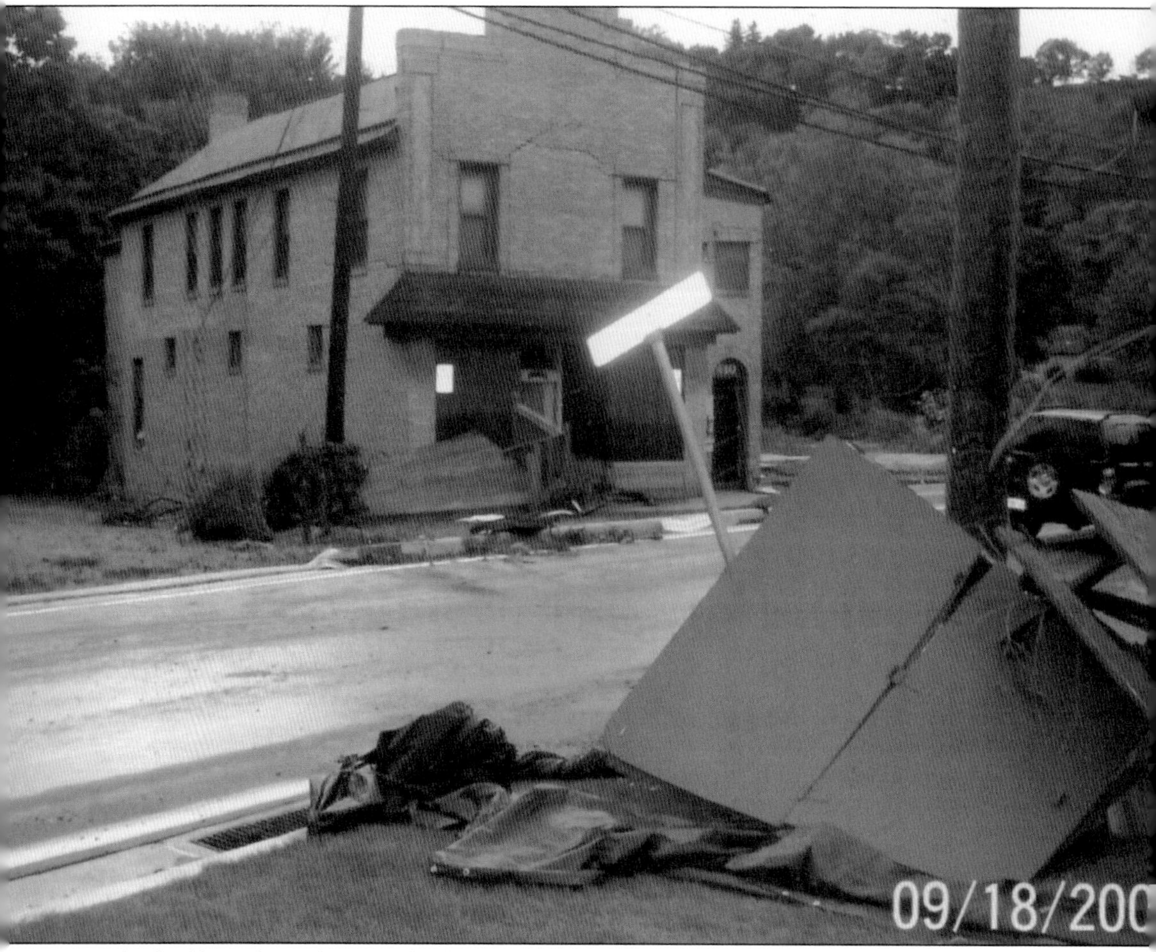

This building, shown here on the day after the 2004 flood, is mentioned in this book as "Quarture's store." It was located at 610 Millers Run Road. Note the structural damage to the brickwork. The building was razed to make way for Cuddy Lane and the Cuddy Business Park.

Seven

South Fayette Township School District

The oldest schoolhouse was built around 1790 on the present location of Robinson Run Cemetery. It was a one-room log structure. The parents of the pupils each contributed his/her share toward the teacher's salary and the purchasing of materials. By 1876, there were six schoolhouses—Pleasant Valley, Centennial No. 6, Southside Oakdale, Mohawk No. 4, Fairview School, and Valley School—and fourteen schools by 1900.

The earliest official minute book of the board of directors of the school district dates from 1909, when an eight-month school term was established and 26 teachers were hired, with most teaching at least four grades. Inexperienced teachers were paid $45 per month; experienced teachers were paid $55. A night school was started in 1909 as well, in Morgan/Treveskyn.

By 1929, only nine primary schools remained—Oakdale, Sturgeon, Federal, Fairview, Gladden, Sygan, Cuddy, National Hill, and Morgan. Mohawk School and Gladden Academy had been turned into residences. South Fayette students traveled by horseback, railroad, or bus to get to high schools in Bridgeville, McDonald, or Carnegie. The township did not have its first high school until Lafayette High was built in 1926 in Morgan.

A school bell sat on top the roof of Sturgeon Elementary. After a fire, Francis "Chip" McFalls, a retired former employee of the school district, salvaged the bell before all the ruins were buried. As a lasting memento of all the township's former schools, Dr. Linda Hippert, superintendent in 2002, had the bell installed on the top of the newly built high school.

Pressure in the late 1950s and early 1960s came from Allegheny County to merge with one or more neighboring school districts, first Upper St. Clair and later Chartiers Valley, but South Fayette has stood firm as an independent and, since the late 1960s, this topic has been dropped. A 105-acre tract on Old Oakdale Road was purchased in 1970. A new elementary school was built there by 1974 next to the 24 acres previously purchased for the new high school in 1957. The entire school district is now located on this property, enlarged to 160 acres, including an elementary school (kindergarten through the second grade), intermediate school (third through fifth), middle school (sixth through eighth) and high school (ninth through twelfth); a stadium equipped for football, track and field, and soccer; a track; administrative offices; two playgrounds; softball field; soccer field; baseball field; parking lots, a bus garage; and a maintenance building.

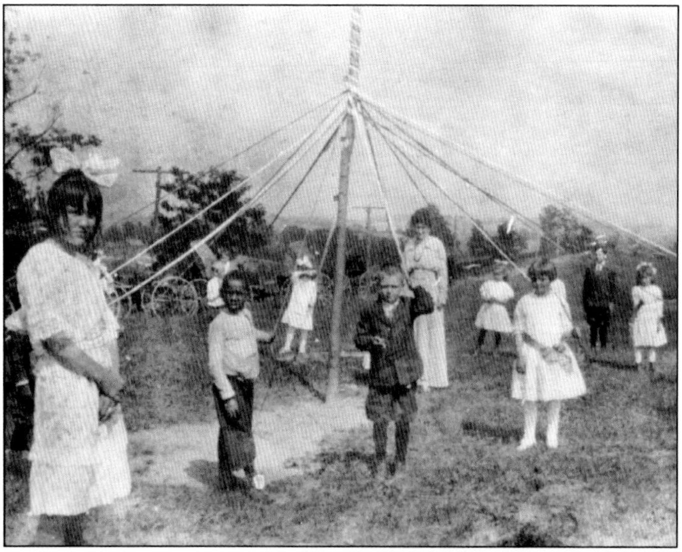

Mohawk School was first built on the Shane property in 1873; it then moved to the Campbell property on Battle Ridge Road in 1898. The school closed in 1929, and the building was later used by Mary Campbell Hastings as her residence. Grace Martin, one of the teachers at Mohawk, left in 1911 to establish Grace Martin's Secretarial School in downtown Pittsburgh. Pictured is the annual maypole dance at Mohawk in the early 1900s.

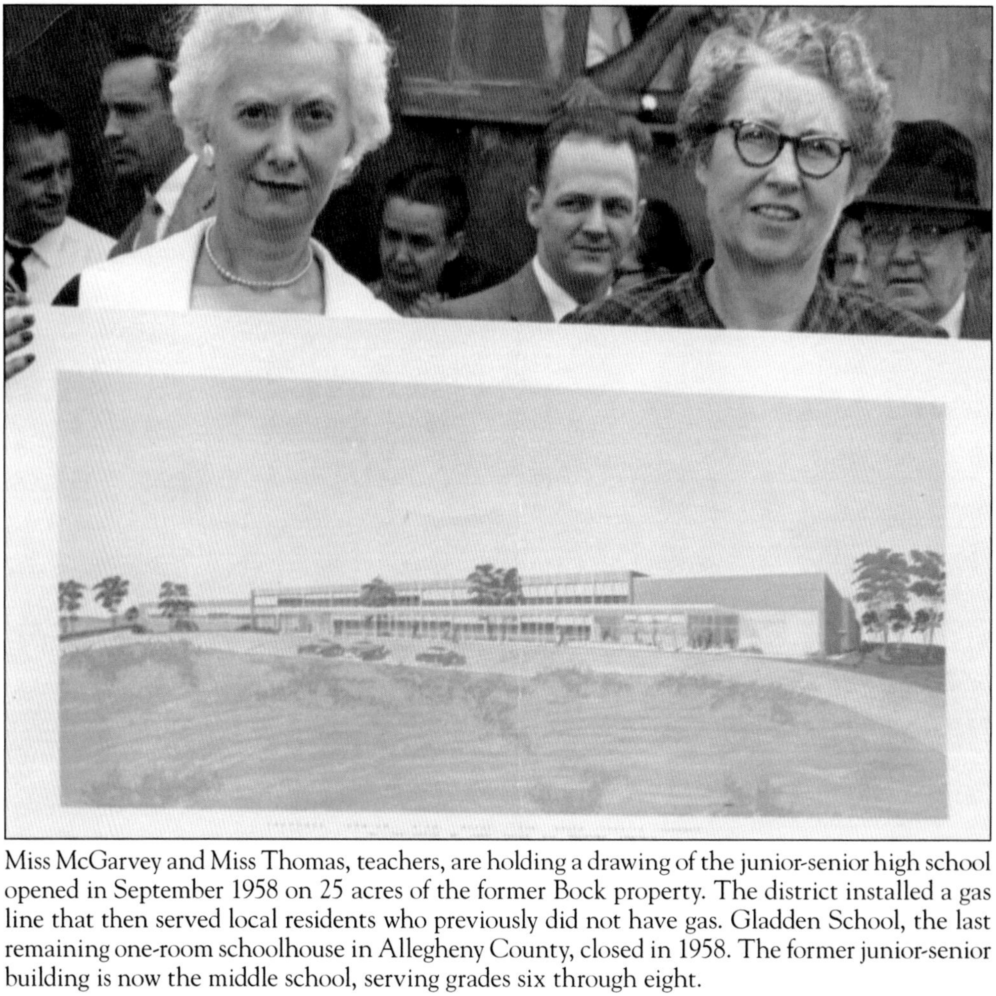

Miss McGarvey and Miss Thomas, teachers, are holding a drawing of the junior-senior high school opened in September 1958 on 25 acres of the former Bock property. The district installed a gas line that then served local residents who previously did not have gas. Gladden School, the last remaining one-room schoolhouse in Allegheny County, closed in 1958. The former junior-senior building is now the middle school, serving grades six through eight.

Pictured are, from left to right, school board members J.S. McDonald, John Czambel, John Townsend, and Leonard Desmet at the ground-breaking ceremony for the new high school. Czambel served on the board from 1942 to 1960, becoming its president in 1947. He worked at Columbia Steel and Shafting Company in Carnegie and would take time off from work without pay to attend board meetings or school events.

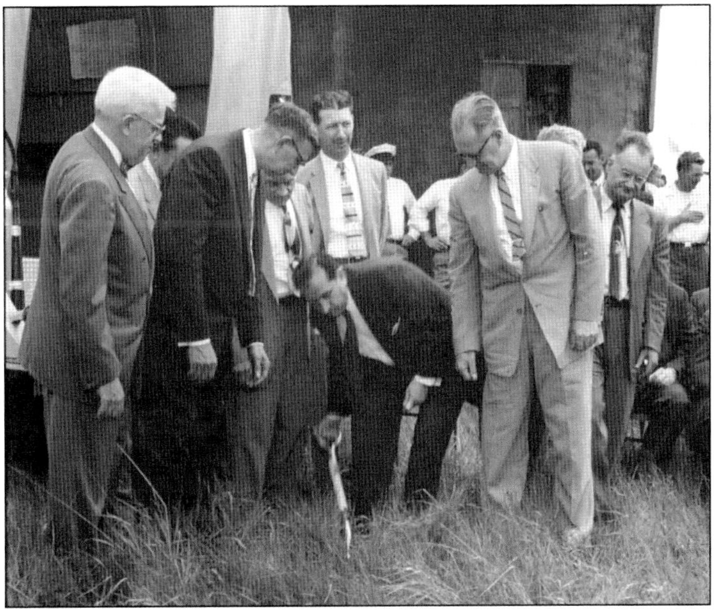

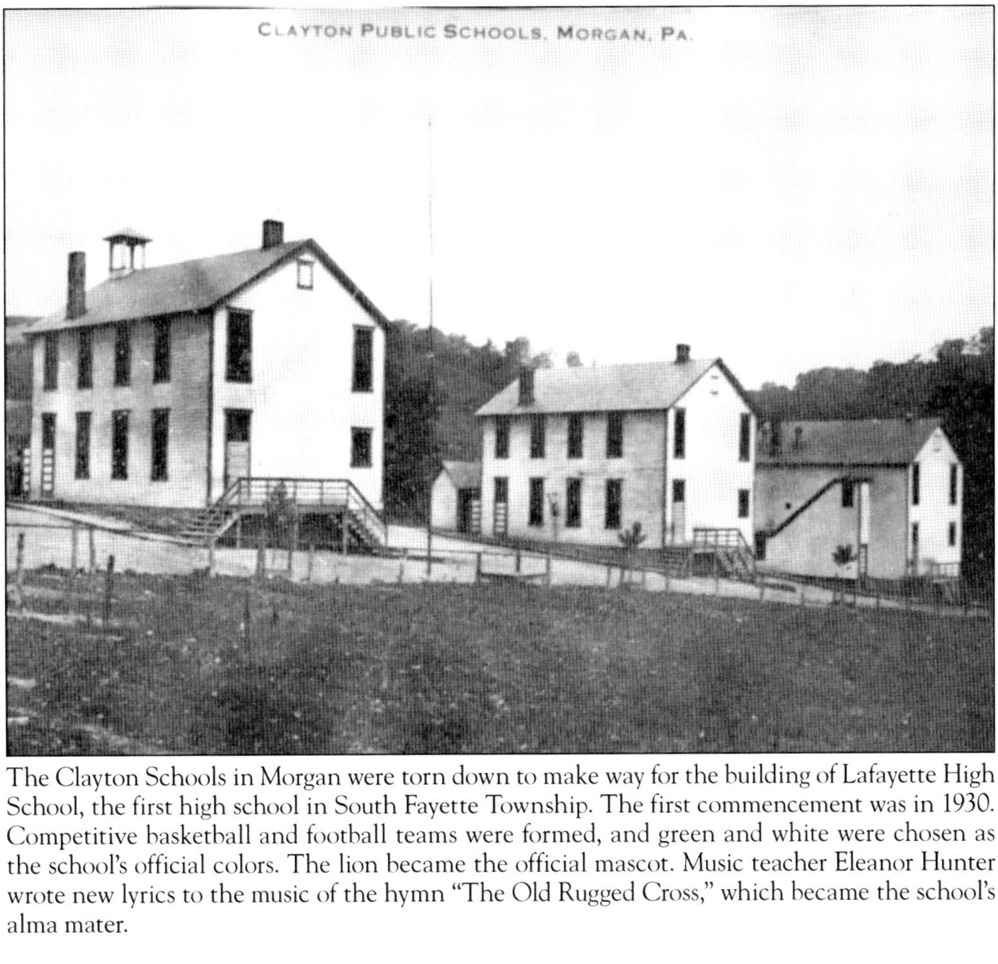

The Clayton Schools in Morgan were torn down to make way for the building of Lafayette High School, the first high school in South Fayette Township. The first commencement was in 1930. Competitive basketball and football teams were formed, and green and white were chosen as the school's official colors. The lion became the official mascot. Music teacher Eleanor Hunter wrote new lyrics to the music of the hymn "The Old Rugged Cross," which became the school's alma mater.

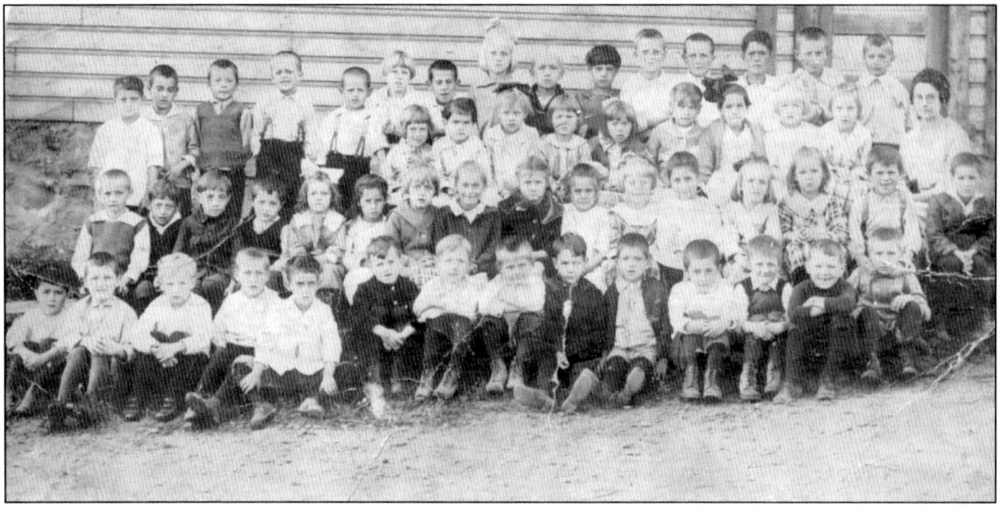

Pictured at the turn of the century are students in front of the Clayton Schools in Morgan.

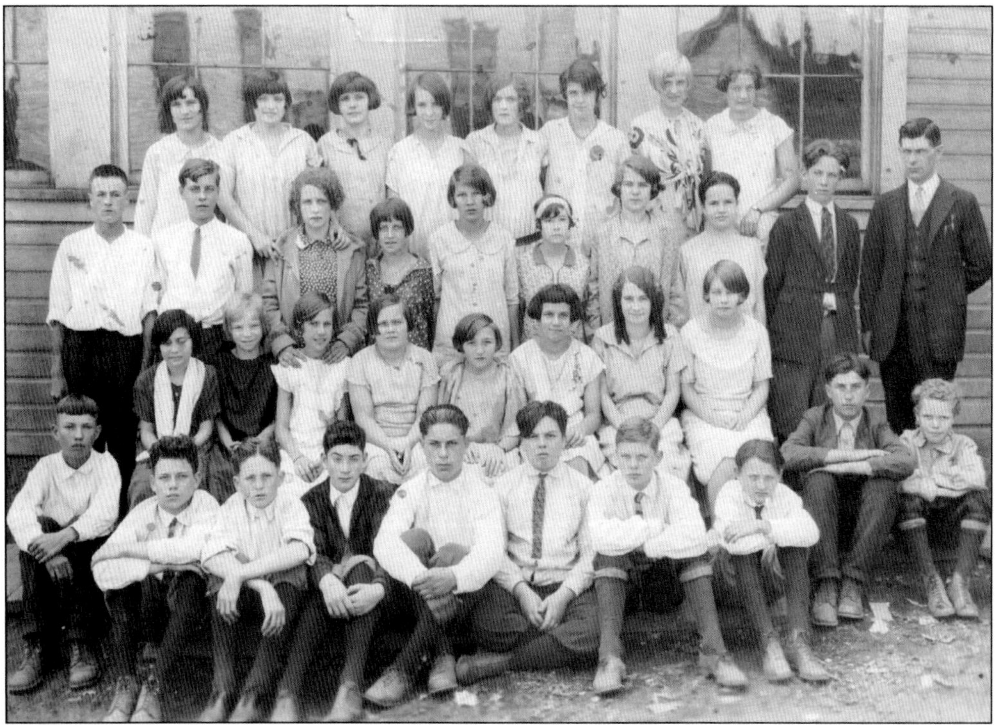

In 1925, these are the students in a Mr. Vance's eighth-grade class, Clayton Schools, Morgan.

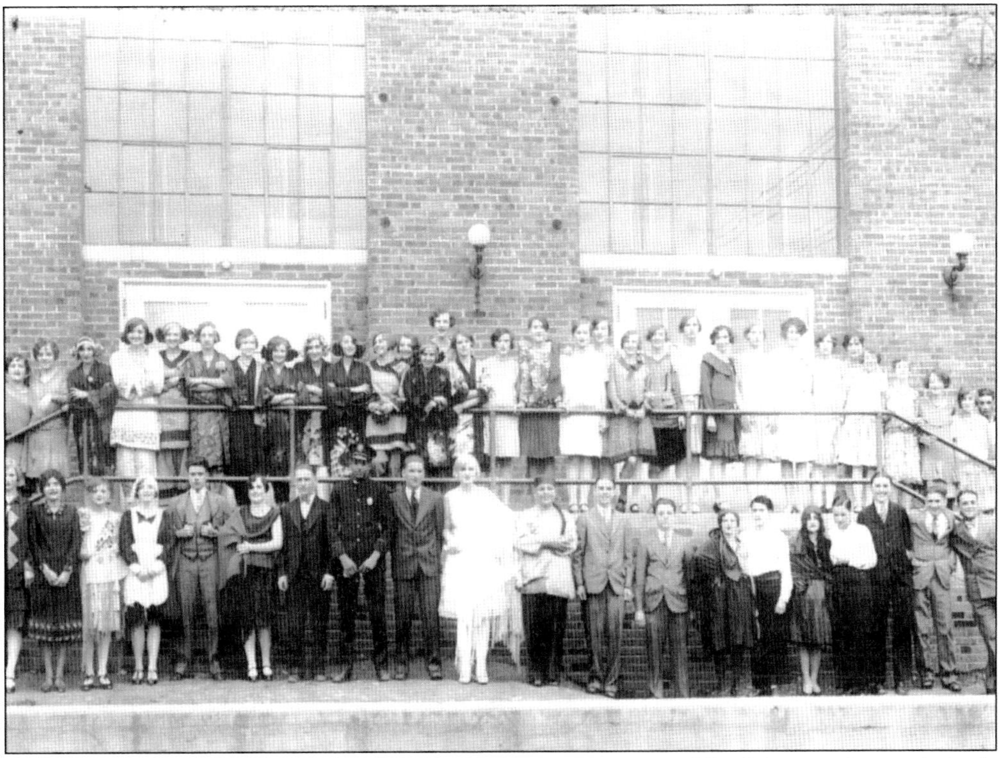

This is an April 1929 picture of the chorus performing *Once in a Blue Moon* at the newly built Lafayette High School, Morgan. The play was under the direction of Eleanor A. Hunter.

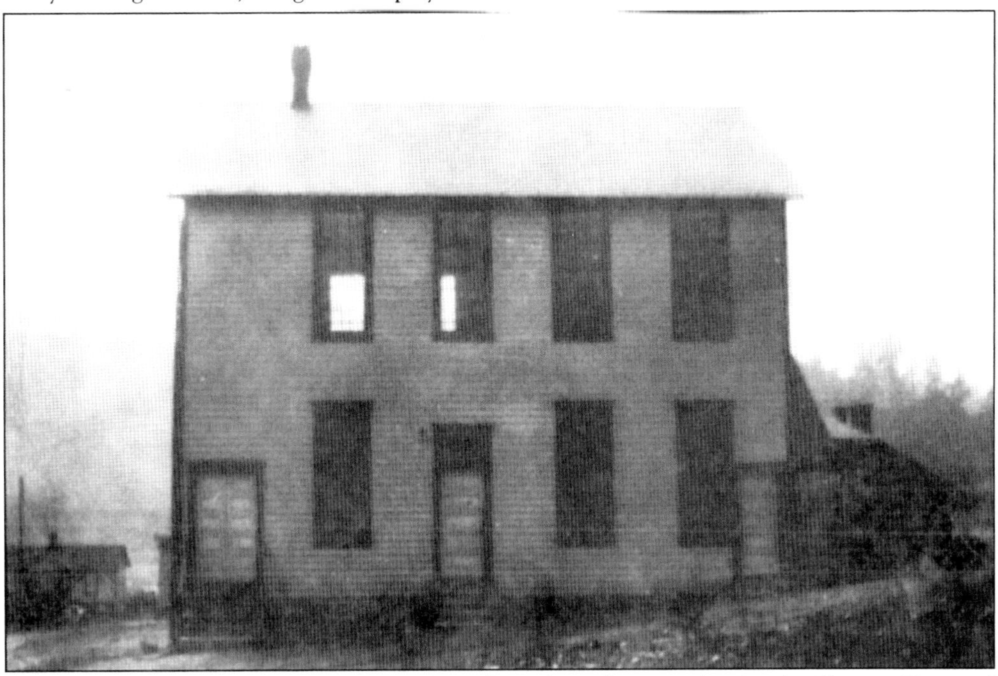

This is the Cuddy School in 1904. Cuddy Hill residents later used it for the Slovene National Benefit Society Club.

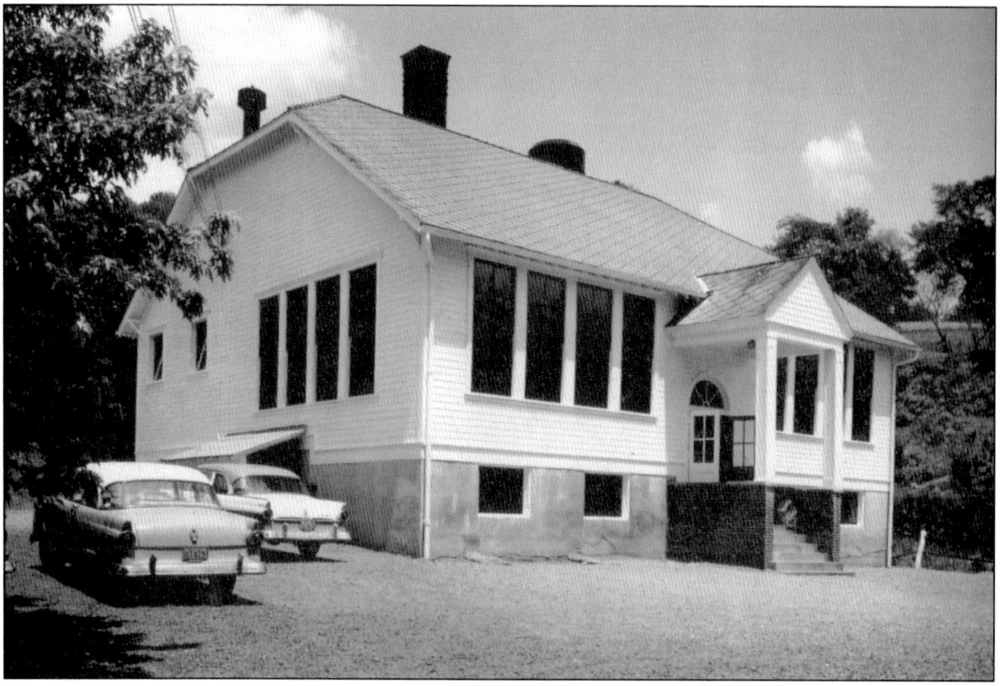

The former Federal School, at 5035 Thoms Run Road, Oakdale, is now the location of Federal Firearms & Supplies.

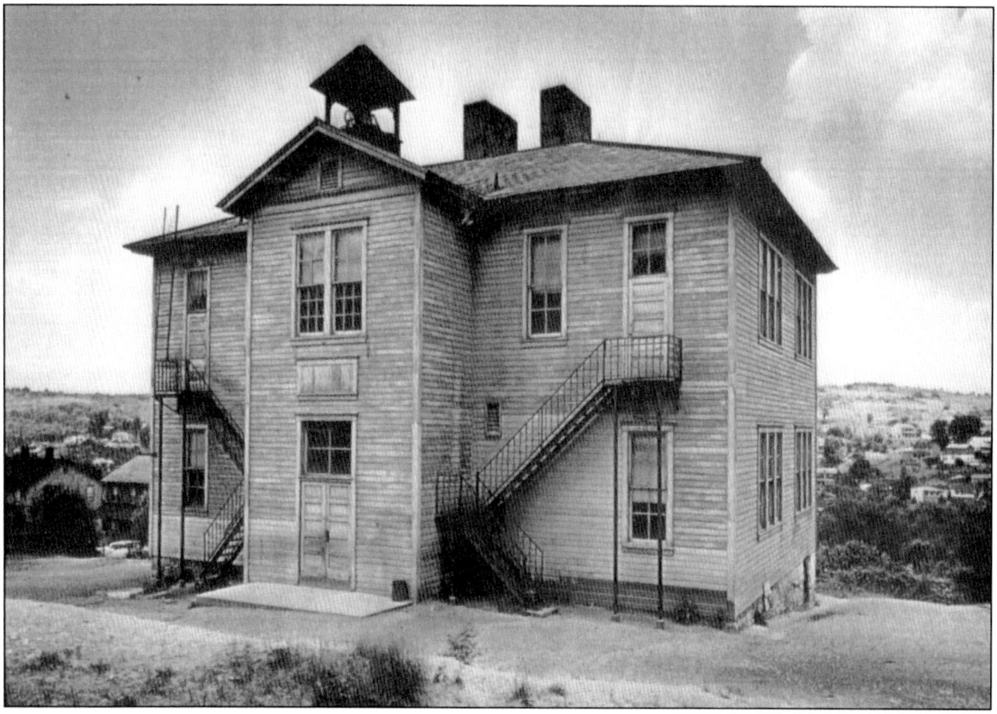

Pictured is National Hill School, which held grades one through six. Classrooms were large, with 35–40 students in each. The school was heated by a large coal furnace in the basement, and at times, students in the upper grades wore their coats in class because it was so cold.

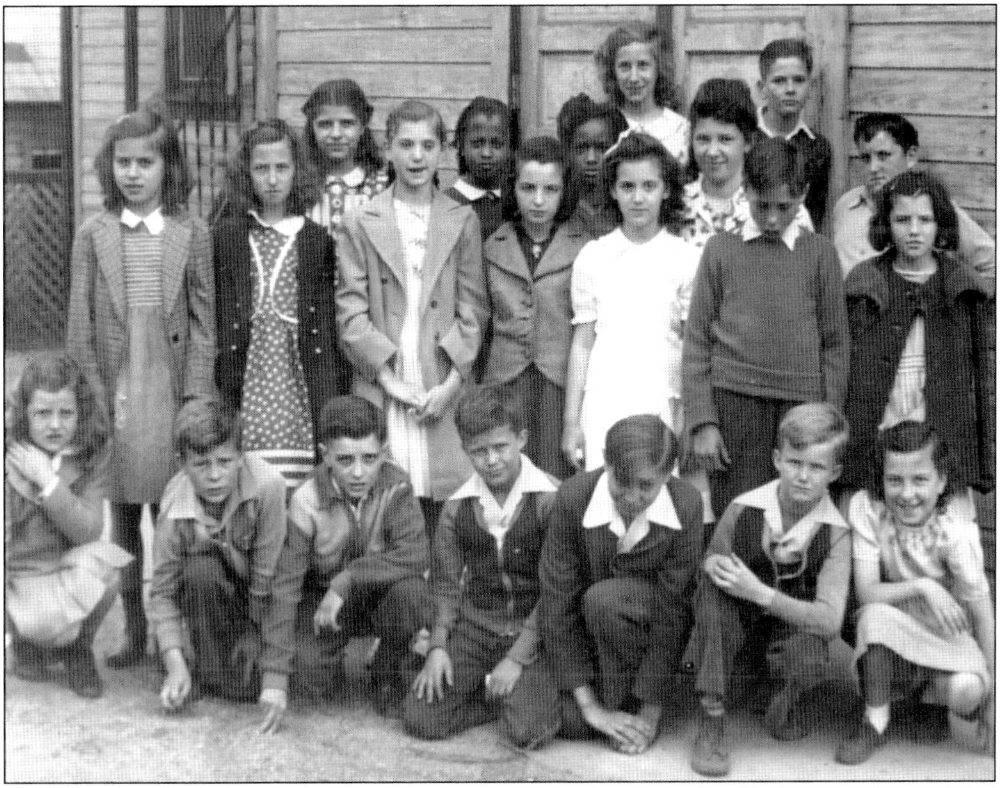

This is the fifth-and-sixth-grade class in 1942–1943 at National Hill. Among the students pictured are Dolores Greer, Donald Brenner, Dominic Petrillo, Francis Walters, Jimmy Kosky, Pat Walters, Dolores Guyaux, Shirley Guc, Blanche Cerzinski, Eileen Kosky, Cassie Weir, Esther Kenneth, Patty Weir, Edith Hepline, Pearl Hodge, Helen Barrett, Emily Nadija, Snuffy Chusta, and Stella Cukrzynski.

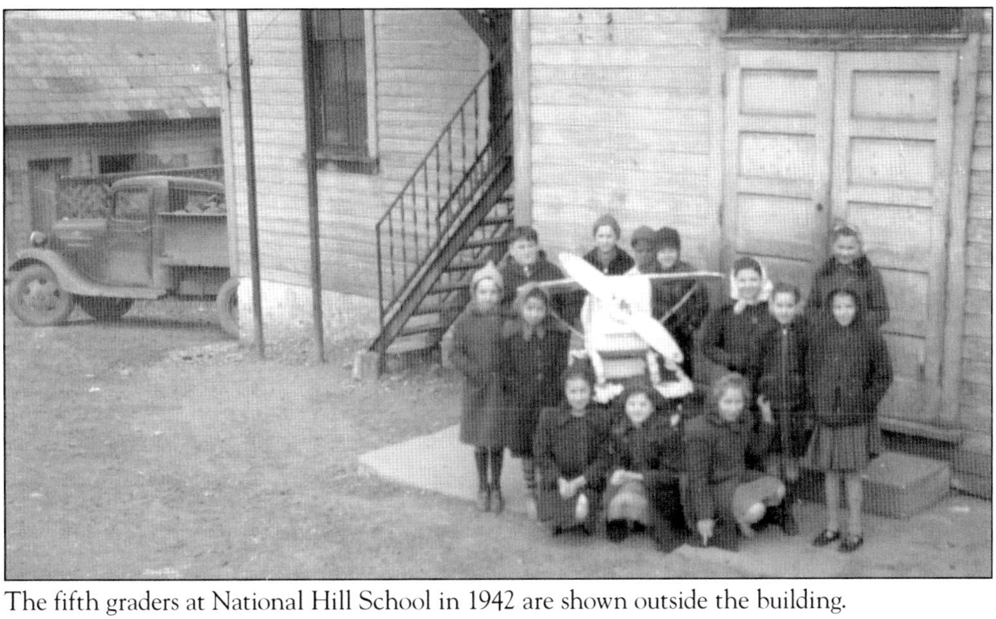

The fifth graders at National Hill School in 1942 are shown outside the building.

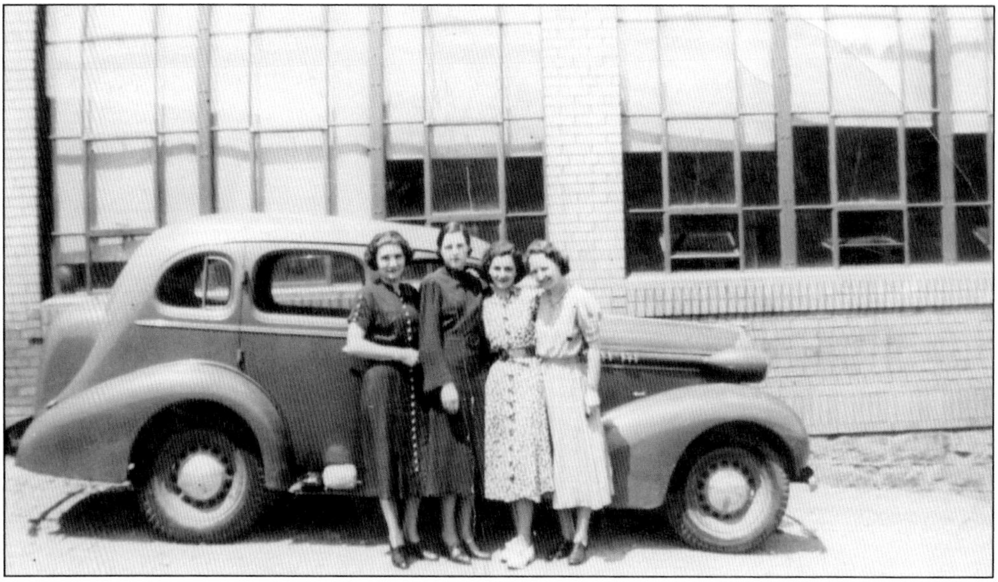

Teachers Miss Bourg, Miss Aubel, Miss D'Andrea, and Miss Painter are posed outside the Sturgeon School in front of a 1938 Chevrolet.

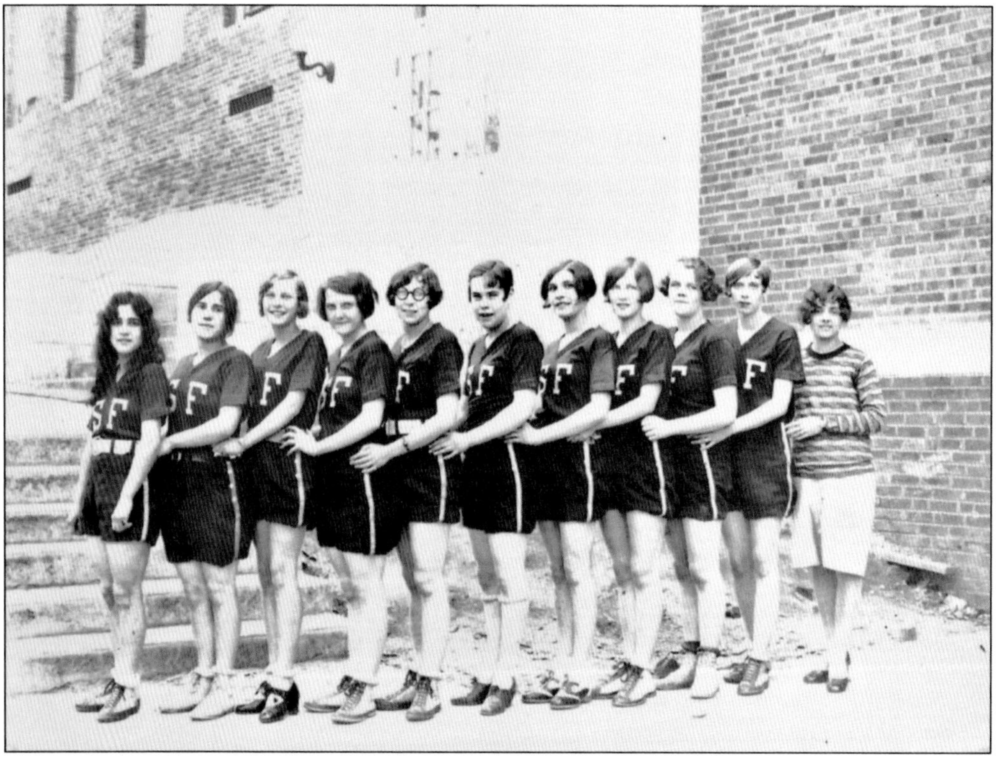

These are the members of the first girls' basketball team and their coach at Lafayette High School in 1929. From left to right are Angelina Valentino, Irene Fornella, Hilda Kvartich, Myrtle Speer, Sara Hickman, Edith Hastings, Regina Bourg, Sara McKissick, Mary Powers, Evelyn Brown (captain), NS Ruth Bowman (coach). Sara McKissick was the school's first valedictorian. Fornella was class salutatorian.

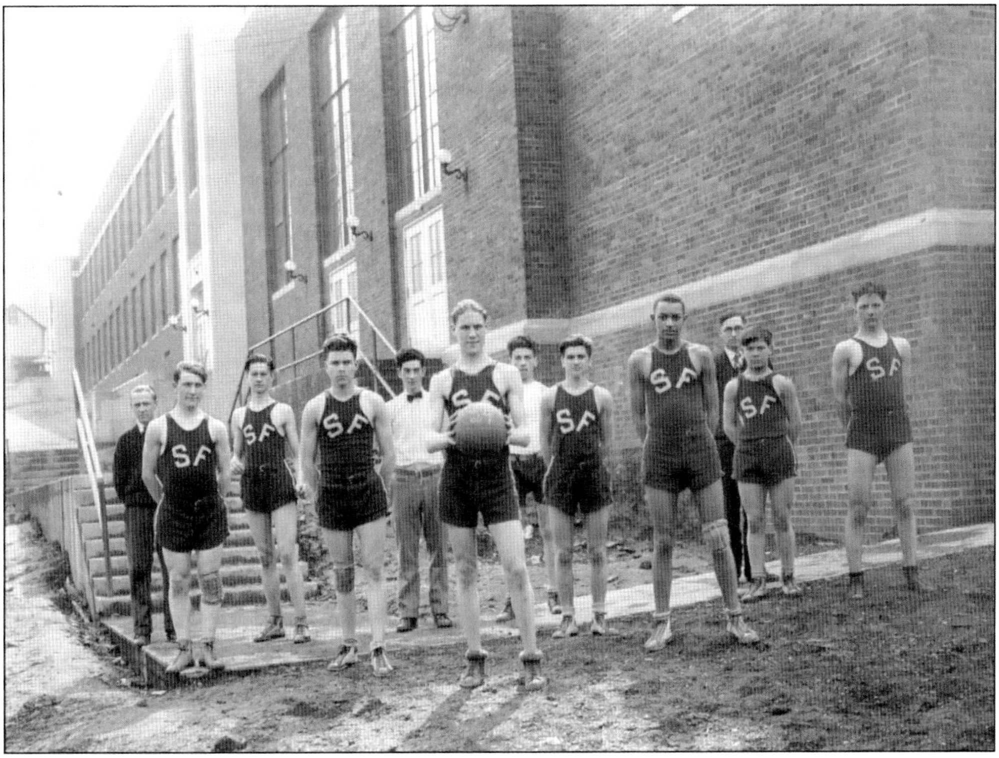

Standing in front of Lafayette High is the first boys' basketball team begun in 1929. From left to right are Thomas McCaffrey, Frank Vezzi, Joseph Stanson, Andrew Fiorentini, James Coleman, Clarence Erbrecht, Joseph Castelli, Raymond Selva, John Harris, coach Myron McGarvey, Albert Danch, and Frank Bogatay.

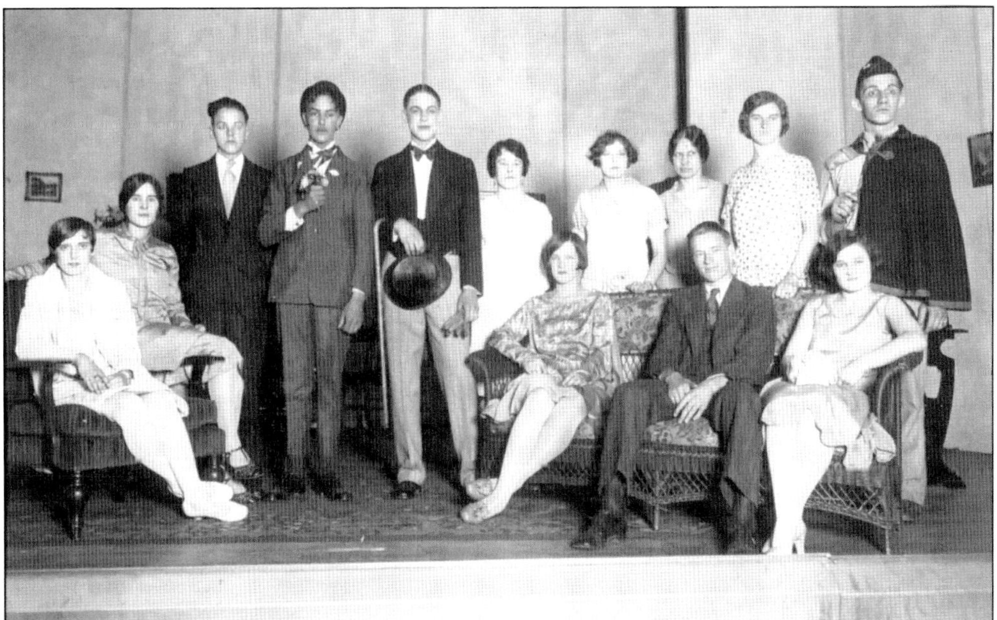

Cast members of the first South Fayette senior class play, *Cyclone Sally*, are pictured in 1929.

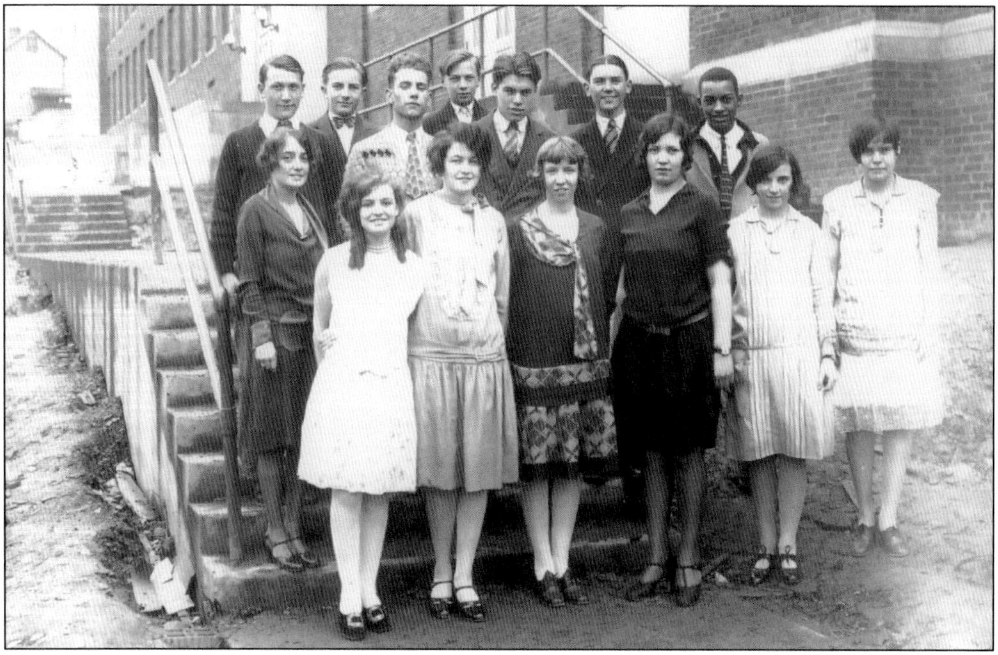

The class of 1930 presented *Second Childhood*. Pictured are, from left to right, (first row) Nokish M. Bean (coach), Rose Catala, Mabel Evans, Genevieve Lawton, Edna Chambordon, Agnes Ferlic, and Edith Hastings; (second row) Frank Vezzi, Sylvester Wirant, James Fornella, Ernest Kvartich, Elmer Kress, Frank Kelminsky, and John Harris.

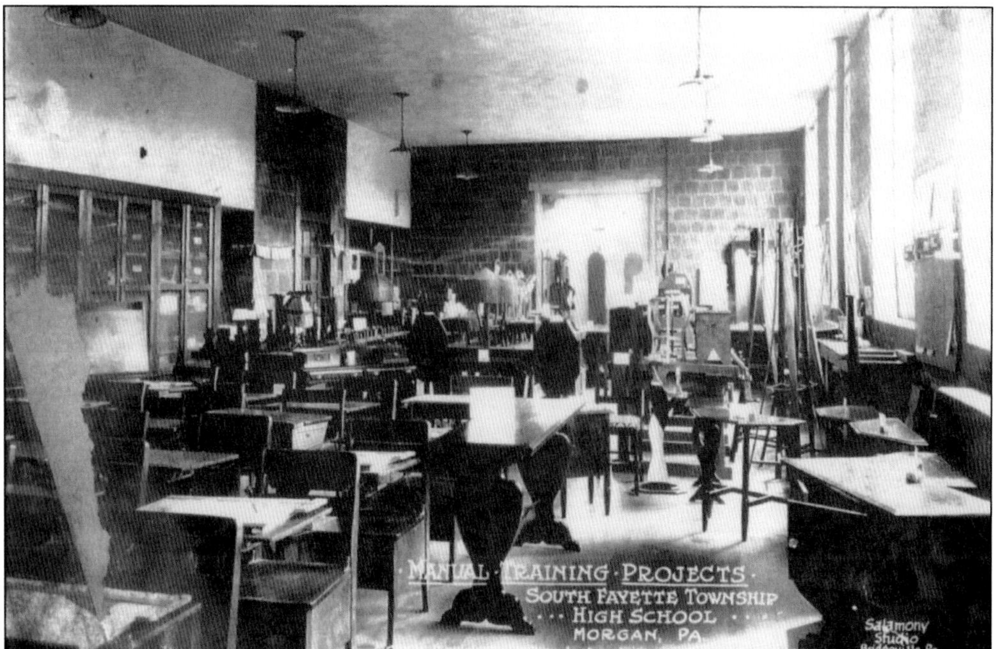

Pictured is the manual training classroom around 1930 at Lafayette High. In 1938, the school added a mining class to prepare the boys to earn a living. The mines at this time were still South Fayette's largest employer.

Pictured are elementary and high school students in front of Lafayette High in 1948.

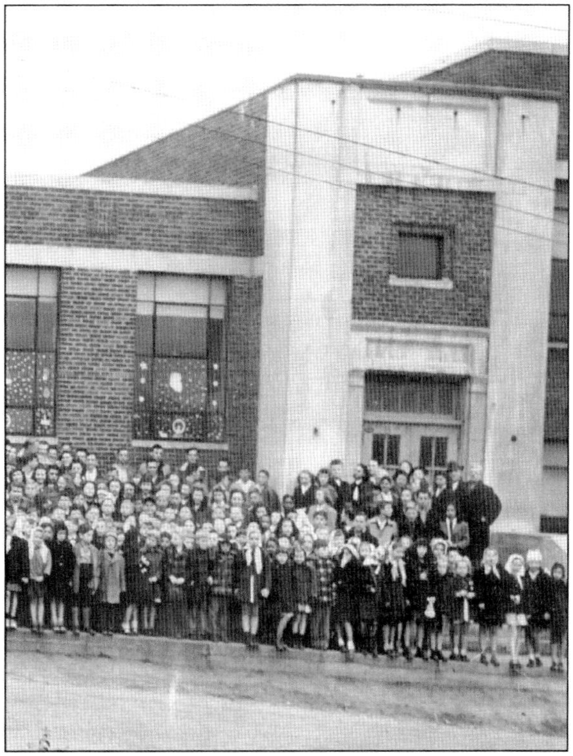

Lunchtime around 1953 at Morgan School meant eating at student desks. Dr. J.S. McDonald is shown with Anna Patterson's first-grade students. McDonald served as supervising principal from 1946 to 1960.

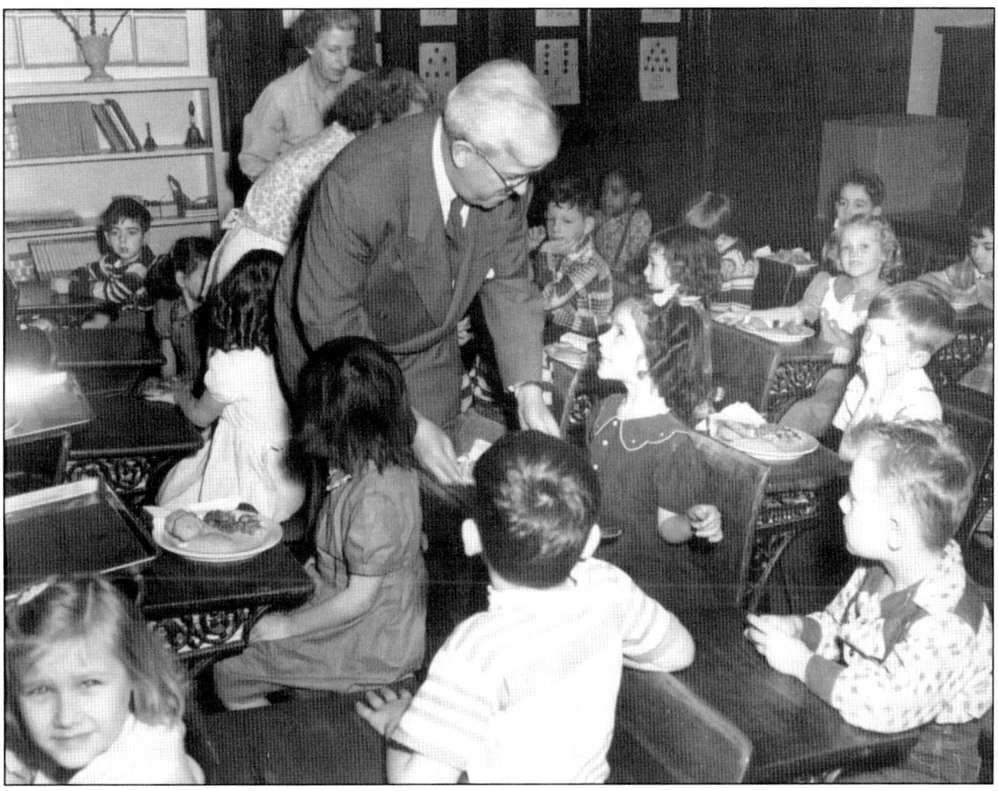

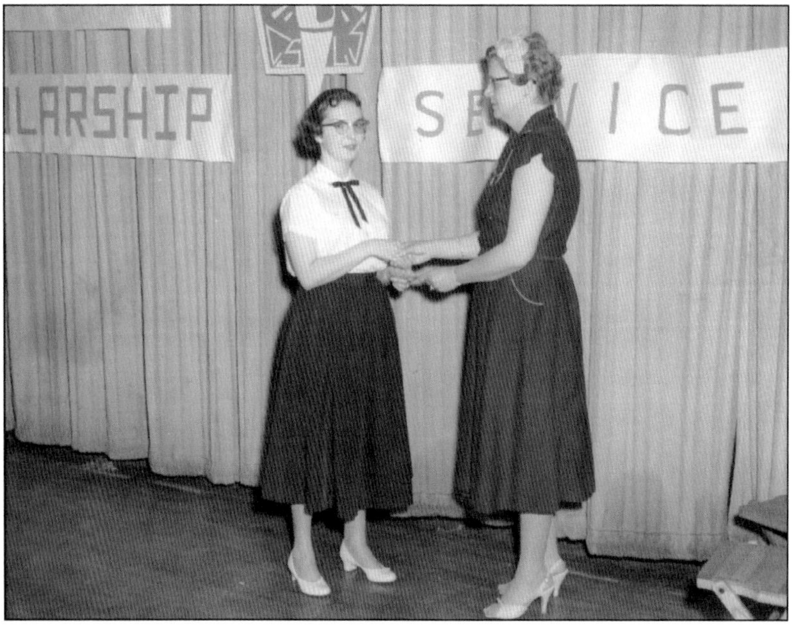

In the mid-1950s, teacher Yvonne Pradines (right) established the first National Honor Society at the high school. The school's Oak Ridge Chapter continues to exist today.

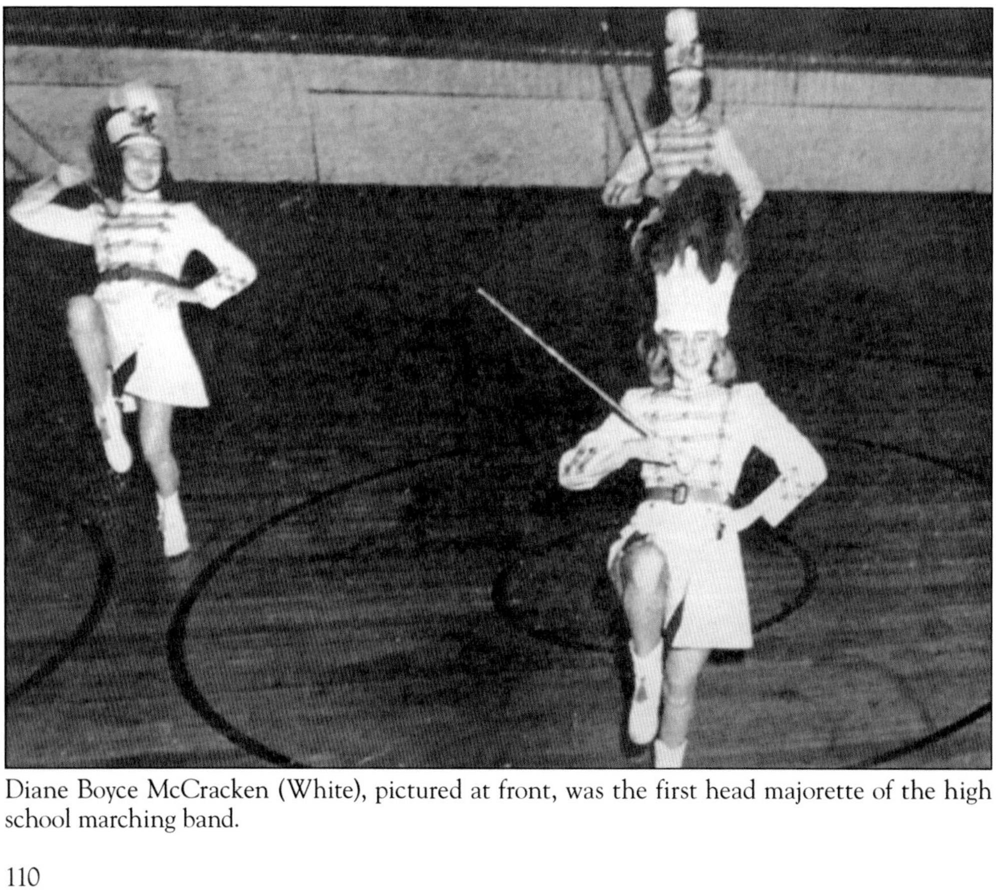

Diane Boyce McCracken (White), pictured at front, was the first head majorette of the high school marching band.

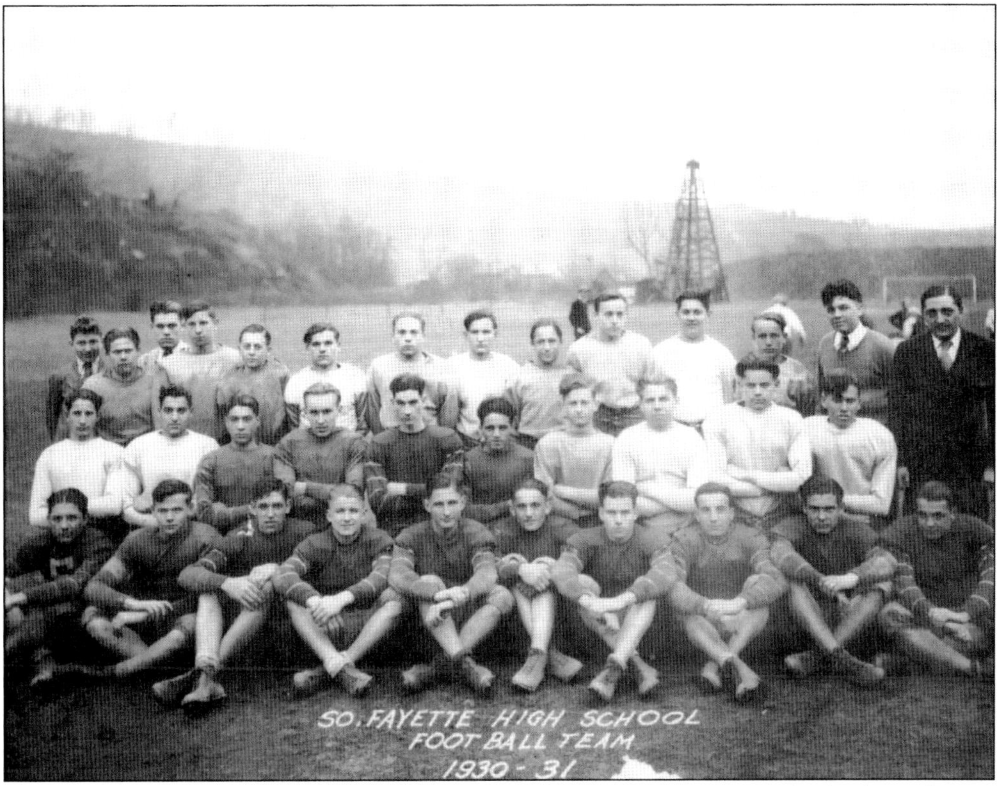

The 1930–1931 high school football team practiced where it could, even in the shadows of an oil well; its rival was Bridgeville High School.

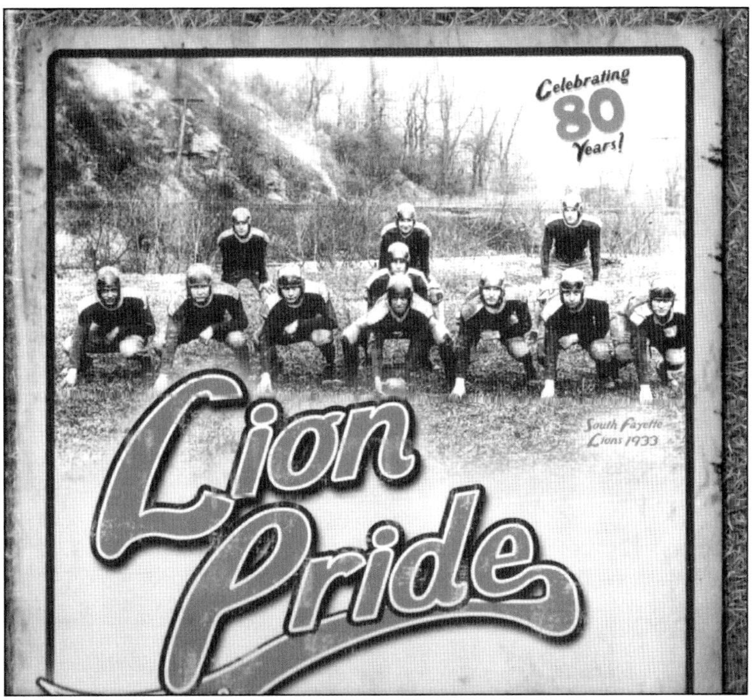

Members of the 1937 team brought the "Class B" football championship win to the township in 1936. The coach was John Donelli. Members included M. Donelli, F. Vezzi, J. Chiappini, A Donelli, J. Koszarsky Jr., P. Henderson, J. Danilo, and four other boys. The six Donelli brothers played soccer and football.

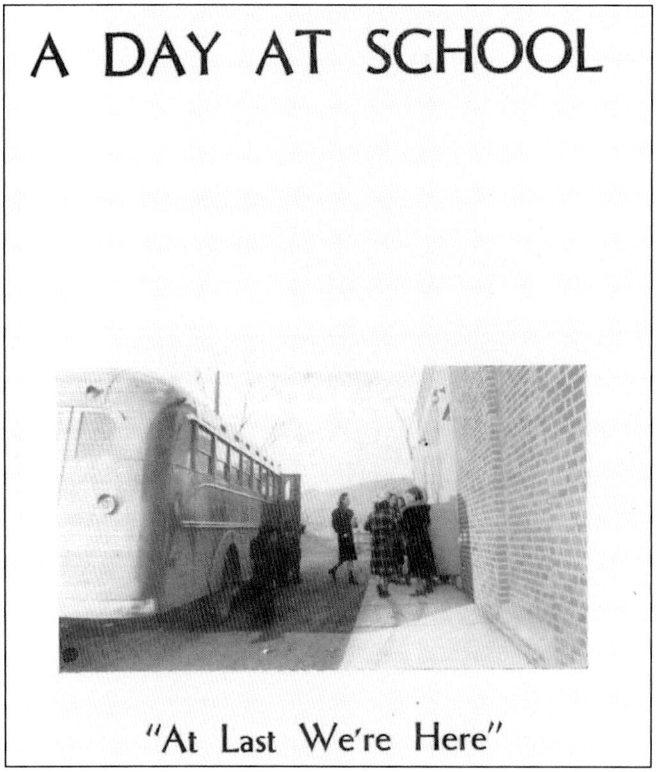

This is the first page of the high school's first yearbook, *The So-Ette*, produced in 1940 under the sponsorship of 10 faculty members. In 1948, the yearbook was renamed *The Lafayette Log*, the name still used today.

Pleasant Valley School, pictured in 1945, was located on what was known as Route 28 next to Old Scotts Pond. In 1960, the road was renamed Route 50. In 1945, Anelita Ferri bought the old school and turned it into a four-unit apartment building. In 1970, when Route 50 was widened, the state tore the building down. Today, Children's South, a division of University of Pittsburgh Medical Center Children's Hospital, has been erected on this site.

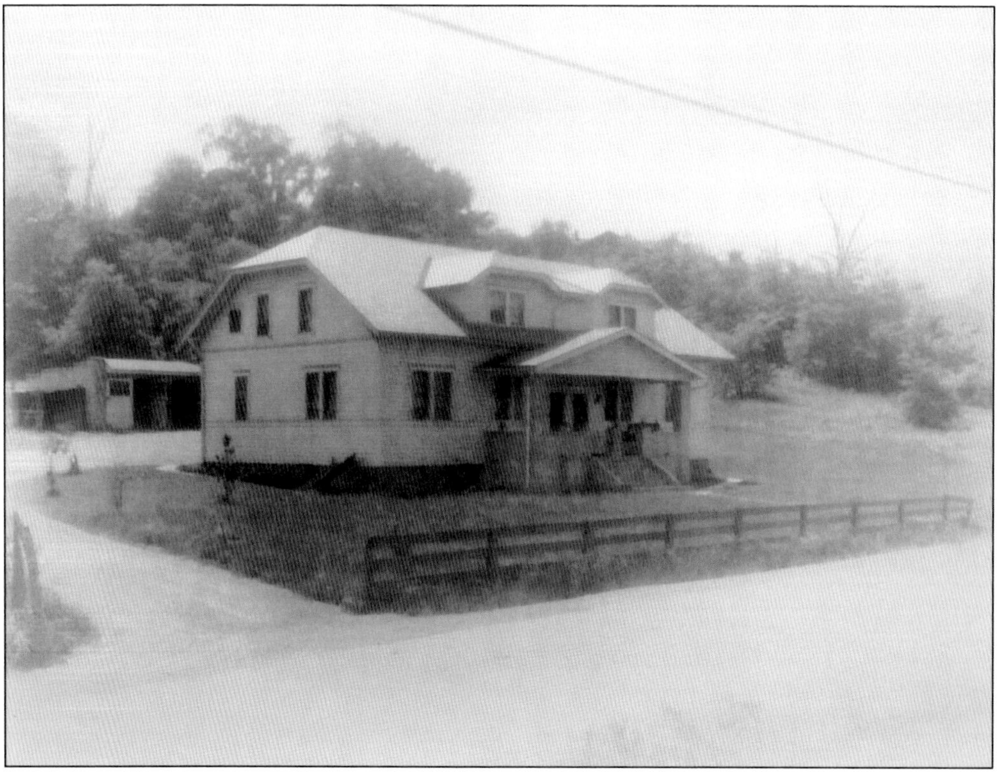

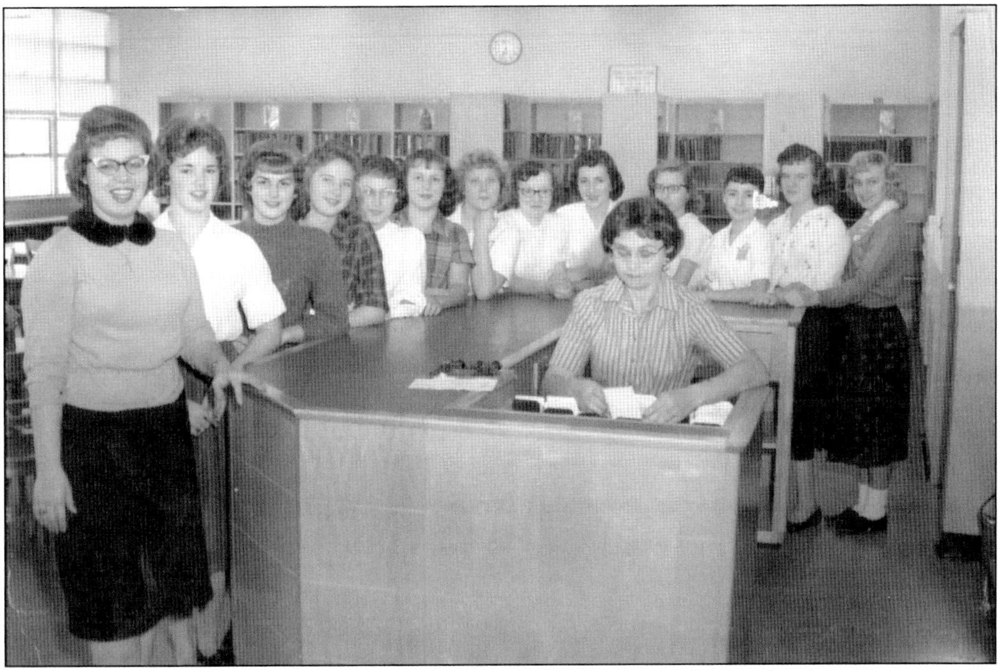

Surrounding Miss D'Andrea in 1960 are the library helpers at the high school.

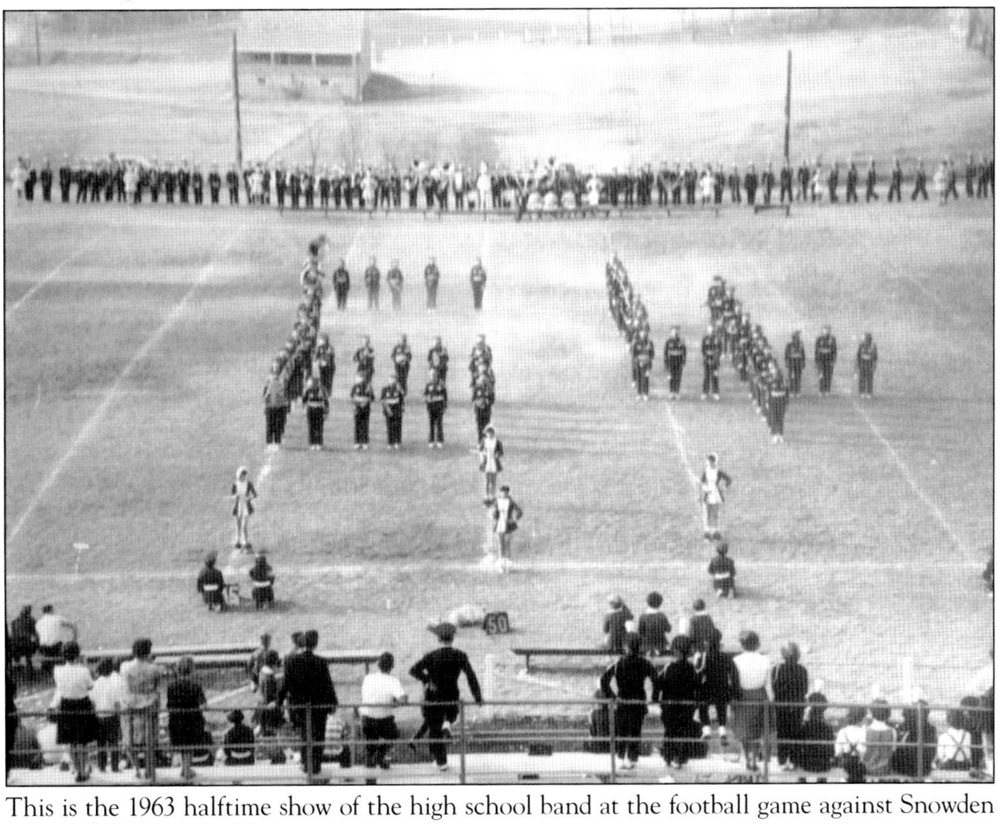

This is the 1963 halftime show of the high school band at the football game against Snowden (now called South Park).

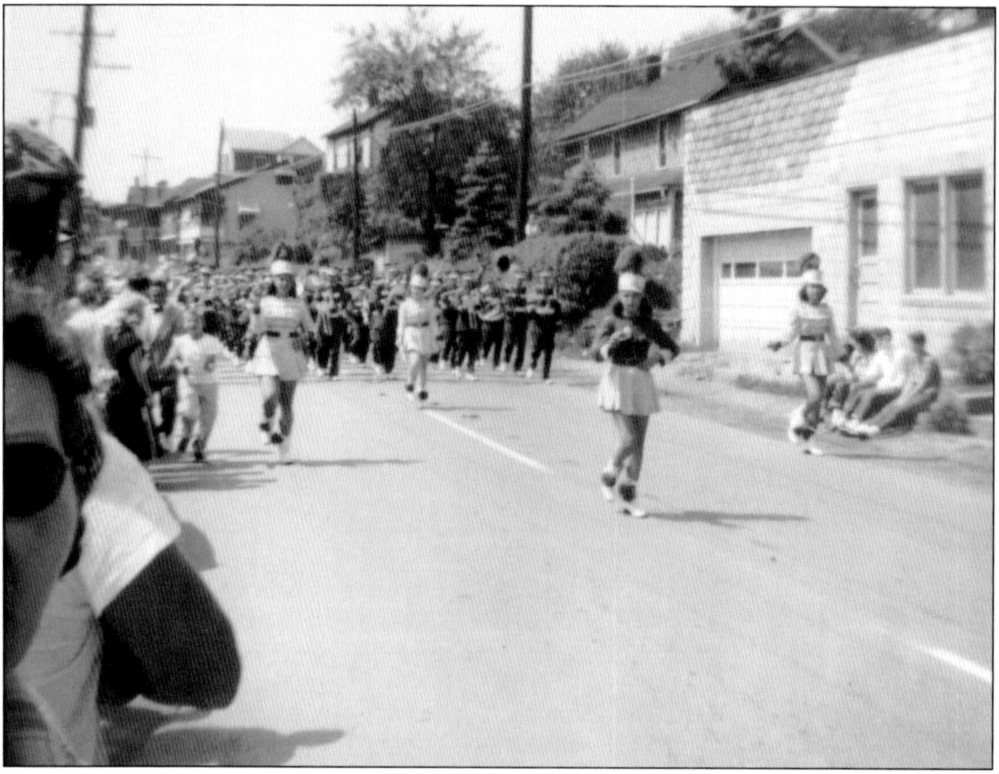

The high school band, pictured around 1958, led many parades throughout the community and continues to participate in the annual Bridgeville Memorial Day Parade.

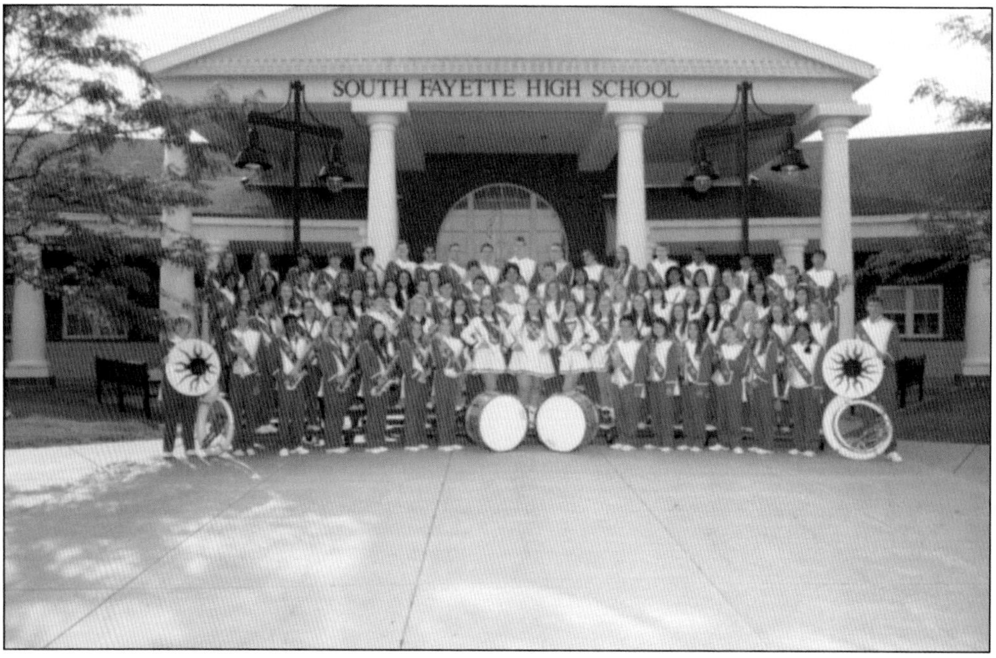

The "Little Green Machine" Marching Band of 2014 poses for a group picture in front of the current high school, built in 2002. (Courtesy of Kevin Sutter.)

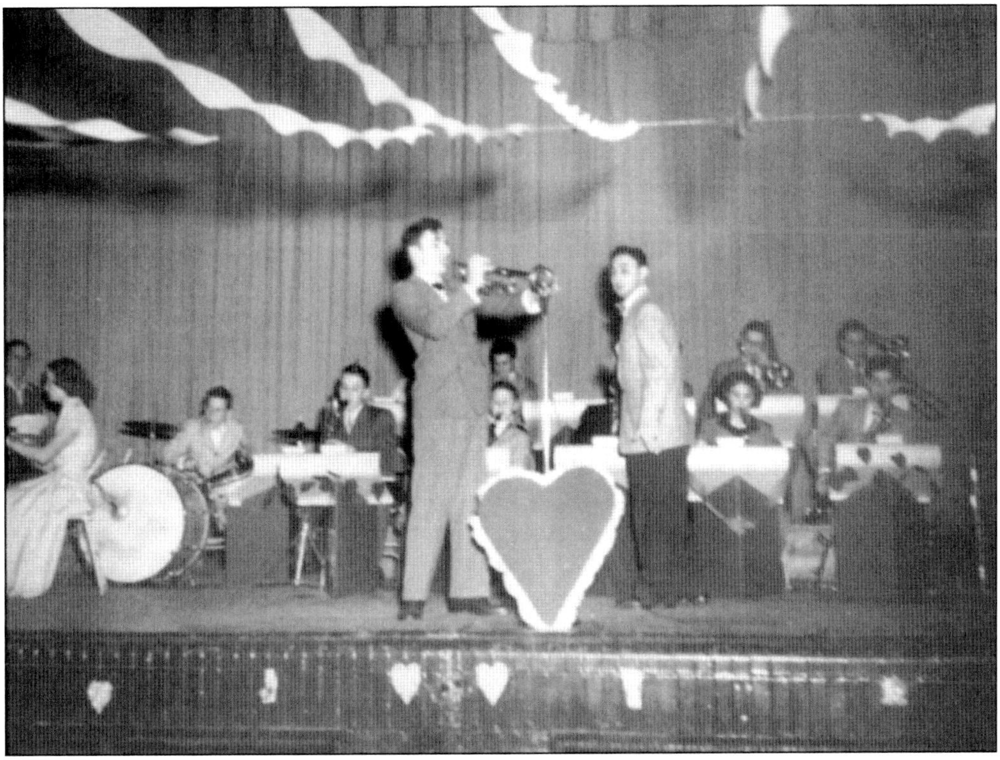

The high school marching band had three directors in its first 50 years of existence: Dominic Scacchitti (called "Sir" by his students), 1948–1962; John Testa, 1962–1990; and Clem Rolin, 1990–2004. Then Scacchitti's grandson Michael Mackey took over the high-energy dance-and-play band, now called the Little Green Machine. Deeply rooted in tradition, the band practices today what originated in the early years: the choreography of dances by the senior class, spot rotations among the "rookie" members, and instrument proficiency requirements for all majorettes. When entering the community, there are signs that read, "Welcome to South Fayette Township: Home of the Little Green Machine Marching Band." Above are Scacchitti and student Paul Rolin, Clem's brother. At right is John Testa.

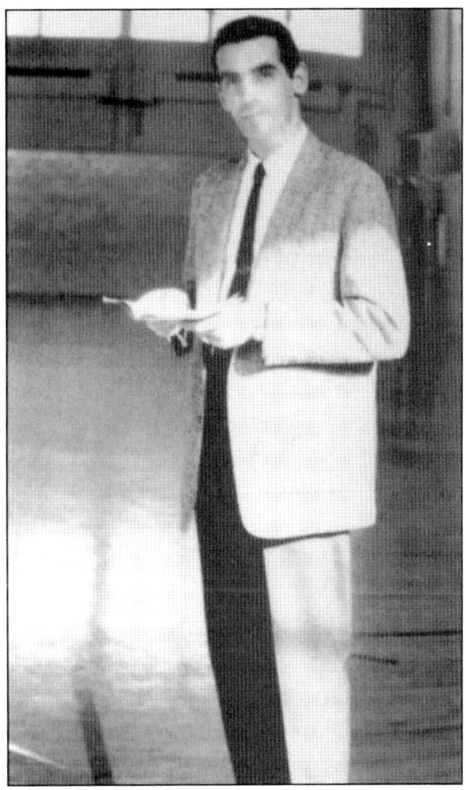

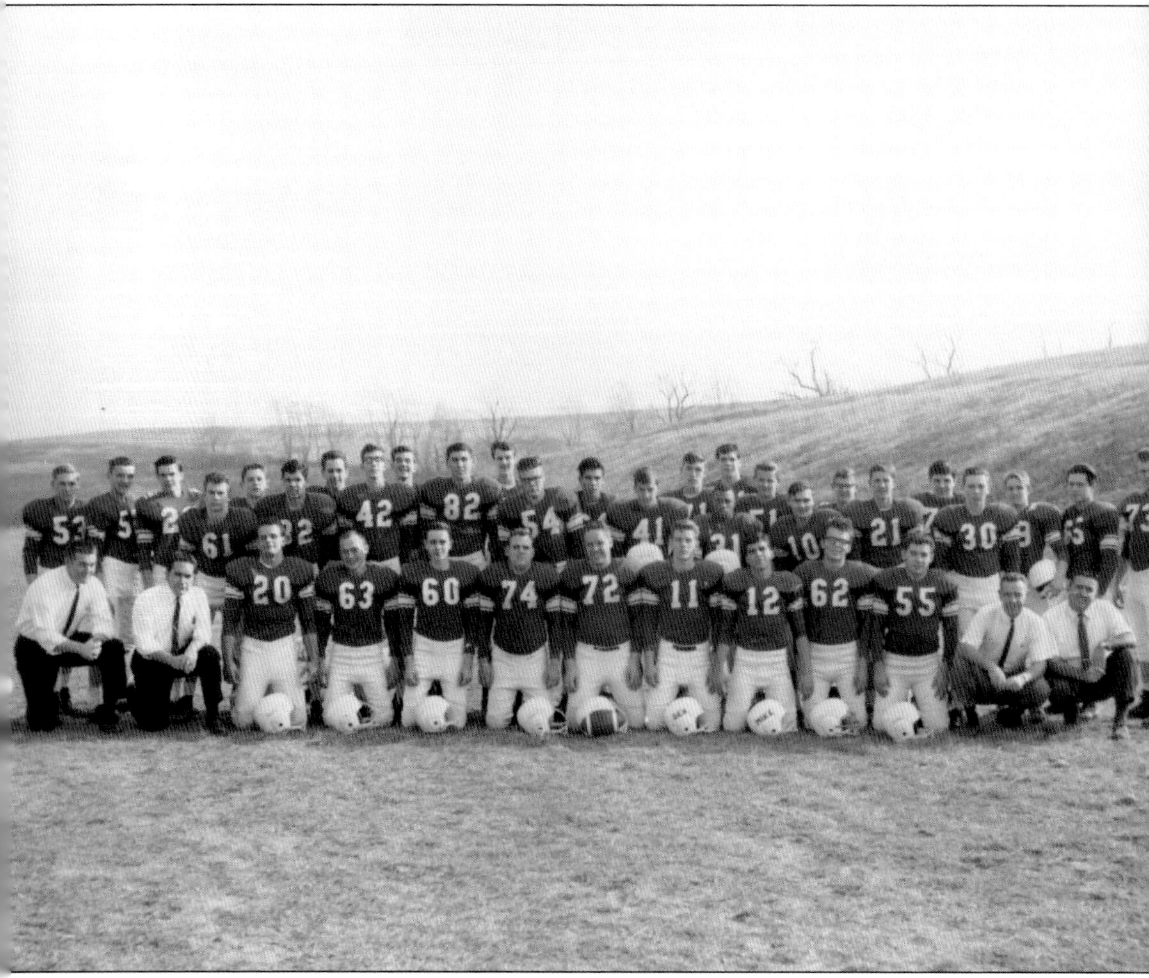

In 1964, South Fayette High School's football team won the Class B championship. Pictured are coaches Jim Balsarini, Sam Ross, Bill Weir, and Joe Basile and players Stan Budzik, Jimmy Papeaka, Allan Aubel, George Emerick, Cliff Kittle, Dennis Carl, Mike Shuck, Kris Aasmo, Hank Mannering, Russell Woleslagle, Jim Sray, Darrell Culley, Bill Klima, Tom Monaghan, Joe Franjione, John Mincin, Leo Longo, Frank Ivancza, Jerry Liberatore, Ron Lengvarsky, Roy Watson, John Martorana, Donald Pradines, and Bill Scott. In their honor, there was a victory parade through town and a holiday was proclaimed. It had taken 28 years to regain the title last received in 1936. In 1967, again coached by Joe Basile and Robert Motte, the undefeated Lions were runners-up for the championship title. In October 2014, the 1964 Championship team held a 50-year reunion during the Lions' football game against Steel Valley High School.

Eight

Today's South Fayette Township

Much of the landscape of South Fayette has changed since 1965. The mines are closed. Most of the former farms are housing complexes and new neighborhoods, such as Hickory Heights, Hunting Ridge, Lakemont, Kingsbrook, Berkshires, Walnut Ridge, Sterling Ridge, and others.

Rakuen Lakes was originally an amusement park, then became Cabana Beach in the 1930s, and now is the site of Lakeview Christian Church. Mariani's Vulcan Station and Universal Oil Co. were on Millers Run Road, serving as the local bus stop and meeting place for the community of Cuddy. Farther up the street in Morgan Hollow was the six-acre bee farm of Alphonse Stankus. Originally a speakeasy in the 1920s, Club 28 Mariani's Restaurant opened after Prohibition, in the 1940s, and became Kam's Restaurant in the 1950s; it was renamed the Lemon Tree Restaurant in the 1970s and still operates today in Sturgeon. The current Iron Creek Bar and Restaurant, at 613 Millers Run Road, was originally a post office and grocery store run by the Chambordon and Invernezzi families, then run by Eugene Malbos, and finally purchased in the 1950s by the Bioni family, who turned it into a bar and restaurant.

Begun in 1999, the Bridgeville/South Fayette Relay for Life is held one day in late May and brings together the community to raise funds for cancer, to remember loved ones lost to the disease, and to celebrate survivors.

The South Fayette Foundation for Excellence was formed as a 501(c)(3) organization in 2010 to raise funds for innovative educational opportunities, awarding yearly grants to district teachers and student scholarships for post-secondary higher education.

South Fayette was in the spotlight in 2003 when Jenna Morasca, class of 1999, won *Survivor: Amazon*, the sixth installment of the hit CBS television series.

The school district's facilities are used additionally as meeting space for Boy and Girl Scouts; township sports teams play games on school fields; the middle school natatorium offers a swim club and lessons year-round; the elementary school offers a summer two-week Little Lions Academy of fun classes such as cooking, rocket making, and earth science. A very active parent-teacher association (PTA) in the elementary/intermediate schools and a parent-teacher organization (PTO) in the middle school sponsor events such as science fairs, movie nights, family bingos, and more. All the school buildings encourage community outreach with Lion Hearts Volunteer Clubs and activities such as the "penny challenge," holiday food and gift collections for the needy, and visits to the local senior nursing facilities.

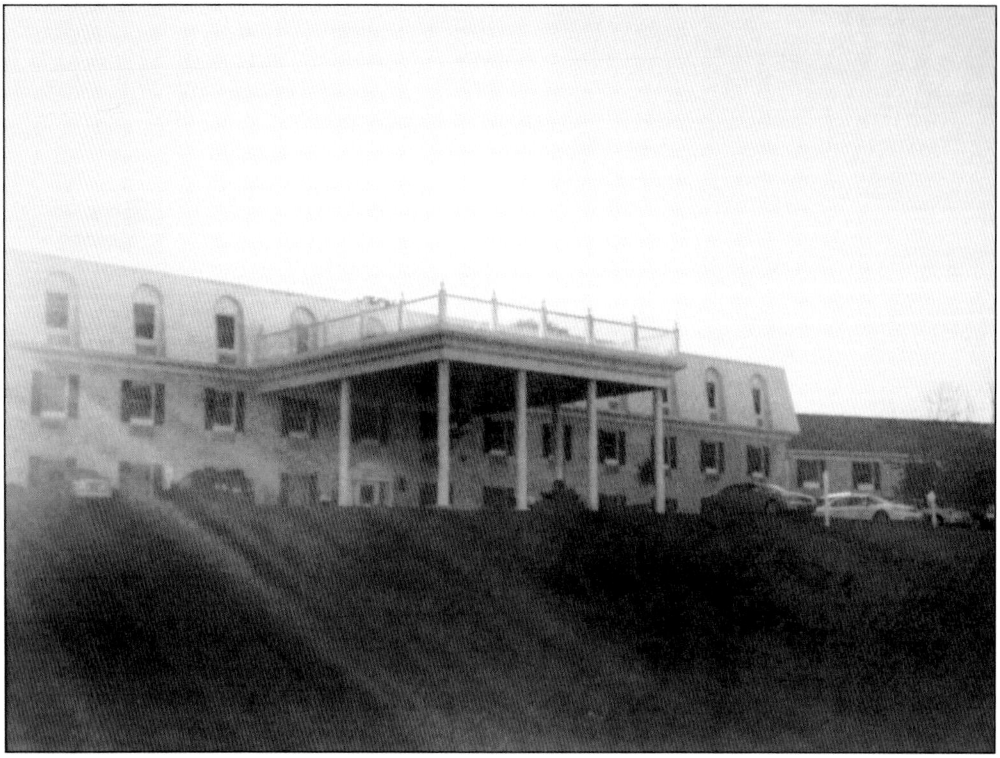

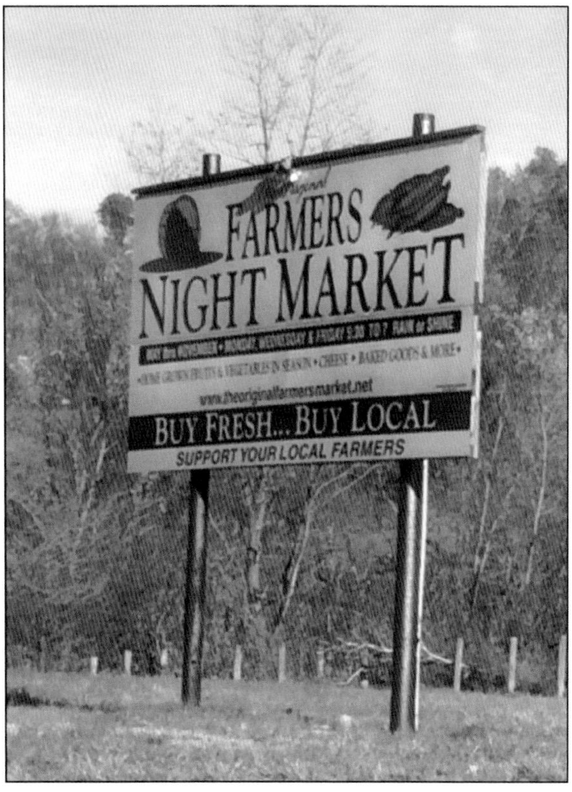

Country Meadows Retirement Community, pictured, sits on 23-acres off Washington Pike. Broadmore Senior Living at Lakemont Farms, also on Washington Pike, has been similarly constructed and offers respite and nursing care as well as senior living options.

The Original Farmers Market began in 1939 with local farmers banding together in the North Side of Pittsburgh. It was relocated in the late 1950s to the Heidelberg Raceway Plaza and, in the 1970s, moved to its present location across from the Gladden Exit on Route 50. It operates from May to October on Monday, Wednesday, and Friday evenings. Local farmers and craftsmen sell their fresh produce, cheese, baked goods, and more to eager customers.

Melissa "Missy" Babish of Cuddy was crowned Miss Teenage America 1969. A 1970 graduate of South Fayette High School, she went on to receive her master's in business administration, taught college statistics, and was administrative director of internal medicine at Mount Sinai Hospital in New York City. She has three children, one grandchild, and is an active Penn State Master Gardener. Missy is pictured when she captured the national crown.

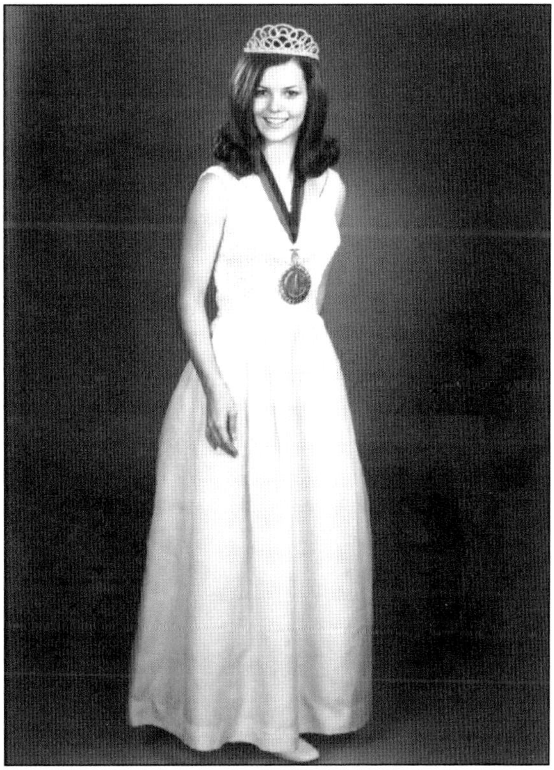

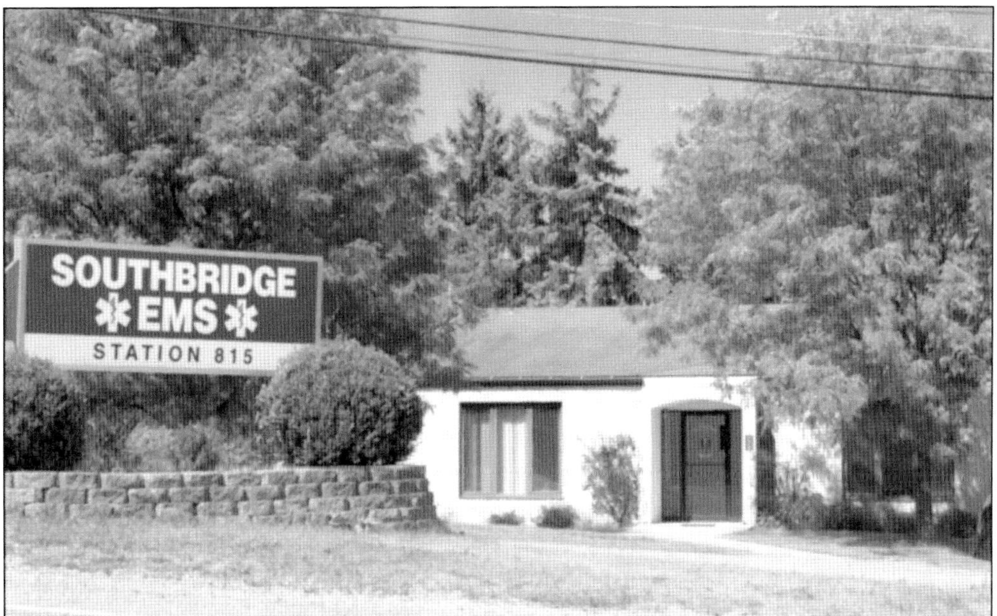

Located at the former site of the Jaycees' "haunted house" on Hickory Grade Road and overlooking the defunct Star City Cinemas (former location of Mulach Steel) is the Southbridge Emergency Medical Services, providing ambulance services to Bridgeville, Cecil, and South Fayette Townships since 1971. (Courtesy of Linda James.)

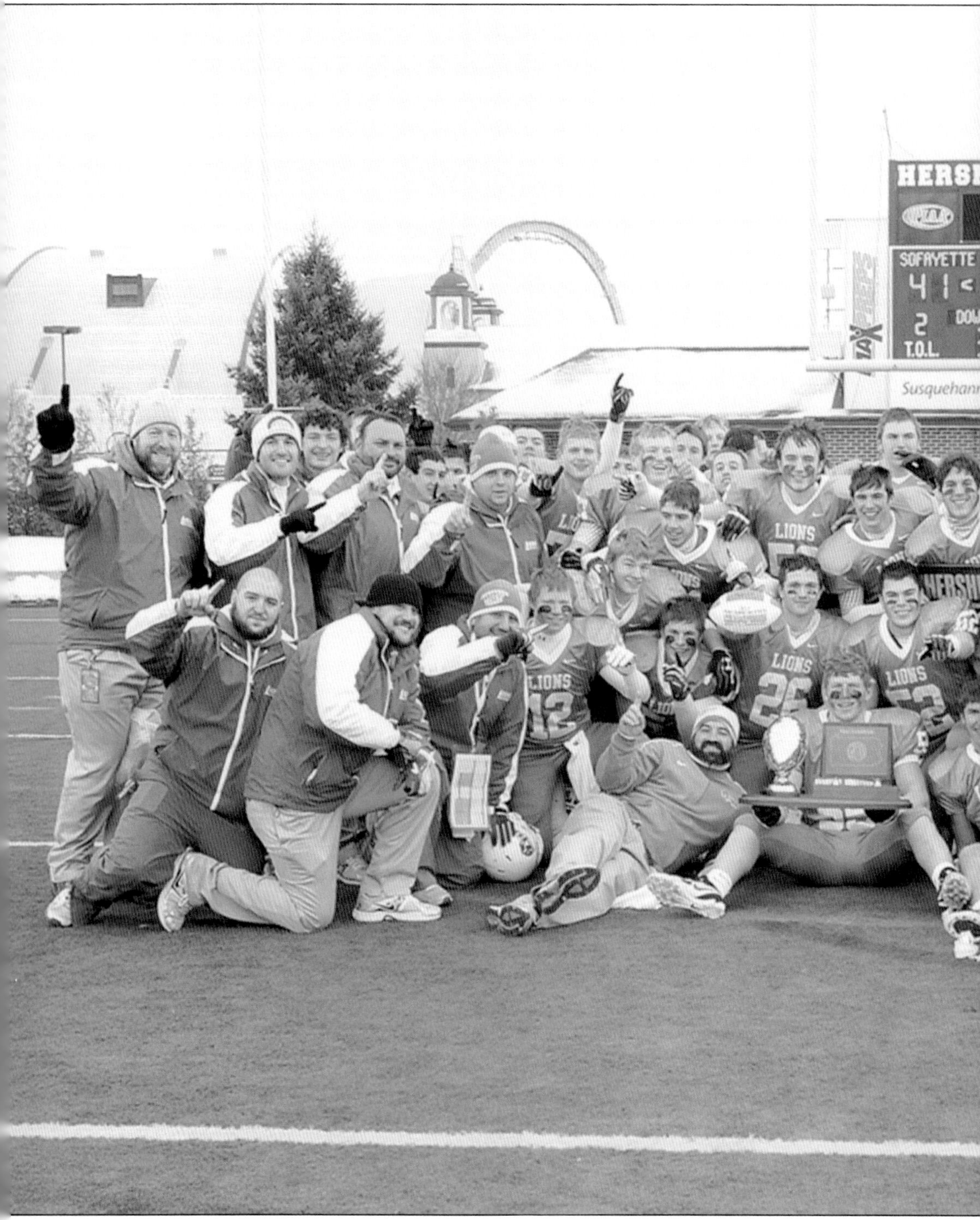

In 2013, the varsity football team was named the Pennsylvania Interscholastic Athletic Association (PIAA) Class AA Football state champion. The Lions were state football champions again in 2014. Other school teams that have earned recent titles include the 1999 Class A boys' baseball Western Pennsylvania Interscholastic Athletic League (WPIAL) champions, PIAA 119-pound

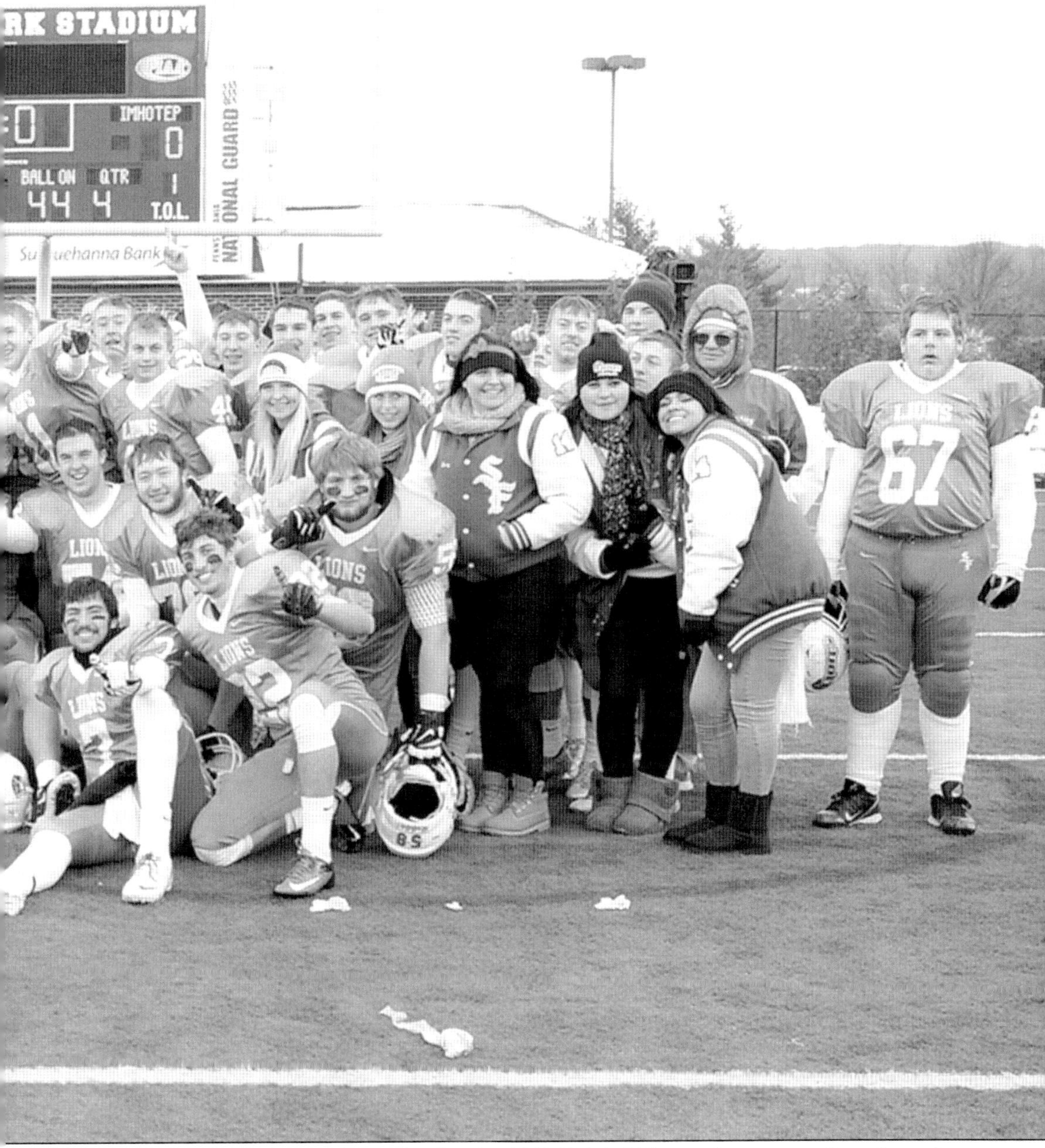

state wrestling champion Mark McKnight, the 2010 PIAA 145-pound state wrestling champion Nick Carr, and PIAA track-and-field athlete Nicole Hilton in 2011, as well as section champs and/or runners-up in track and field, cross country, golf, soccer, and volleyball over the years. (Courtesy of Kevin Sutter.)

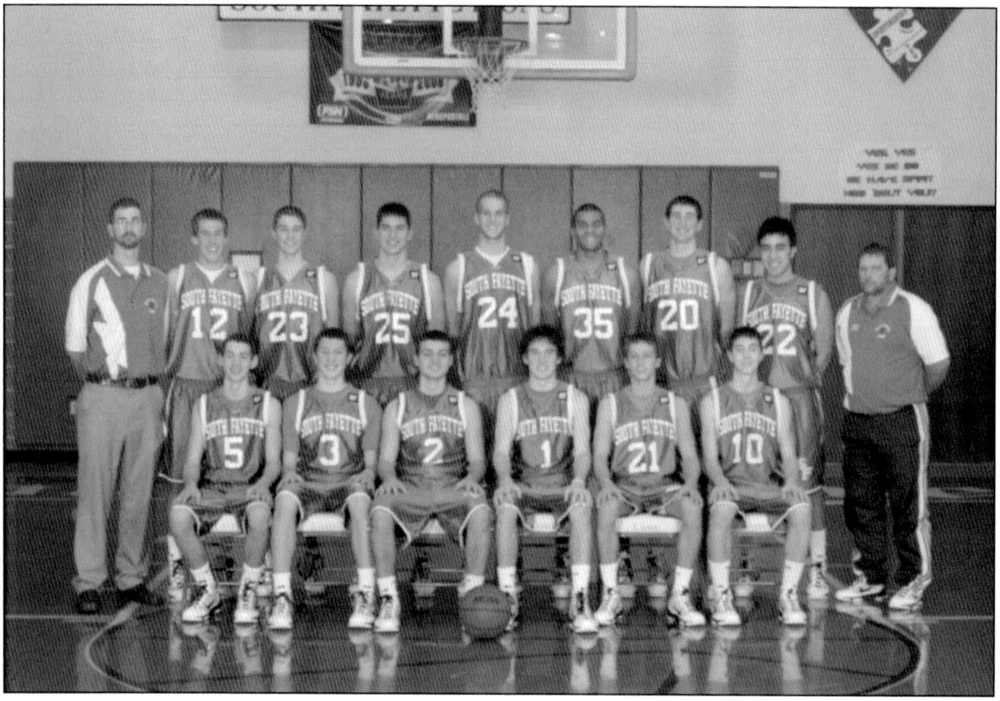

In 2010, the boys' varsity basketball team celebrated winning the title of PIAA Class AA boys' basketball state champions. Pictured are, from left to right, (first row) Luke Brumbaugh, Tyler Patterson, Patrick Zedreck, Tyler Henry, Nick Elder, and Adam Silko; (second row) coach Mark Keener, Josh Patterson, Zach Challingsworth, Tanner Courtad, Michael Lamberti, Michael Burroughs, Christian Brumbaugh, Shane Davis, and coach Rich Bonnaure. (Courtesy of Kevin Sutter.)

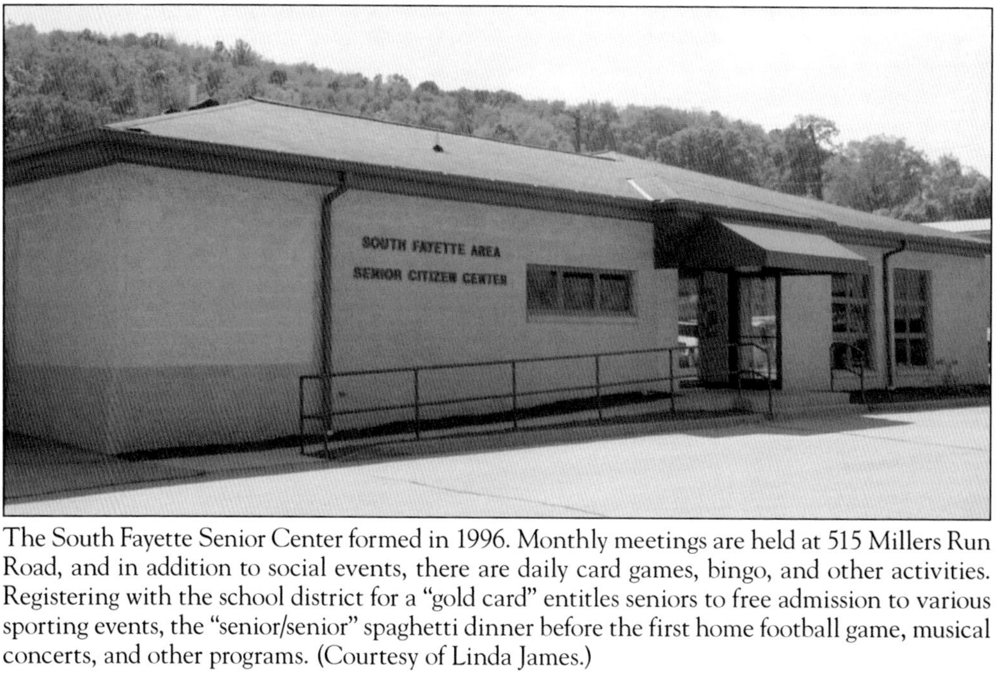

The South Fayette Senior Center formed in 1996. Monthly meetings are held at 515 Millers Run Road, and in addition to social events, there are daily card games, bingo, and other activities. Registering with the school district for a "gold card" entitles seniors to free admission to various sporting events, the "senior/senior" spaghetti dinner before the first home football game, musical concerts, and other programs. (Courtesy of Linda James.)

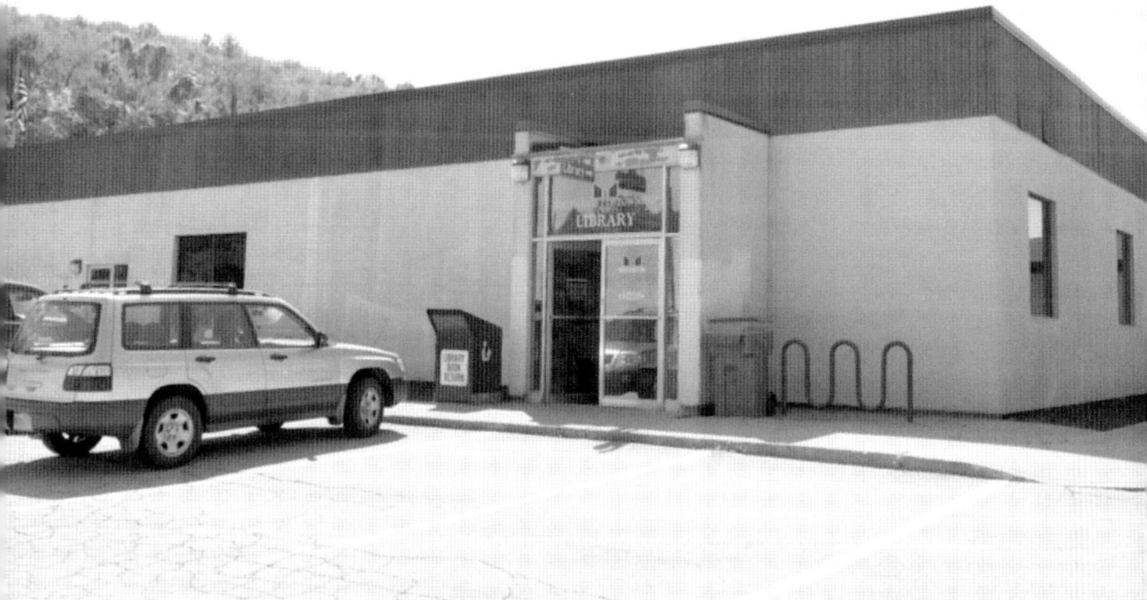

Next to the South Fayette Senior Center is the township library. It began in 1994 with a mainly donated collection in two rooms (roughly 900 square feet) in the municipal building. The municipal building's extensive renovations in 2005 allowed the library to grow in space to include children's and teen programs, 12 public access computers, enhanced reading and studying space, an extensive and ever-improving collection, and an outdoor educational garden. (Courtesy of Linda James.)

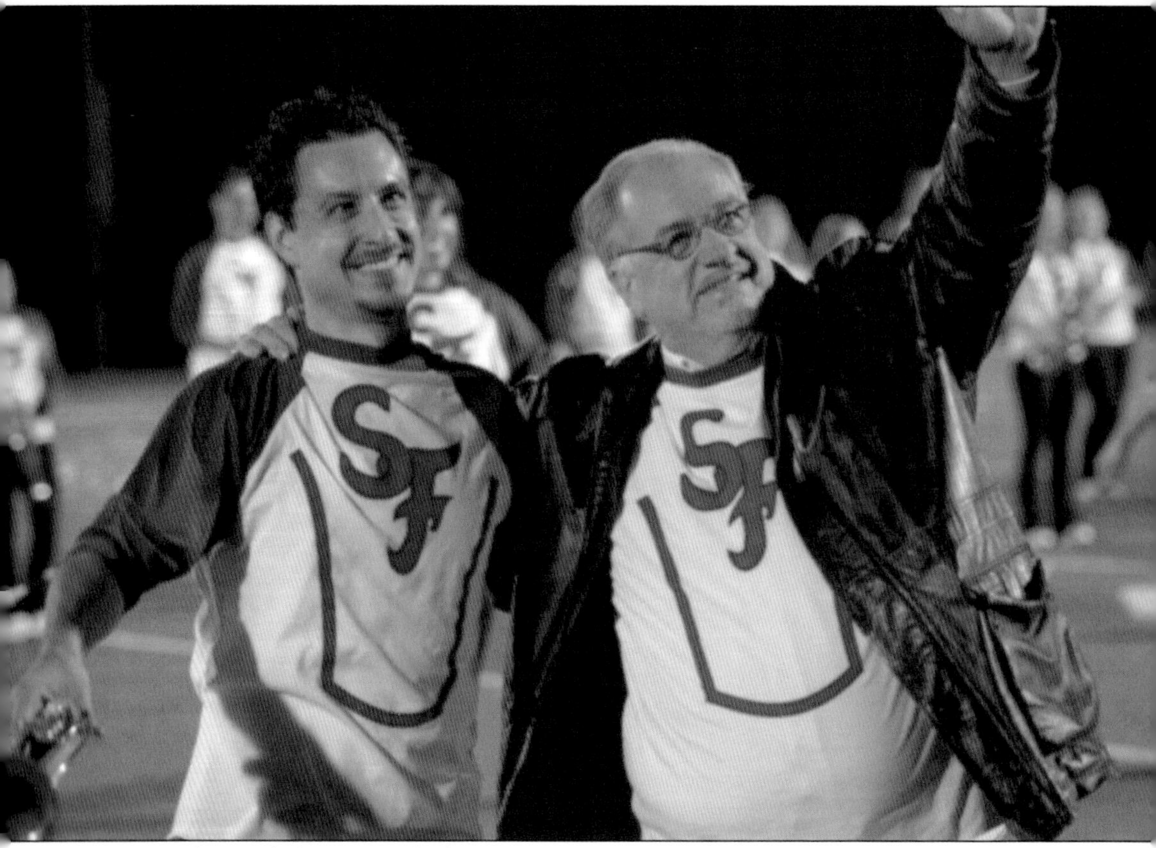

In 2011, the South Fayette Band Alumni Association was formed by Ryan Wolf, Marylee Ainsworth, Lenore Buchta, and Flo Rolin to maintain and preserve the history and tradition of the Little Green Machine and to support the current instrumental program of the school district. Since then, the alumni association raises funds and gives out the Scacchitti-Testa Scholarship (named in memory of the first two directors of the high school band) to a graduating member of the Little Green Machine Band. In September 2012, more than 70 alumni—from classes 1957 to 2012—took part in the first alumni band concert on the football field at South Fayette since 1997. Pictured are Michael Mackey (left) and Clem Rolin, fourth and third directors of the band, who directed the alumni performance. Eryn Carranza has been the Little Green Machine director since 2011.

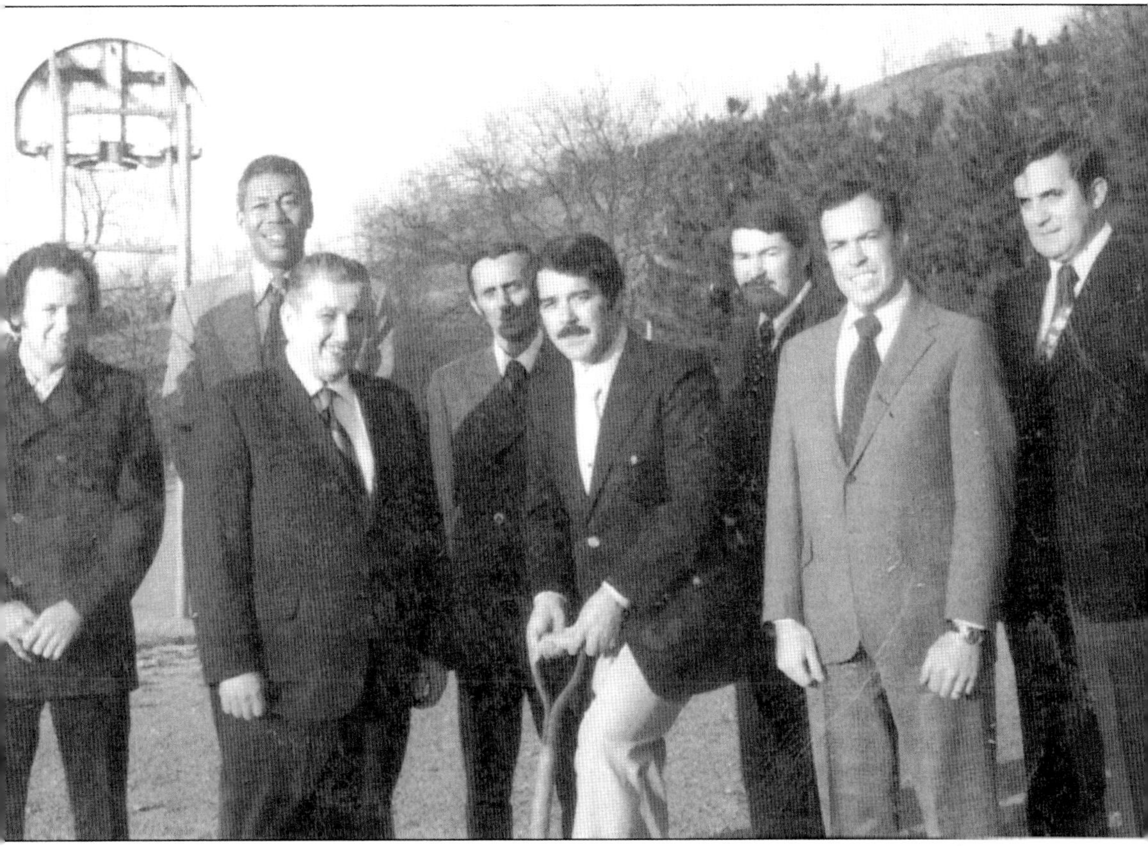

The township's first parks and recreation board was formed in 1976 with Jewett Hayes as chairman. Pictured are, from left to right, Fred Mannering, Hayes, Michael Kachuriak Jr., Frank Slovick Sr., Harold Chappel, James Balsarini, Kurt Gairing, and George Gillespie. Other official committees that were formed over the years included a planning commission, civil service commission, municipal authority, zoning hearing board, and an environmental advisory committee.

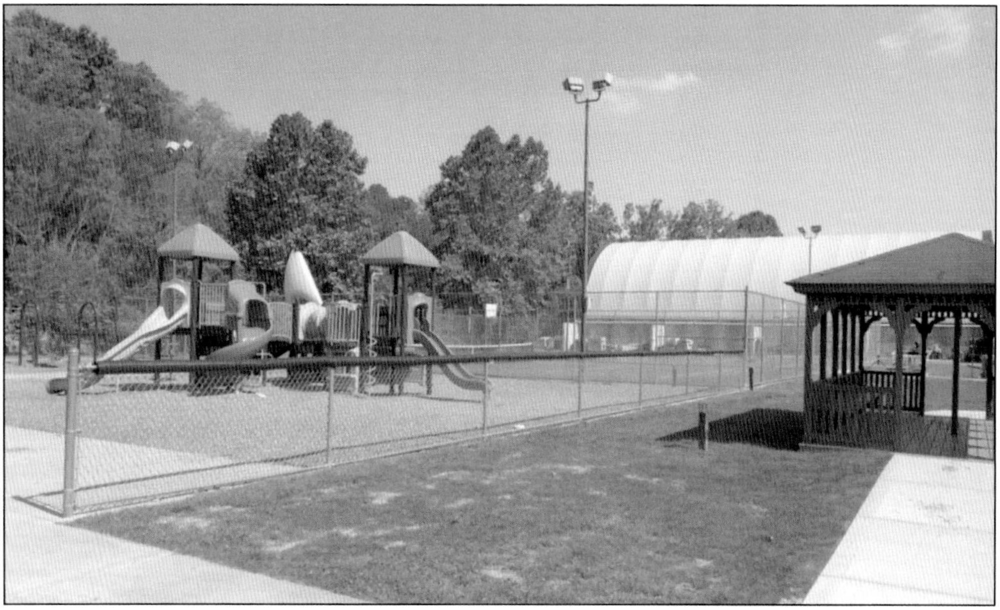

South Fayette residents enjoy their outdoor spaces. Fairview Park, with 125 acres, has walking trails, baseball fields, picnic facilities, tennis and basketball courts, and a dog free-run zone. Morgan Park (pictured), completely renovated after the 2004 flood, has batting cages, baseball fields, tennis and basketball courts, and a playground. The Boys Home Park has a pavilion, walking trails and a tot playground. El Rancho Park and Koppers Field have soccer fields. Sturgeon Park has a baseball field and a tot lot. The Panhandle Trail has walking and biking trails. Township athletic teams consist of youth lacrosse, boys' and girls' recreational basketball, swimming, adult baseball, youth cheerleading, hockey, soccer, men's softball, and youth football. The township also sponsors a three-day Disabled Sportsman Hunt for South Fayette residents and nonresidents who hold a Pennsylvania Game Commission permit for hunters with disabilities. (Courtesy of Linda James.)

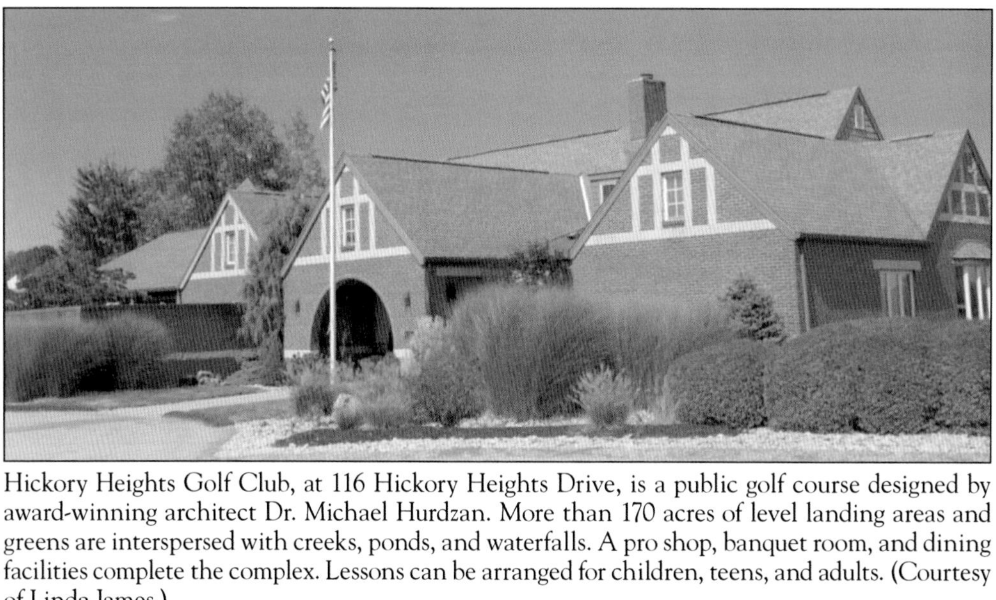

Hickory Heights Golf Club, at 116 Hickory Heights Drive, is a public golf course designed by award-winning architect Dr. Michael Hurdzan. More than 170 acres of level landing areas and greens are interspersed with creeks, ponds, and waterfalls. A pro shop, banquet room, and dining facilities complete the complex. Lessons can be arranged for children, teens, and adults. (Courtesy of Linda James.)

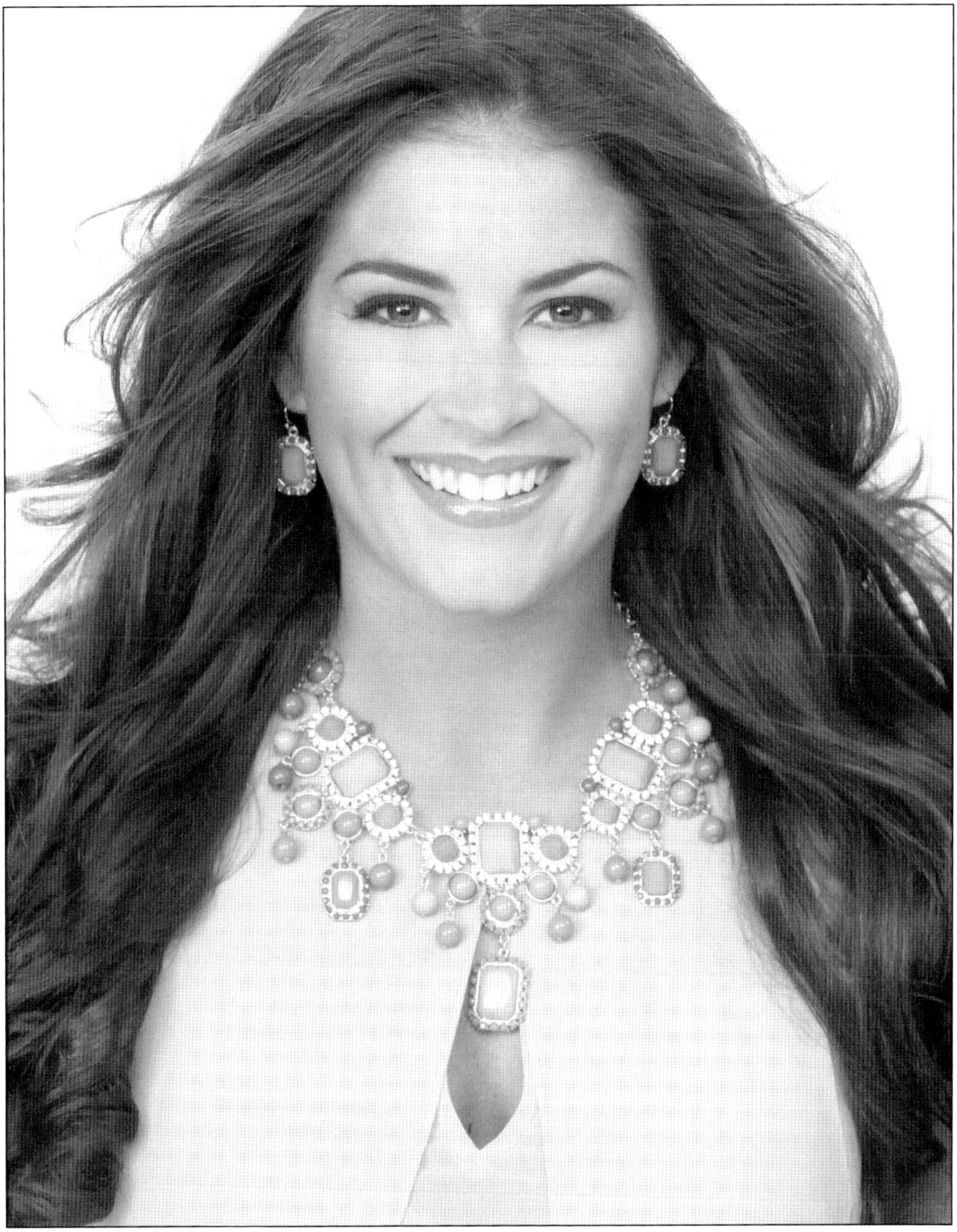

Ashley Schmider graduated as the class valedictorian from South Fayette in 2009 and summa cum laude from Duquesne University in 2013. She is a supporter of Strong Women, Strong Girls mentoring program and has made this her platform, along with the Children's Miracle Network, while being involved with the Miss America Organization. She was crowned Miss Pennsylvania 2015 and went on to compete in the Miss America pageant on September 13, 2015, in Atlantic City, New Jersey.